"Gregor Craigie blends clear writing, deep research and deeper compassion in this essential study of the housing crisis that affects us all—but especially society's most vulnerable people. By applying a global lens to a national crisis, he highlights realistic ways to solve one of the most urgent problems of our time."

Josh O'Kane, author of *Sideways: The City Google Couldn't Buy*

"In this **insightful and accessible blueprint**, Craigie navigates readers through the crisis of the Canadian housing landscape with national and international examples, that include both failures and innovative solutions. Written like a novel, each micro-chapter transports readers to the location of the story and into the lives of the characters. However, unlike fiction, **this book provides copious facts, advice, and moments that tug at your heart and inspire action. While the alarm rings loudly, Craigie's calm and expertly crafted narrative provides a beacon of hope.** With compelling clarity, he empowers policy makers, and others, to embrace these transformative insights and breathe life into much-needed solutions. Don't miss this essential read; the future of Canadian housing depends on it."

Celina Caesar-Chavannes, author of *Can You Hear Me Now?*

"To solve Canada's housing crisis, Gregor Craigie roams the globe seeking answers in twenty disparate places. . . . Astonishingly, he finds individuals in every location willing to share intimate details of how they are coping with upheaval. . . He warns that Canada's housing crisis is just beginning, offers a list of 37 measures to address the emerging nightmare, and, in 'Craigie's Index,' even adds a touch of statistical whimsy. *Our Crumbling Foundation* is **a transformative tour de force.**"

Ken McGoogan, author of *Searching for Franklin*

"This is **an exhaustive look at one of the most important issues facing this country right now.** With impeccable timing, Craigie presents a thorough analysis of the mechanics of housing affordability, and just how far off the path we've gone."

Daniel Foch, co-host of *The Canadian Real Estate Investor* podcast

"*Our Crumbling Foundation* **documents the harrowing human costs of Canada's severe undersupply of housing.** Other advanced countries build far more housing per person than Canada, and thus many of these tragedies are avoidable. Why can't we accept more housing in our neighbourhoods?"

Eric Protzer, Senior Fellow, Harvard Kennedy School

"I needed to read this book! *Our Crumbling Foundation* is a captivating mosaic of housing need across Canada. You travel when you read this book. Gregor Craigie draws from his journalism roots to illustrate the housing struggles of a diverse group of Canadians. . . . He brings to life solutions being implemented around the world: the huge co-op movement in Berlin, La Samaritaine and the public housing project Bois-le-Prêtre in Paris, tiny home and modular construction in Ireland and Oregon, even 3-D printing homes in Mexico.

The solutions are at hand!"

Cathy Crowe C.M., Street Nurse, Visiting Practitioner at Toronto Metropolitan University

"*Our Crumbling Foundation* **is a must read, not just for policy wonks but for anyone affected by a housing crisis that knows no bounds.** With a focus not just on the problem, but also tangible solutions, Craigie provides numerous paths forward. . . . From Duncan to Paris with many stops in between, *Our Crumbling Foundation* **explores the multitude of factors that got us into this housing mess, and how we can get ourselves out of it, by bringing to life the** housing frustrations of real people and a range of policy solutions tried around the world."

Jill Atkey, CEO, BC Non-Profit Housing Association

"Gregor Craigie's *Our Crumbling Foundation* has nailed the issue of the moment with its overview of the housing crisis causing so much anxiety in cities around the world, especially amongst young people. Gregor's weaving of stories of real people and their real struggles to find suitable and affordable housing, makes this book accessible to the reader and demystifies a complex and perplexing housing crisis. . . . Gregor provides practical solutions that have worked elsewhere . . . and leaves us with hope that governments will formulate policy that will create the conditions to build more housing that is urgently needed now."

Mitzie Hunter, Former MPP Scarborough-Guildwood and Ontario Minister of Education

"Author and journalist Gregor Craigie delves into the heart of the housing crisis in this latest work, exploring the diverse struggles faced by individuals across Canada in their pursuit of affordable and adequate housing. Through compelling storytelling, Craigie not only navigates the challenges but also unveils global insights, highlighting both triumphs and setbacks worldwide. Ultimately, Craigie presents a comprehensive list of 'repairs' for our crumbling foundation. A must-read for those seeking understanding in the face of this complex societal change."

Carolina Ibarra, Chief Executive Officer, Pacifica Housing

"Gregor Craigie's *Our Crumbling Foundation* is a deeply reported look at Canada's ever-growing housing crisis. It's also so chockful of solutions that it makes you want to shake politicians and policymakers and ask: 'When are you going to act?'"

André Picard, author of *Neglected No More*

OUR CRUMBLING FOUNDATION

OUR CRUMBLING FOUNDATION

How We Solve Canada's Housing Crisis

GREGOR CRAIGIE

RANDOM HOUSE CANADA

LIBRARY AND ARCHIVES CANADA CATALOGUING IN PUBLICATION

Title: Our crumbling foundation : how we solve
Canada's housing crisis / Gregor Craigie.
Names: Craigie, Gregor, author.
Description: Includes index.
Identifiers: Canadiana (print) 20230474179 | Canadiana
(ebook) 20230474233 | ISBN 9781039009387 (softcover) |
ISBN 9781039009394 (EPUB)
Subjects: LCSH: Housing policy—Canada. | LCSH: Housing—Canada.
Classification: LCC HD7305.A3 C73 2024 | DDC 363.5/5610971—dc23

Cover design: Kate Sinclair
Text design: Kate Sinclair
Typesetting: Erin Cooper
Image credits: C.J. Burton / Getty Images

Printed in Canada

246897531

Penguin
Random House
RANDOM HOUSE CANADA

*This book is dedicated to everyone whose life is on
hold because they cannot find a home of their own.*

CONTENTS

AUTHOR'S NOTE

WHILE THIS IS A BOOK about housing, it inevitably deals with those who have none, which raises the question of what people without housing should be called. I use the words *homeless* and *homelessness* in this book, but I also use some of the other terms that are becoming more common, such as *unhoused* or *people experiencing homelessness*. While some housing advocates object to the word *homeless*, arguing it now has negative connotations, I have interviewed many people who are sleeping on the streets, and the vast majority of them have described themselves as homeless. As a result, I am comfortable using the term. When the Associated Press updated its style guide in 2020, it said *"homeless* is generally acceptable as an adjective to describe people without a fixed residence." However, the guide urged AP writers to "avoid the dehumanizing collective noun *the homeless*, instead using constructions like *homeless people, people without housing* or *people without homes."*

There is also the question of what exactly constitutes "housing." In this book, I use the term broadly to cover home ownership, rentals, shared living arrangements with roommates, and even less traditional living arrangements, such as living in an RV. That's not to say that everyone who lives in a recreational vehicle wants to live in one—indeed, many do not and I describe that in more than one chapter. However, housing can take many forms, and I use the term accordingly.

On currency—costs and prices are in Canadian dollars unless stated otherwise.

And one final note on anonymity. I have used the real names for the people who are quoted in this book, with a few exceptions where a person needs to maintain anonymity for personal or professional reasons, or for reasons of safety.

INTRODUCTION

Just the Beginning

CANADA IS CAUGHT in a housing crisis. It's been obvious in Toronto and Vancouver for years, as the sight of homeless people on the streets became as common as news stories about record-high home prices. But in between the two extremes of multi-million-dollar homes and people with no homes at all, there's a huge and growing segment of society whose lives are dominated by the difficult question—where will I live? Some simply give up on their dreams of buying a home. Others spend their free time looking for a better place to rent. Some have been evicted by landlords cashing in on those high prices. Others are plagued by panic attacks every time a rental application is rejected and are terrified of ending up homeless. And for those experiencing homelessness, of course, every day is a crisis.

Stories like these aren't new. Housing affordability in Canada has been a concern for some people for years. What is new is the scale of the problem. In 2022, Canada's first Federal Housing Advocate,

Marie-Josée Houle, put it bluntly: "housing and housing affordability is becoming more and more out of reach for most Canadians." Many are young, employed, and well-educated. But those things don't mean what they used to mean in Canada. The old rule that going to school and getting a good job would allow you to buy a home doesn't apply anymore for many young Canadians. There are many reasons for this. Perhaps the most obvious is that incomes haven't kept up with rising housing costs. Between 2001 and 2021, the average price of a single-family home in Canada more than tripled, while the cost of everything else rose only 43 percent. The result is that homes are too expensive for many Canadians. On top of that, there just aren't enough of them. The Canada Mortgage and Housing Corporation estimates that by the end of this decade Canada will need an extra 3.5 million homes. That's on top of the more than 2.3 million new housing units already predicted to be built by then. But this crisis is about much more than just supply and demand. Single-family zoning, divestment from social housing, decades of low interest rates that encouraged the commodification of housing, and short-term vacation rentals have all contributed, along with many other factors. British Columbia and Toronto have recently eliminated most single-family zoning in an effort to increase the housing supply. But if Canada is going to make housing more affordable, or at least attainable, then it will need to make many more changes. That's why I wrote this book. After reporting on this issue for more than twenty-five years, I want to see more people move into secure housing.

I've reported on housing and homelessness more times than I can remember. I've interviewed hundreds of people about this— renters, landlords, buyers, sellers, developers, real estate agents, homeless people, housing advocates, builders, building inspectors, market analysts, economists, municipal councillors, mayors, hous- ing ministers, premiers, and prime ministers. It's not that I'm obsessed by the issue of housing—though it has always interested me—so much as the fact that the issue has dominated life in British Columbia for as long as I've lived here. And it's only got worse, both here and across a lot of the rest of the country. It took many years before it finally dawned on me exactly how big the problem is.

It may seem counterintuitive, but this epiphany came to me not at work but at home, when my wife and I received our 2021 property assessment in the mail. The number seemed to scream out at me as soon as I ripped open the envelope: *$1.3 million!* Our 110-year-old, ramshackle wood frame house was worth a fortune. I felt a brief moment of jubilation, and even heard the Barenaked Ladies singing in my head. *If I had a million dollars . . . I'd be rich.* But my momentary elation at our new-found wealth on paper was eclipsed almost immediately by a sobering realization—there is no way I could afford to buy my house today. I thought back seventeen years to when we bought our first house in Vancouver. I remembered the nagging suspicion that the $305,000 price tag would lead us to financial ruin. Little did we know it would be the best financial decision we'd ever make. Sure, we have another decade or so of mortgage payments in front of us, but we're extremely lucky. Today, my journalist salary combined with my wife's teacher salary simply wouldn't be enough to buy that house, or the one I now call home. I thought of my young colleagues who won't have the same opportunity I had, simply because they were born too late. Then I thought of my kids. How will they ever afford homes of their own? And where? If these sound like the middle-class concerns of someone who's relatively fortunate, well, that's because they are. I own a safe house in a beautiful city. It's walking distance to schools, shops, and the beach. Everyone should be so lucky. And I know my kids will likely be able to rely on at least some financial help from their parents in the future—a factor that matters more and more these days, and only exacerbates intergenerational inequalities. But this book isn't about me or my family. It's about the millions of Canadians who are struggling with unaffordable housing, and the impact it is having on both them and the country as a whole.

This book tells the stories of Canadians who are suffering due to the lack of affordable housing in this country. It also profiles people in other countries who have benefited from changes that could work here. As a journalist, I've heard countless tales of struggle over the years. But in writing this book, I've heard many success stories too. They've convinced me that there is no single measure that will fix this problem. Instead, most or even all the solutions presented in this book will be needed. Of course, many measures have already been introduced in Canada, like co-op housing, which has been around for decades, and the recent two-year ban on non-Canadians buying residential properties here. But much more is needed.

It's tempting to think we might just do nothing and wait this all out. While house prices smashed records during the first two years of the COVID-19 pandemic, they started to drop in 2022. But make no mistake, housing is still too expensive for millions of Canadians. In fact, rising interest rates made mortgages more expensive, which effectively cancelled out any benefits to buyers of lower prices. In the third quarter of 2022, housing in Canada was more unaffordable than ever. A Royal Bank report estimated the share of the average household income needed to cover the ownership costs of an average home had risen to 62.7 percent—an all-time high. In Toronto, the average house cost 85.2 percent of pre-tax income. In Vancouver, it cost 95.8 percent. "The current decline in house prices will not save us," Benjamin Tal, deputy chief economist at CIBC, said. "By any stretch of the imagination, this is not the end of the housing crisis. This is just the beginning."

1

PRICED OUT

_____

Vancouver

WHEN MARTIN AND NICOLE Chiu got married in 2011, Martin's parents invited them to move into their house. The newly-weds took over the two-bedroom suite on the lower level, while Martin's parents occupied the three-bedroom suite upstairs. In many ways, the house was perfectly designed for multi-generational living. It was a Vancouver Special—the familiar style of single-family house that's a more common sight in the city than Starbucks outlets or rainy days. The utilitarian two-storey design first appeared in the late 1940s and took advantage of local zoning laws to maximize floor space and reduce building costs. It was panned by architecture critics but proved extremely popular with many immigrants between the 1960s and the 1980s. Roughly ten thousand were built, especially on the city's working-class Eastside.

Martin and Nicole paid his parents a reduced rent, and over the next decade they saved enough money for what they hoped would be the down payment on their first home. They were still saving when their first two children were born—the oldest, Jacob, and his little sister, Chloe, four and a half years later. In 2019, when baby Nate arrived, the young family of five moved upstairs into the three-bedroom suite, while Martin's parents moved downstairs. Their nest egg was growing—thanks to disciplined saving and the low rent. But in January 2021, a For Sale sign went up across the street that made them realize their bank account would never catch up with Vancouver.

Panned by architecture critics, the Vancouver Special proved popular with many new residents for its utilitarian design, which effectively maximized affordability and living space for extended family.

It was an old three-bedroom bungalow with no garage, listed at just under $1.3 million. The price tag did nothing to deter would-be buyers and real estate agents seduced by a new listing like raccoons by an open compost bin. A telltale parade of new Audis, BMWs, and Land Rovers started cruising down East 37th and hammered home just how far out of reach the Chius' home ownership dream really was.

"This is supposed to be East Van," Martin lamented. But times had changed in the traditionally working-class neighbourhood, and the couple realized they would have to change too. Their savings would allow them to pay a 20 percent deposit on a home up to $300,000. That might have given them a fighting chance at a detached house in East Vancouver back in 2004. Just. But in January 2021 it wasn't even close. One look at the benchmark price (the term used by Canada's five largest real estate boards, who claim it provides a more accurate estimate of typical home prices than average or mean prices) made that obvious. The benchmark price of a detached house in Metro Vancouver was more than $1.5 million that month, while the benchmark price for an apartment was more than $680,000. If the Chius wanted to buy, they'd simply have to look elsewhere.

So they went online and entered a maximum price of $300,000. Nothing showed up in Metro Vancouver, so they zoomed out. Way out. "We kept going and going," Martin remembers, "and we didn't find anything we could afford until we got to Williams Lake." The small city is a six-and-a-half-hour drive away from Vancouver, in good weather, and would make an ideal home for many outdoor enthusiasts. But the Chius had decided they wanted to live in a bigger city for a number of reasons, including the need for reliable high-speed internet because Martin worked from home for a major bank. So they kept looking farther and farther from Vancouver, and were surprised to find several townhouses they could afford in Calgary.

They booked flights to the other side of the Rockies and set off in search of a new home.

The Chius weren't alone. Across Vancouver, thousands of families were feeling the financial squeeze of high housing costs. Stories of dozens of desperate buyers competing for homes became commonplace. Houses, townhomes, and condominiums were routinely sold in bidding wars for hundreds of thousands of dollars over the asking price. Some house hunters got what they were looking for, along with a lot more debt than they had planned to take on. Others had to adjust their expectations, opting for a townhouse instead of a detached home, or resigning themselves to a suburban commute instead of living near the city centre. Some had to give up on home ownership entirely, and continue renting.

Of course, some people are happy to rent. They prefer the freedoms it offers them or they've calculated it's a better financial choice than buying. But as property prices skyrocketed in 2021, rents started to rise in a way they previously hadn't. Then, in 2022, when house prices started to fall, rents kept rising. Like many jurisdictions, British Columbia has legislation that restricts rental increases to a few percent a year. In fact, rents were frozen for much of the pandemic. But BC has no restrictions on landlords raising rents between tenancies. With many property owners who were tempted to sell their rental properties to cash in on record-high prices, a growing number of tenants were starting to worry about their future.

In 2021, approximately 77,000 households in the city of Vancouver were unaffordable, unsuitable, or inadequate, according to a housing report prepared for city council. That doesn't include any of Vancouver's suburbs, which add up to more than half of the metropolitan population. Martin and Nicole Chiu knew they were relatively lucky living in the shared house with Martin's parents, despite watching prices rise out of their reach. They could easily find people who were much worse off, as some of their friends struggled with much higher rents or evictions. The city's housing report pegged the number of homeless in the city of Vancouver at 2,000, with an additional 7,000 people living in single-room occupancy (SRO) hotels—usually dilapidated old buildings in Vancouver's infamous Downtown Eastside. Across the city there was a growing disquiet that the heartbreaking poverty and social dysfunction of Canada's poorest postal code was starting to spread.

Bob Rennie, a real estate marketer who made millions from Vancouver's hot housing market and became known to many as the Condo King, started writing op-eds and speaking in community forums on housing affordability. "We have to do something or we'll have civil unrest if we can't get people into shelter," he said during a panel discussion hosted by the *Vancouver Sun* in 2022. "We're going to have people that are earning minimum wage who are not able to find rental or housing."

Rennie may have been understating the problem, because the housing crisis affects more than just low-income earners, at least among young Vancouverites. Tom Davidoff sees that at the University of British Columbia. An associate professor who specializes in real estate and finance at UBC's Sauder School of Business, he teaches a lot of students who are likely to make elite incomes after they graduate, but even they are anxious about housing in Vancouver. "When I ask a class of students if they're worried about affording a good home, all of them raise their hands." Prices have gone so high in Vancouver, Davidoff says, that "the luxury is having a housing unit at all."

Yes, housing prices have shot up across the whole of Canada. But in Vancouver they've outpaced just about everywhere. In January 2001, the price for a detached house in Metro Vancouver was $345,260. By January 2021, when Martin and Nicole Chiu gave up on their dream of owning a home in their hometown, that price had jumped to $1,576,800. That's an increase of more than 350 percent, while the average cost of all the items measured by Statistics Canada for the official inflation rate went up by just 43 percent over the same period. But there was worse to come. The prices just kept soaring, with the benchmark for a detached house finally peaking at $2,139,200 in April 2022—more than six times what it was in 2001. Even apartments cost a fortune in Vancouver, peaking at $844,700. That's more than nine times the median annual household income in Metro Vancouver of roughly $90,000. More difficult to calculate is the number of young would-be buyers who gave up on their dream of owning a home, or the number of low-income renters evicted because their landlords decided to cash in on record-high prices.

To some extent, this is nothing new. Housing has been expensive in Vancouver for decades because newcomers arrive every year— both immigrants from overseas and migrants from the rest of Canada. Many are drawn by the allure of tranquil ocean currents, old-growth forests, and snow-capped mountains floating above a green city that usually looks as though it's just been washed. Some long-time residents simply shrug off the latest surreal numbers as the cost of living in paradise. Others view the prices as yet more proof the Vancouver housing market is totally disconnected from reality. Of course, many homeowners rejoice to see confirmation that their primary investment continues to grow in value. But others see trouble ahead—more people priced out of the market, more renovictions (the handy new term for the troubling trend of renters being evicted for renovations), and more homelessness.

Homeless encampments have a long history in Vancouver. During the Great Depression, the city became known as the Hobo Capital of Canada. In 1931 as many as twelve thousand people reached the end of the railway line without finding the jobs or fortunes that made them travel in the first place. Instead, they found themselves living in makeshift camps, christened "hobo jungles" by local newspapers. City officials eventually used a typhoid outbreak as the excuse to break up the camps. They sent the men, under threat of arrest, to so-called relief camps, where they provided cheap labour for federal projects like roads and airports. Before they were sent packing, many of those men slept in improvised shelters on the edge of the city dump, where Strathcona Park is now located, and where history was destined to repeat itself.

Martin and Nicole Chiu lived a fifteen-minute drive from Strathcona Park. By the time the couple started to think about leaving Vancouver, hundreds of people were sleeping on the site of the long-forgotten hobo jungle. Many had moved there the previous summer after being forced out of smaller encampments in other parks. Strathcona Park was estimated by some to be the biggest homeless encampment in Canada during the pandemic; it grew into a small city of tents and other makeshift structures. Its residents had to endure cold winter rains, at least one big dump of wet snow, considerable crime, and a fair bit of angry sentiment from some of their housed neighbours. With city parks turning into homeless camps and "tear-down" homes selling for millions of dollars, is it any wonder that housing is usually the main topic of conversation in Vancouver?

Even before he became premier in 2022, David Eby found himself in the unenviable position of having to move beyond talk and actually do something about the crisis. A human rights lawyer who once headed the BC Civil Liberties Association, Eby was named housing minister in 2020. In many ways it was a natural fit. Housing was one of the province's most difficult and pressing issues, and Eby was one of the government's most capable ministers. The lanky lawyer is quick on his feet in interviews. He was also worried about housing before many of his political colleagues came to the issue. That may be natural, given that Eby came of age just as Vancouver's housing market was really starting to rise out of the reach of many in his generation. Furthermore, he was elected in Point Grey, one of Canada's most expensive neighbourhoods. The leafy area of stately single-family homes, comfortable condos, cafés, and beaches has long been out of reach for most people of modest means. But the latest surging prices were shooting the local housing market into the stratosphere. At the peak of the market, in the spring of 2022, single-family houses in Point Grey ranged from a century-old two-bedroom house (listed as "a unique opportunity to kickstart the dream of owning land in one of Vancouver's most desired neighbourhoods") for $1.9 million all the way up to a 19,000-square-foot mansion priced at just under $39 million. The most expensive condominium was listed at $6.9 million, while the bottom end featured a handful of apartments in 1970s co-op buildings that were on the market for half a million dollars each.

In many ways, Vancouver's housing market was a disaster, but Eby was worried it would get worse, even if prices were finally flattening out. He pointed to new statistics that suggested a perfect storm of housing unaffordability: the lowest number of homes for sale since records began, the highest in-migration of people to the province in thirty years, and a national survey that ranked British Columbia as the top pick for Canadians thinking of moving to a new province. Prices in his own neighbourhood were out of control, but that was nothing new. Now the contagion was spreading. In the Fraser Valley, east of Vancouver, the average price of a home had just increased by a jaw-dropping 42 percent in a single year. And prices were rising rapidly in smaller towns too, as many people who'd been forced to work from home during the pandemic realized they could cash in on their expensive big-city houses to work from home in more affordable communities instead.

While some lucky homeowners relocated to greener pastures,

a growing list of cities and towns across the province were seeing homeless camps established by people with nowhere else to go. Strathcona Park and Vancouver were far from alone in witnessing this phenomenon. Victoria, Nanaimo, Surrey, Maple Ridge, Abbotsford, Kelowna, Kamloops, Prince George, and others all saw encampments formed in parks or vacant lots. Some consisted of only a few dozen people. Others had hundreds.

The numbers went up and down as people came and went. Many moved into temporary shelters, including motels the provincial government purchased during the pandemic, a similar strategy to the one being used in Toronto at the same time. While many people had become homeless because of addiction and mental illness, Premier Eby saw a clear link between tent cities and rising house prices. "The reality is if people have more income they just displace lower-income people from the lower-rental housing available through renovictions and demovictions, and the vulnerable end up out on the street."

Eby acknowledged there were many factors contributing to the affordability crisis: years of low interest rates, the rise of short-term vacation rentals displacing long-term renters, an influx of foreign buyers purchasing Canadian properties as long-term investments, criminals using property purchases to launder their money, and suddenly rising interest rates. He was frustrated that many of those problems would need to be addressed by the federal government. But he also realized they all boiled down to one simple equation: too much demand and not enough supply. "What we really need," he concluded, "is to increase the supply of affordable housing."

That's long been a standard refrain in more business-friendly political circles. But David Eby represents the left-of-centre social democratic NDP, which tends to shy away from the mantra that a problem can be solved simply by increasing production. With prices continuing to climb, though, Eby decided that both the government and the private sector would need to supply more housing. "Government can't build all of the housing that we're going to need to house everybody. We need private sector developers to be building housing as well. And they need to be able to do it more quickly and in a more understandable and transparent process that supports city planning and livable communities."

While he was still housing minister, Eby decided the main fix should be to build a lot more housing, and to do it quickly. In his direct line of sight—municipal governments. Eby was convinced that one of the biggest impediments to new construction was municipal zoning regulations that made it either fiendishly difficult or downright impossible to build more housing. Leaving municipal governments free to block so much new construction for so long was an "unforced error," according to associate professor Tom Davidoff, comparing the province's housing strategy to a struggling tennis player. "We've now realized it's untenable for the province to delegate full control of land use to municipalities," he says.

The new premier agreed. "I can understand you don't want a shadow on your property," Eby said, alluding to residents of single-family homes who don't want towers being built nearby. "Or you're concerned about parking. But at the same time . . . you're wondering why your local stores are struggling, and you wonder why your taxes are going up because the expansion is happening out in the suburbs instead of downtown areas, and you wonder why we can't get climate change emissions under control because people have to commute longer and longer distances to work. Well, we're in a real crisis of not building enough housing in the cities, and we're going to need larger systemic solutions."

While Premier Eby focused on supply and demand, some housing advocates insisted he was missing the real problem. Developers build enough housing, they said, but not enough of what they build is affordable. And they pointed to a giant development in Vancouver as proof. The Oakridge Park development is big enough to cover twenty-one soccer pitches, and will create 3,300 individual housing units right in the heart of Vancouver. It took a decade for the developer, Westbank, and the city of Vancouver to settle on a final plan. The city decided to upzone the property—a process of increasing the allowable density on the site. When that was done, the developer was allowed to build more than 3 million square feet of residential space. But only 9 percent of that was set aside for social housing, and 4 percent for what the city considers affordable housing. In the end, 87 percent of the homes in this sprawling new development were priced beyond the financial means of most people in Vancouver who do not already own a home. Housing advocates were critical of Vancouver city councillors for not demanding a higher proportion of both social and affordable housing in the mix. But the deal is done, and luxury condos in the development have been marketed to overseas buyers in Dubai, Shanghai, and beyond. With construction costs soaring and investors lining up, the price of a 1,000-square-foot two-bedroom condo was predicted to be well above $2 million.

Andy Yan, the director of Simon Fraser University's City Program, says developments like this one show what the marketplace is good at, and where it falls short. A registered professional planner, Yan was born and raised in Vancouver and has been studying housing affordability in the city for years. "Yes, Vancouver has a supply problem," he says. "But governments have to understand that the market economy won't provide housing for everybody." Developers are good at building luxury homes, he points out, as well as many studio and one-bedroom condos. But they fall considerably short when it comes to affordable housing and middle-income housing of two and three bedrooms for families in some cities. So while municipal governments must make it easier for developers to build more private market housing, he says the federal government must also make major reinvestments in building public housing—something the federal Liberals all but abandoned when they slashed the budget in 1994. Until all levels of government do more, Yan predicts young families like Martin and Nicole Chiu will continue to leave Vancouver in droves.

In the end, the Chius did find their first home—in Calgary. They bought the three-bedroom townhome for $287,500. "We never thought we'd get to this point," says Nicole, who had all but given up on the dream of owning her own home. Shortly after moving to Calgary, she gave birth to their fourth child, baby Clarke. Leaving Vancouver meant more than saying goodbye to mild winters, the smell of salt air, and a short stroll to Starbucks for coffee. The couple also made the difficult decision to part with grandparents who helped with child care, other family, and friends. But the Christian couple found a church in their new city, and realized they could afford to have Nicole stay at home with the kids full-time. For the Chius, that was the biggest reason to chase their dream of buying an affordable home: it allowed them to live the way they want. "If a couple is working in Calgary," Martin says, "they can get that down payment together. But in Vancouver, it's just crazy! And if you're working those two jobs, how are you having a life as a family, spending time with your kids or your spouse? Can you even have a social life, or community, or a faith community?"

While thousands of other families follow the Chius out of Vancouver, the city is still growing by leaps and bounds. Tom Davidoff at UBC says recent measures by the provincial government will likely provide some much-needed relief, but only to an extent. "Now things will only get somewhat worse, instead of much worse." Davidoff says that's not surprising, given how many factors have contributed to Vancouver's housing woes, and how few of them are directly within the provincial government's control. "They're swimming against a pretty powerful tide, because more people are entering the housing market than the number of new homes being built." With the federal government setting record immigration levels for the next few years, and with more Canadians choosing British Columbia over other provinces as their destination of choice, the squeeze looks likely to continue for years to come.

But while Vancouver is growing, Andy Yan wonders who is staying. "Growth doesn't mean stability," he says. "You look at how many people are able to set [down] roots in Vancouver, and the fact of the matter is that it has become increasingly difficult to do. Vancouver has become the inverse of that song 'Hotel California.' You can come, but you can't stay."

2

PRICED IN

Tokyo

FRI MCWILLIAMS CALLS HERSELF a digital nomad. A professional interpreter based in Tokyo, her work went online during the pandemic, and she can now do a lot of it from anywhere that has a good internet connection. That's left Fri (pronounced "Free") wondering where she should live. Born in Japan in the 1970s to a Japanese mother and a Canadian father, she spent her first fourteen years in Japan before moving to Vancouver to attend high school. She still has many good friends there, and while there isn't as much work for her in Vancouver as in Japan, the digital migration of much of her work has made her think about moving back to Canada. But one of the things that makes her hesitate is the huge difference in costs between the two cities. Simply put—Vancouver is much more expensive than Tokyo.

"My cost of housing would double if I moved to Vancouver," she estimates, based on her experience as both a renter and a homeowner. Fri has called Tokyo home since 2008 and has rented several apartments there for much less money than she'd pay for similar places in Vancouver. Her first apartment was a two-bedroom unit about an hour from central Tokyo that cost less than $900 a month. After the 2011 Tōhoku earthquake she moved to a small studio apartment closer to the centre of the city, costing a little less than $1,000 a month. Not all Tokyo apartments are cheap. Fri once rented a three-bedroom apartment on the thirty-sixth floor and split the rent of roughly $2,800 with her then husband. But paying that much was a choice. If she needed to, Fri knew she could move to a different prefecture and find a clean, safe rental for less than half of what she was paying.

Eventually, Fri decided to buy an apartment. Not because she'd spent years saving, but because prices were so low that it just didn't make sense not to buy. She found a one-bedroom apartment in Tokyo at an affordable price and qualified for a mortgage with a super-low interest rate of 0.9 percent for the first five years, then 1 percent for the duration of a thirty-year mortgage. Some buyers could have qualified for the apartment with no down payment. As a freelancer, Fri was considered higher risk and therefore needed to pay a down payment of $10,000. The monthly mortgage payments cost Fri about $1,000 a month, but she now rents her apartment out for $1,500 a month—a financial spread that's possible because her apartment is in a nice area and because buyer incentives are so generous. The end result is considerable financial freedom that has allowed Fri to embrace her new identity as a "digital nomad." She divides her time between the ski cabin that she inherited in the mountains of Nagano, short stays in a Tokyo hotel, visits to Vancouver, and even a few trips to France. All the while knowing she can either move back into her Tokyo apartment or find an affordable place to rent there. "There's much more choice in Tokyo," she says, "not just a few places that everyone is fighting over."

Fri acknowledges that it's difficult to compare Tokyo and Vancouver because almost everything about the two cities is so different. "Apples to oranges," she says. Or, as one expat on the "Canadians in Japan" Facebook page called it, "apples to concrete." Transportation, apartment size, appliances, furniture, administrative costs, rental customs, and many other housing characteristics are different from one side of the Pacific to the other. The differences are so remarkable that some people who've lived in both say there's no point comparing the two. But Fri knows both cities, and she's confident that "for the same lifestyle it would cost me double to live in Vancouver."

One of the many things that Fri finds remarkable about Tokyo's relative affordability is that rents have stayed essentially the same since she moved back to Japan in 2008—something that's unheard of almost everywhere else. She's kept in touch with old friends from Vancouver and watched from afar as they faced higher and higher housing costs. "It goes through my head a lot," she says, "because I think of going back to Vancouver frequently."

Susan Chen is another Tokyo resident who's thinking of moving to Vancouver. An artist and executive coach who works in English, Japanese, and Mandarin, Susan has no problem paying the $800 monthly rent on her one-bedroom apartment in a Tokyo suburb. She's lived in Tokyo for eight years, but her parents still live in Canada, and her American spouse would like to move to Vancouver to enrol in a post-secondary education program there. So Chen has been scouring rental listings on the other side of the Pacific, and growing more and more appreciative of just how affordable Tokyo is by comparison. "It's very inexpensive," she says. "My rent is just one-quarter of what it would be if I moved to Vancouver."

While she doesn't think she'll stay in Tokyo much longer, Susan says she and her spouse think about it occasionally, and the primary reason is affordability. They sometimes scroll through the @cheap-housesjapan Instagram page to marvel at the inexpensive homes that can be bought there. The account lists hundreds of clean, if dated, Japanese homes for sale, with prices that haven't been listed next to similar Canadian properties in decades. A two-storey cottage in Hachimantai, Iwate—just six kilometres from the nearest ski hill—was listed in late 2022 for US$14,000. A modest one-storey house in the rural town of Tagawa, Fukuoka, was listed for US$19,000. Even in Tokyo, some old homes are listed for less than US$100,000. "It's crazy," Susan says with a laugh, "because when you look at the prices there, sure there might be a range in quality, but if we were willing to renovate an old house, we could buy a house within Tokyo without even a down payment. You can invest as easily as buying a car, that's how easy it is to live in Tokyo!"

It hasn't always been this way. Japan used to be much more expensive than Canada. That was certainly the case when John Hozack followed his girlfriend from Vancouver back to her home in Japan in 1998. "When I first arrived, the cost of living in Japan was much, much higher." That didn't bother John too much at the time. He was in love, and he had a plan. "I chased her over there to marry me, then I'd bring her back and start a career and a family in Canada." John accomplished most of his goals. He married his girlfriend, started a career as a teacher, and had a family too. But two kids and two cats later, he's still in Japan. "I wouldn't come back and live in Canada, because I made a home here. Prices have no effect on me." Still, John can't help but notice the stark differences between costs in Canada and Japan. "I can buy a pint of beer here for five bucks. Meat and vegetables are not much different. Taxes are less here as well. And the health care is far better and cheaper." But the comparison that really jolts John Hozack—and one he feels in his bank account too—is the astonishing difference in housing costs. John and his wife own a new house they built in the industrial city of Amagasaki. They also rent an old house in Yokohama, where John teaches in a private Japanese school. The mortgage payments on their Amagasaki house are about $750 a month, while the monthly rental in Yokohama costs them $600. But they also have to pay rent for their son in Vancouver, where he's a student at the University of British Columbia. That three-bedroom suite costs John's son and his roommates $3,000 a month in total—more than twice their total housing costs on both homes in Japan. "Outside of Tokyo," John Hozack concludes, "Japan is vastly more affordable than Canada."

But even in Tokyo, housing can be much cheaper. Chris Corday has seen that first-hand. The CBC journalist and his Japanese wife moved back to Tokyo from Vancouver in 2021, with their young son, leaving behind the new two-bedroom, two-bathroom condo they'd bought in the swanky downtown neighbourhood of Yaletown— "about the smallest you'd ever want to live in with a kid." They moved to Tokyo in the middle of the COVID-19 lockdown, for Chris's two-year assignment with the Japanese public broadcaster NHK. After enduring a fifteen-day quarantine in a hotel room with their four-year-old son, they moved into a larger home in Tokyo than the one they left in Vancouver. The three-bedroom apartment cost them about $2,400 a month. Chris and Keiko had rented in Tokyo before and knew they could pay less. So, a year later, they downsized to a two-bedroom apartment that cost a little less than $2,000 a month in a nice part of Tokyo, about a fifteen-minute bike ride from the busy Shibuya train station. Like Fri McWilliams and Susan Chen, Chris could find much cheaper rental accommodation if he needed it, and he agrees housing is more affordable in Japan. "I think people here worry a lot less about rent than they do in Canada. I hear it a lot less in conversations." That's not to say the Japanese are without their worries. Wages have stagnated for years in Japan, and

Chris sees members of his wife's family struggle financially. Still, it's difficult to avoid the fact that even with wage concerns, most people in Tokyo and the rest of Japan can keep a roof over their heads. "Some of them are not ideal, and you may have to move an hour away on the same train line, but you can always find a cheap place to live in Tokyo."

If only things were so easy in Vancouver. When his two-year posting at NHK ended in 2023, Chris and his family moved back to Vancouver, and while they counted themselves lucky to have been able to buy the condo before prices hit their peak, they realized that Vancouver wouldn't offer them the same flexibility to move that they enjoyed in Tokyo because there's so much more choice of housing in Japan. "We've talked about selling our Vancouver condo and moving into a townhouse, but where would you move?"

Of course, the obvious question is, why? Why is housing in Tokyo and the rest of Japan so much more affordable than it is in Canada? The simple answer is that Japan has more homes than it needs. Japan's population has been falling for more than a decade now, and it's expected to decline steadily for decades to come. In 2018, Japan had roughly 8.5 million empty homes. Home prices declined steadily from the early 1990s until 2008, and have remained largely flat since then. And while the @cheaphomesjapan Instagram account lists inexpensive homes for sale, other rundown houses are given away for free. The ski cabin that Fri McWilliams inherited was valued at just $10! This demographic situation stands in stark contrast to Canada, of course, which is experiencing record population growth of more than 1 percent a year, due largely to immigration. And while Canada still has many empty dwellings used as secondary homes or vacation properties, our supply isn't keeping up with demand.

So can Canada learn anything from Japan when it comes to housing affordability, given that one country's population is shrinking and the other's is booming? Maybe not at the national level. But Tokyo is another story. While many Japanese towns and cities were emptying out, Tokyo continued to grow. The population in Japan's capital kept growing until 2018, before starting to inch downward in 2019. So how did a megacity that kept adding people keep housing prices flat? The most popular explanation is that Tokyo kept building new homes, and that it built a lot of them. In 2021 Japan recorded more than 850,000 new home starts, a measure of the number of new housing units on which construction started that year. By contrast, Canada had 271,000 new home starts. Japan's population is a little more than triple Canada's, so on a per capita basis the numbers of new homes under construction was similar—one new home per 141 people in Canada, one new home per 146 people in Japan. But remember, Canada is growing at a record pace, and Japan is in a long, slow decline. Yet Japan keeps building new homes, year after year after year.

So how does Japan do it? One popular explanation ties it to a relaxation in development rules across the country in 2002 to make it easier and cheaper for property owners and developers to build new homes. The Urban Renaissance Special Measure Law followed a spectacular housing boom in the 1980s and then bust in the 1990s. Restrictive zoning made it difficult to repurpose vacant office buildings, which in turn made it more difficult for the Japanese government to address a financial crisis brought about by bad loans to building developers. Hiroo Ichikawa, an urban planner and professor at Meiji University in Tokyo, explains, "To help the economy recover from the bubble, the country eased regulation on urban development. If it hadn't been for the bubble, Tokyo would be in the same situation as London or San Francisco." Or Vancouver. Or Toronto. According to a press release from the Japanese prime minister's office, the Urban Renaissance Special Measure Law was designed to "promote measures promptly and in a prioritized manner for the revitalization of urban areas." Put another way, the central government took zoning control away from local governments in one fell swoop. Building and planning laws are now set nationally, leaving local governments with little control over development.

Redevelopment in many Canadian cities often involves years of public hearings and protests from local residents, followed by either significant changes to the proposal or scrapping it altogether. In Tokyo, most developments go ahead as long as they meet the national standards. The end result is more housing, built relatively quickly and cheaply. It's also "spectacularly ugly," according to some visitors, who lament the lack of coordination and the relatively lax building codes. "Some of Tokyo's older apartment buildings give industrial Siberia a dystopian run for its money," Robin Harding of the *Financial Times* moaned. Still, if it's supply you want, then Tokyo has it.

But, once again, Canada and Japan are extremely different. Houses in Japan are much smaller on average than they are in Canada. And in many cases the building standards are lower in Japan. The one notable exception is that seismic requirements in the earthquake-prone nation are second to none. In many ways housing is seen as a disposable commodity in Japan; more people aspire to live in new buildings, and it's more common to replace old buildings with new ones. That's partly due to Japan's ever-evolving seismic standards, and the paramount importance placed on making buildings as safe as possible with new seismic technologies, even if it means tearing down a lot of older buildings.

André Sorensen is a professor of geography and planning at the University of Toronto who has studied urban development in Japan since the 1990s. He believes zoning regulations have played less of a role in making Japan affordable than the country's declining population. And like anyone who's spent a lot of time in both countries, he cautions against trying to make too many simple comparisons between the two. "It's a very different history and economic and demographic context." Still, Sorensen points to another key factor that has helped keep housing in Tokyo affordable, and that he believes is inadequate in Canadian cities like Toronto: public transportation. "One of our real failures in Canada is that we didn't invest nearly enough in transit over fifty years, commensurate with our urban growth." Sorensen says the end result is that housing costs in large cities rise because people can't travel longer distances easily to find cheaper housing. "There's no question a high-speed transit that's highly effective and frequent can have a big impact on availability of lower-cost housing." And that, Sorensen says, is one thing Japan has done exceptionally well. "Their public transit and the railway system are so convenient. It opens up lots of sites. Even if you're in a big city, you can get to where you need to be conveniently and cheaply."

Viewed from Japan, life in Canada's big cities looks neither convenient nor cheap. Jonathan Wakrat lives with his wife and young child in a pleasant two-bedroom apartment in Setagaya City. The peaceful residential area is full of parks, museums, shops, and places to eat. "The food is excellent and cheap! A set lunch costs just ten bucks!" A healthy *onigiri* (Japanese rice ball) for his daughter costs less than a toonie. As for getting around, Jonathan says it's easy. He lives a twelve-minute walk from the subway and can always find an affordable e-bike or e-scooter to rent if he's in a rush. Jonathan and his wife pay more in rent than most Tokyo residents—about $2,200 a month. But that gives them a good apartment with ample space in a nice neighbourhood. They know a lot of people in Tokyo who pay a lot less. While Jonathan and his wife can afford a comfortable lifestyle in Tokyo, they can also afford to have one of them spend most of their time at home with their daughter. When his wife goes to work, Jonathan gets their daughter out the door to go to the local free daycare. Trained as a teacher, with a master's degree in education, Jonathan now spends most of his time with his family or doing occasional gigs as a stand-up comic in Tokyo's English-language comedy clubs. He grew up in Montreal, and has lived in other big cities like Shanghai and Toronto. "I was angry in Canada a lot because of what I had to pay. They nickel and dime you hard in Toronto!" Jonathan grew up thinking Tokyo was the world's most expensive city, but now he looks back home and wonders if he could afford to return to Toronto.

Despite the high costs of housing in Canada, Jonathan would like to come home. Japan isn't home for either him or his wife, who is from Taiwan. As much as Toronto's prices make him mad, he appreciates how multicultural the city is, and he says his wife found it extremely welcoming. Fri McWilliams also likes Canada's more open cultural mix. "I don't always feel welcome here in Japan. I get told in Japanese to go home. But in Vancouver there's just an assumption that everyone has a different background." Similarly, Susan Chen feels unsure about staying in Tokyo. A self-described "third culture kid," she's well acquainted with feeling uncertain about where, exactly, home is. Her parents still live in Canada, but "it's almost like nowhere would ever be completely home because everywhere you are, there will be people that you love and care about who aren't there." All of them are drawn to the good things about Canada. But all find the rising costs of housing hard to accept. "I just don't understand why I'm paying a premium for Toronto," Jonathan Wakrat jokes. "The juice isn't as good as the squeeze!"

3

SHATTERED DREAMS

Golden Horseshoe

POORNIMA MALISETTY LIVES in a comfortable detached house in Brampton, one of the small towns that grew into a big Toronto suburb in the 1950s as the city stretched over the surrounding countryside. Now home to more than 600,000 people, Brampton is one of Canada's fastest-growing cities. But Poornima didn't mind all the construction because of the opportunity it provided her family. She lives with her husband, their two children, and her husband's two aging parents. Her in-laws were finding it more and more difficult to walk up and down stairs, and as Poornima watched all the building around her, she had an idea. Maybe they could find a new house with a ground-floor suite for her parents-in-law. When pre-sales for a new subdivision in west Brampton hit the market in the fall of 2021, Poornima and her husband took the plunge and committed to a pre-purchase agreement for a new house. It was part of a new development called Valley Oak. The builder, Paradise Developments, boasted of "luxury detached homes" in an established infill community. Poornima's previous house had been built by the same company; she was impressed with the quality, and so was drawn to the new development.

The new house wouldn't be finished for another year and a half, and it wouldn't be cheap. The total price they agreed to pay was $1.9 million. But the couple had money in the bank thanks to two "upper-middle-class" salaries and some of the proceeds from the sale of their first home. They paid a deposit of $250,000—"our life-time savings"—and looked forward to the day they would move into their new home. "It was a lot of money, but at that time, at that rate, we thought it was affordable." Poornima was especially excited about the ground-floor suite for her in-laws. "They would be able to live in the in-law suite on the main floor, because they cannot climb stairs. So that's why I bought this house."

The couple had another reason for wanting to buy: their kids. The area is known locally for its good schools. But Poornima was also thinking about their adult years, and her growing concern that they might never be able to afford homes of their own if prices kept rising the way they had been. "We thought, if we don't buy it now, our kids will never be able to buy for themselves in the future."

If that seems like an irrational fear, remember that home prices in the Greater Toronto Area were going through the roof in 2021. The Toronto Real Estate Board reported intense demand and a record-high average selling price of $1,095,475—an increase of nearly 18 percent in just one year. And that was just the latest in many years of price rises. Across Ontario, the average price of a home went up 180 percent in ten years—while average incomes grew just 38 percent. Not surprisingly, those rising prices led to lower rates of home ownership, especially among young people. Only 25 percent of Torontonians in their thirties own homes, compared with roughly two-thirds of all Canadian households who owned their home in 2021.

There's also a glaring discrepancy along racial lines, with Black and Indigenous home ownership rates being less than half of the provincial average in Ontario. Rapidly rising prices weren't going to fix that.

At the peak of the market, in early 2022, the average price of a detached house in the Toronto area surpassed $1.5 million. It was a seller's market, to put it mildly. Homeowners who listed their properties for prices that would have seemed preposterous just a few years earlier received multiple bids over the asking price. Bidding wars generated dozens of competing offers, with final sale prices hundreds of thousands of dollars over the asking price. Poornima wasn't the only one who worried her family would soon be priced out of the market entirely. But the timing of her decision to buy a house that hadn't yet been built couldn't have been much worse.

Less than five months later, the Bank of Canada raised its overnight lending rate from 0.25 to 0.5 percent, citing "the unprovoked invasion of Ukraine by Russia" and the corresponding rise in oil and commodity prices as a "major new source of uncertainty." That single rate hike was manageable for most Canadians. But by the end of the year, the Bank of Canada had hiked rates six more times, and more would follow in the new year. The interest rate had soared from 0.25 percent at the start of the year to 4.25 percent by the end. For Poornima Malisetty and her husband, it was just too much. "Now we are in serious trouble."

She wasn't the only one. In that one development alone, about one hundred other buyers were caught in a similar financial dilemma. The rapid rise in interest rates had hit them in two ways. First, it raised their monthly mortgage payments. "I work and my husband works and we have two kids," Poornima explained. "So with the interest rates now, the monthly payments will come out to $10,000. I'm just not sure how we can afford that." Second, the rising rates brought resale prices down and assessment values along with them, all of which meant financial institutions would suddenly loan homeowners a lot less. The house that Poornima and her husband had agreed to buy for $1.9 million in their purchase agreement was now assessed at $1.6 million. As a result, the bank decided it would shrink the mortgage it offered the couple by the same amount. That left them searching for an additional $300,000 on top of the $10,000 monthly mortgage payments they couldn't afford to pay. "Even if we won the lottery," she sighs, "we wouldn't be able to close." With their life savings of $250,000 hanging in the balance, Poornima and her husband were consumed with worry. "We are not able to sleep. We are not able to eat. It's been six months since we all slept properly." Other buyers had similar struggles. Poornima befriended a pregnant woman who told her the stress over the purchase had proved too much for her husband, who had asked for a divorce. "I feel like crying when I see her there with her toddler, and there she is with a baby in her tummy!"

Another buyer, real estate agent Gurpreet Sander, heard similar stories. One man told him his home's appraised value had dropped by $400,000. Once again, the bank cut the total amount of the mortgage, leaving the buyer to find an additional $400,000, on top of the $400,000 down payment he'd already paid. "It's an extremely difficult situation for everyone." Gurpreet organized dozens of buyers into an informal group that asked the builder for a price reduction. But the builder wouldn't budge. "Paradise Developments makes business decisions, enters into contracts with suppliers, hires employees and commits to the contracting of numerous building trades based on agreements we have signed," the company said in a statement.

The homebuyers didn't hear a lot of sympathy coming from the general public either. When Toronto media reported their story, Poornima and other buyers faced a backlash on social media. "Everybody is saying that we are greedy and that's why we bought this house, and that it is our fault to agree to such a high price. But we were thinking if we don't pay this higher amount right now, our children might not be able to buy a house ever in their lives."

The response was even nastier for other buyers. One young father who was working two jobs told me that many online critics called him a criminal because he could afford to buy a new house. "There were so many videos and comments online [saying] that I must be a drug dealer," he recalled. "My wife was worried and I was worried because we thought that could get us in trouble."

While the Valley Oak buyers tried to negotiate with the developer, local real estate agents were quick to point out that pre-construction purchases are especially risky because of the potential for prices to drop before the house is built. Of course, many real estate agents frown on pre-construction purchases because agents are often not necessarily required in transactions between buyers and builders. But even existing homeowners were going under.

Mortgage broker Elan Weintraub saw it in many clients who bought existing homes with variable rate mortgages. "They bought in March and thought, 'My monthly payments of $2,000 are fine.' But then, nine months later, it's grown to $3,500, and they're saying, 'Holy shit!'" Elan admits the market turned into a frenzy in 2021. But he says many buyers felt exactly like Poornima Malisetty—if they didn't buy now, they might never get another chance. "People were thinking, 'If I don't buy today for a million, it's going to be $1.3 million and I'll never be able to afford a property in my life.'" Despite the frenzy, Elan says he saw many buyers who acted as prudently as possible under the circumstances. But when interest rates went up, and kept going up, there was nothing they could do. "It just went up beyond belief."

Across southern Ontario, homeowners were going under. In Newmarket, another satellite city of Toronto, Syed Mubarak and his wife had to renew their fixed-rate mortgage in December 2022.

Their $4,000 monthly mortgage payments ballooned to $6,500, two-thirds of which went straight to interest. Mubarak took on a second full-time job to cover the extra costs, working eighty hours a week. Syed and his wife had hoped to start a family when they first moved in, but decided to wait because of rising mortgage costs. "When am I going to really have time to spend with my child?"

In Richmond Hill, another suburban city of Toronto, Mehdi Amari and his wife were approaching the end of their four-year fixed-term mortgage, and were shocked to learn the higher rates would cost them an extra $1,200 a month. The couple could have broken their mortgage earlier, but that would have cost them $18,000 in penalties. They decided to wait and hope for no further interest rate increases. In the end, that decision cost them more.

In London, Kartik Soni watched his variable-rate mortgage rate jump from 1.54 percent to 3.79 percent in just a few months. His monthly mortgage payments rose from around $1,900 to about $2,500, just as his monthly grocery bill increased by several hundred dollars. Kartik has a good job at a bank and hoped his wife could find a similar job to help them deal with rising costs. "So keeping my fingers crossed, if she gets a good job or maybe a decent job, we'll be able to survive. Otherwise, it will be really difficult."

In Toronto, Rebecca Cossar had locked in her mortgage at a low rate of less than 2 percent in early 2021. Two years later, when she had to renew, her payments nearly quadrupled. "Which means everything you pay down in a month, instead of going to capital, is just going to interest. So you're just literally standing still. It's very depressing. And I'm not young. I've had my mortgage for years."

While many long-time homeowners worried about simply paying interest, others worried about losing their homes entirely. In Kitchener, 62-year-old Anita Gupta and her husband realized they couldn't afford the higher payments that would follow their mortgage renewal. Anita has fibromyalgia, and neither her disability support payment nor her husband's pension would cover the higher costs. The only option, she said, was to sell their house.

Jeff Dakers faced a similar situation in Barrie. Jeff had owned homes for years, and saw prices and rates go up and down as he watched his kids grow up. But 2022 was different. "This change came on so fast that it blindsided us." Jeff and his wife still had a mortgage, after borrowing against the equity in their home several times over the years. "It's almost like a trap," he laments. Still, he had a good job selling high-end windows to big property developers, and the couple's house was nice. The four-bedroom home included a two-bedroom suite, a finished basement, and a two-car garage. It backed onto a green space in a nice neighbourhood, and its value had been rising steadily for years. So Jeff and his wife thought they were okay. But it quickly became obvious they were not.

As interest rates kept rising, For Sale signs started popping up around the neighbourhood, just as the couple's one-year mortgage was coming up for renewal. Because Jeff is self-employed and is paid on commission, he wasn't eligible for a mortgage from one of the big banks. That meant he had to turn to so-called B lenders, who offer about 20 percent of all mortgages in Canada. They're typically aimed at borrowers with more risky income, and are usually shorter and more expensive. That was the case for Jeff. The mortgage agreement he signed in 2021 was pegged at a little less than 3 percent. A year later, it looked as though he might have to pay as much as 9 percent. That would translate into monthly mortgage payments of $5,500, on top of monthly taxes of $500. "Yeah, I started to freak out a little bit, you know? I thought, well, we're going to have to change some things." The couple thought carefully about what to do next, but they didn't wait long. Before their mortgage term expired, they signed on with a local real estate agent and put their house up for sale. Jeff says they priced the home about $50,000 lower than what they thought they might get, to generate interest. It worked. They had three offers in just a few days, and sold the house to an investor for a few thousand dollars over the asking price. The buyer then agreed to rent the house to Jeff and his wife. After a few months of living in the home as a renter, Jeff was philosophical. He no longer had to worry about doing repairs himself, and his monthly housing costs had actually gone down a little. On the other hand, he no longer had the home equity that once comforted him. "But then again, what equity we did have was starting to disappear quickly."

While thousands of homes went on the market in Ontario in 2022, they couldn't hide the essential problem that the province doesn't have enough homes. The Ontario government said 100,000 new homes were under construction in 2021, the highest number since 1987. But several studies showed the province needed anywhere between 471,000 and 650,000 more homes that year, and that the shortage would only get worse. Canada Mortgage and Housing Corporation forecast Ontario would need more than 2 million additional houses by 2031 to balance supply and demand. The Housing Task Force set up by the provincial government put that number at only 1.5 million. And a study from the Smart Prosperity Institute at the University of Ottawa agreed 1.5 million new houses would be needed. But even 1.5 million new homes in a decade is an extremely aggressive target. By comparison, Ontario added only 620,465 new private dwellings (which include detached homes, apartments, and everything in between) from 2011 to 2021, according to census figures.

It's worth noting that it can be difficult to estimate future housing needs. At least, it can be more difficult than simply predicting population growth. That's because population and the number of households in any given community don't always have a tidy relationship. If a family welcomes a new baby, for instance, the population rises but the total number of households does not. Conversely, when an eighteen-year-old leaves home, the total number of households goes up while the population remains the same. To make matters more complicated, when demand is significantly greater than supply, it's difficult to calculate how many unrealized households there are. How many grown children have simply resigned themselves to living with their parents and given up on any desire to have a home of their own? Still, reasonable estimates of future housing demand can be made. But Mike Moffatt, the lead author of the Smart Prosperity Institute report, says all three levels of government have fallen short. Moffatt is also an economist and assistant professor at the Ivey Business School. He says the Ontario housing market was reasonably affordable until 2015, when the province's population growth started to surge due to a significant increase in immigration.

In its final year in office, Stephen Harper's Conservative government started to welcome more newcomers, and Justin Trudeau's Liberals followed suit when they formed government. In 2014–15 Canada welcomed 240,763 immigrants. That increased to 323,192 the following year. By 2021 Canada saw 492,984 new arrivals. In 2022 a million people arrived—an all-time record. This had a pronounced effect in Ontario—which already received more immigrants than any other province—because the surge in immigration started at the same time as a serious downturn in oil prices that made many immigrants choose Ontario over Alberta and Saskatchewan, and made many Ontarians who'd moved west go back home. Mike Moffatt says Ontario's population growth rate "almost doubled overnight, but we really didn't change how we were building housing. That led to the shortage we have today." He points to the official community plans in many Ontario cities that call for the construction of only half the new homes that will be needed by 2031, and describes that disconnect as a classic Canadian problem where different levels of government are working at cross-purposes. "We have three levels of government, all kind of operating on their own, and the whole system lacks coordination." The end result is a lack of decisive action on new home construction.

If nothing else, the federal government at least acknowledged the scale of the problem in its 2022 budget. Finance Minister Chrystia Freeland—whose Toronto riding of University-Rosedale has some of the most expensive homes in the country—said the "core problem" is a lack of housing stock across the country. And she went a step further, acknowledging the role that the rising population had in soaring house prices. "We cannot have the fastest growing population in the G7," she said, "without having the fastest growing housing stock." Freeland even acknowledged some of the panic that many parents felt about their children's future, and the fear that they might not be able to buy a home of their own in the future, calling it an "intergenerational injustice." The 53-year-old said, "We had a better shot at buying a home and starting a family than young people today, and we cannot have a Canada where the rising generation is shut out of the dream of home ownership." Over the next few months, the federal government promised to spend tens of billions of dollars on several initiatives designed to double construction over a decade with several initiatives, like the Housing Accelerator Fund. A year later it pledged $15 billion in new low-cost loans for affordable apartment construction starting in 2025. It remains to be seen how much those will accomplish, and as Mike Moffatt noted, all three levels of government have a key role to play on housing.

A few weeks after Chrystia Freeland tabled the federal budget in 2022, the housing crisis was back in the spotlight in Ontario's election campaign. Polling showed the issue was among voters' biggest concerns. Doug Ford's Progressive Conservatives campaigned for re-election on a promise to build 1.5 million new homes over ten years by "cracking down and punishing land and housing permit speculators who are artificially choking the supply of new homes and driving costs up." The PCs were returned to office in an election that saw the lowest voter turnout in Ontario history, giving Doug Ford another four years to do something about the housing crisis.

A few months later, Premier Ford and Housing Minister Steve Clark announced they had found a partial solution to the housing crisis that would accommodate the construction of 50,000 new homes. The problem was that it was located in the Greenbelt, the essential ribbon of protected land that winds its way from Niagara Falls up to Peterborough through farms, forests, wetlands, and watersheds. The Greenbelt Plan was created in 2005 by provincial government legislation in an effort to guard against urban sprawl into environmentally sensitive land. Some 810,000 hectares had been off limits to development for years, but the province now wanted to pull about 3,000 hectares out of the Greenbelt in the Greater Toronto and Greater Hamilton areas. In the past, Ford had promised not to touch the Greenbelt, and the announcement set off a series of protests.

Nonetheless, the province moved quickly on the plan, while acknowledging the significant opposition. "There was strong support for continued Greenbelt protections," a government statement conceded, "and broad opposition to any removals or redesignation of lands . . . numerous submissions asserted that the proposal is contradictory to the vision and goals of the Greenbelt Plan."

Opposition politicians accused the Ford government of being more interested in its wealthy donors—property developers who could build expensive new homes if land was taken out of the Greenbelt—than in the many Ontarians who were desperate for an affordable home. The province's auditor general investigated, and found the process of deciding which land to pull out of the Greenbelt was heavily influenced by a group of well-connected developers who stood to make a fortune. "The process was biased in favour of certain developers and landowners who had timely access to the housing minister's chief of staff," Bonnie Lysyk concluded. Less than two weeks later, the housing minister's chief of staff, Ryan Amato, resigned. Ontario's integrity commissioner J. David Wake concluded the process of selecting lands to be removed was marked by "unnecessary hastiness and deception," and Steve Clark resigned as housing minister less than a month later. Premier Doug Ford eventually reversed his government's decision to remove land from the Greenbelt, calling it a mistake and saying he was "very, very sorry." The new housing minister, Paul Calandra, went a step further by introducing legislation to return the land to the Greenbelt and requiring any future changes to be made through legislation instead of regulation, which would make it more difficult to change Greenbelt boundaries in the future. But that didn't put the matter to rest. Two weeks later the RCMP revealed it had launched an investigation into the Greenbelt land swap. While police looked for answers, a troubling question remained in this region whose population is projected to keep growing steadily for decades: Would building badly needed new homes make it necessary to cut down more trees and build over more farms? Environmentalists insisted the answer was no. "There is not the slightest hint of evidence or any reason to expect that bulldozing the Greenbelt land will do anything to reduce the housing shortage, let alone home prices," Phil Pothen, with the advocacy group Environmental Defence, said. Gil Peñalosa—an urban planner and runner-up in Toronto's 2022 mayoral election—agrees there is still enough urban land to house many more people, without touching the Greenbelt. He called for a "renovation revolution" that would create more housing on existing lots by ending single-family exclusionary zoning and replacing it with the right to build as many as six housing units on every lot. That could add a lot of housing, while protecting a lot of nearby farmland at the same time. That's no insignificant point. Between 2016 and 2021, Ontario lost roughly 319 acres of farmland every day. Apart from feeding millions of people in a growing region, the province's farms provide habitat for species at risk as well as jobs for more than 860,000 people.

The Ford government's own Housing Affordability Task Force—the same one that concluded the province would need 1.5 million more homes by 2031—said a shortage of land in southern Ontario is not the problem. "Land is available," the report concluded, "both inside the existing built-up areas and on undeveloped land outside greenbelts. We need to make better use of land. Zoning defines what we can build and where we can build. If we want to make better use of land to create more housing, then we need to modernize our zoning rules." Instead of building on protected land, the Housing Task Force said it agreed with the many planners, municipal councillors, and developers who said "as-of-right zoning"—the ability to bypass long consultations on zoning bylaw amendments—is the most effective tool to address housing supply. That message is starting to get through at both the municipal and provincial levels. In 2023, the cities of Toronto and Victoria made significant changes that would essentially end single-family zoning, and the British Columbia government imposed similar measures on most larger municipalities in the province. It's too soon to say whether the changes will increase supply to the extent that is needed. But other cities in other countries have already made these changes, as we will see, and their experiences offer valuable insights for Canadians. Whatever means end up being the most effective, Ontario's provincial Housing Task Force insists the end goal is crystal clear: "If we want more Ontarians to have housing, we need to build more housing in Ontario."

4

DREAMS RENEWED

Paris

CATHERINE CORTINOVIS FELT OVERWHELMED when she moved into her brand-new studio apartment in central Paris. "When I visited for the first time, I cried." Catherine is a retired executive assistant who worked with business elites for many years but could never afford to live like one herself. There was no reason to think that would change on her modest retirement income. But things have been changing in Paris in recent years, in a big way. That's why Catherine could move into a beautiful new studio apartment above a luxury department store. It's not big—31 square metres (333 square feet). But what it lacks in space, it makes up for in amazing views from both the large bay windows and the long balcony. It's also affordable. The monthly rent is €700, which includes all utilities and fees. An apartment that size would typically cost more than €1,000 in the private market, though one with such impressive views would cost much more. "Without social assistance, I could never afford such an apartment." The social assistance Catherine refers to is a renewed focus on public housing that's transforming the French capital and the lives of many of the people who live there.

Catherine's new home is one of ninety-six affordable units that were built on top of La Samaritaine. The iconic Parisian department store occupied a prominent position in the heart of the French capital for more than a century. But by 2005 it was well past its prime and was closed for "safety reasons." It took sixteen years to renovate the monumental institution. But when it reopened in 2021, La Samaritaine symbolized more than just the rebirth of a luxury retailer. It was an inadvertent reflection of a building boom that is rejuvenating Paris's housing market, and a demonstration of how an old city can reimagine itself for the future.

Rising up from the banks of the Seine and stretching back to the rue de Rivoli, La Samaritaine occupies four buildings just a block away from the Louvre. The store's name came from an ancient water pump on the nearby Pont Neuf bridge that featured a sculpture of a Samaritan woman pouring water for Christ. But while a good Samaritan would have represented charity to the city's many church-going residents, La Samaritaine department store symbolized opulence, wealth, and privilege. The store's name was etched across its exterior wall on giant enamel panels featuring brightly coloured letters that beckoned shoppers inside the eleven-storey retail destination. Once inside, they could test the store's motto—*On trouve tout à la Samaritaine* (One can find everything at La Samaritaine)—and marvel at the building itself. A riveted steel frame supported an enormous glass roof decorated in the art nouveau style. The different sections of the sprawling retail complex were joined by an array of facades built from steel, glass, and glazed lava stone. The store was remodelled in art deco in the 1920s, just as it surpassed one billion francs in total sales. It remained an institution in France for the rest of the century and was even named a UNESCO World Heritage Site in 1991. But by that point the *grand magasin* had been losing money for twenty years, and would continue to do so until its closure.

When it finally reopened in 2021, La Samaritaine boasted almost every luxury imaginable in a modern retail experience—coats, cosmetics, spas, salons, gloves, hats, watches, jewellery, and much more—as well as beautifully renovated historic architectural fixtures and a giant new undulating wall of glass. It also featured ninety-six brand-new affordable apartments for average Parisians to call home.

La Samaritaine, the iconic Parisian department store, now with new affordable homes on the top floors.

There's no denying that a luxury department store and affordable housing are a strange pairing. After all, La Samaritaine is now owned by luxury goods company LVMH—whose chair, Bernard Arnault, was listed as the world's richest person in 2023, with a net worth of $164 billion. The company didn't need affordable housing to pay for the renovation. It did, however, need to offer housing for average Parisians in order to win government approval for its renovation plans. For the lucky residents—who include a garbage collector, an interpreter, and a teacher—the new apartments and stunning views of the Eiffel Tower, the Louvre, and Sacré-Coeur seemed a miracle.

Zina Hadjab couldn't believe her luck to be moving into such a nice new home with her husband, Julien, and their two teenaged daughters, Sefora and Camellia. "We had a lucky star!" Zina had applied for public housing five years earlier, just as new construction in Paris was beginning to pick up. "I never would have imagined living in the centre of Paris," she says. "I was expecting an apartment in the 18th, 19th, or even 20th arrondissement." Zina works as a nursing assistant in the neurology department at Saint-Antoine hospital, about four kilometres away from her new home. She used to live in the suburb of Noisy-le-Grand, roughly twenty kilometres away from the hospital, and spent about two hours a day commuting. Moving to central Paris meant she could sell her car. But Zina says her commute isn't the only improvement. Her new home is what's known in Paris as a T4, which typically contains one living room and three bedrooms. It's about 80 square metres (about 860 square feet) and includes a bright loggia, essentially a covered balcony, that is 20 square metres (about 215 square feet). "It's another life for us and our daughters. We have the feeling of being alone in the world up there, and everything is nearby." Zina's monthly rent is an affordable €1,400, which is more than the average rents her neighbours pay, due to her higher income category. Her only complaint—the near-constant temptation of delicious fresh-baked pastries on every corner when she steps outside.

For a cleaner named Fouleimata, her new home in La Samaritaine changed her life. Before she moved there, she shared a tiny studio apartment in the suburb of Clichy, just outside the 18th arrondissement, with her husband and three children, aged eleven, three, and sixteen months. Not only does her family now enjoy the added space and views of the Louvre, but Fouleimata believes her children will benefit from good local schools. "It is indeed a chance for us, for the education of our children too."

One of Fouleimata's neighbours, Nadia, is equally excited about what her new home and its location will mean for her teenaged daughters. "I had just divorced, and although I'm a teacher, I was facing real precariousness and difficulty finding stable housing." As a mother, Nadia also appreciates living in what's considered a safe neighbourhood. "In this district, I have complete confidence when my daughters go out."

On average, tenants of these subsidized homes paid €430 a month for a studio apartment and €929 for three-bedroom units. A quarter of the ninety-six apartments were set aside for people coming from precarious living arrangements, half were reserved for people with very low incomes, and the final quarter were made available to people who make too much money to qualify for social housing but not enough to afford local rents in the private market.

You might wonder whether the ninety-six affordable apartments built on top of a luxury department store are simply a strange quirk, and not reflective of any wider trend. But while the development is certainly unique, those affordable apartments are part of a much bigger building boom in and around Paris that started in 2015 and has flooded the market with hundreds of thousands of new homes.

Paris is still an expensive city. The average monthly rent for a 50-square-metre (538-square-foot) apartment was €1,200 in 2021. But after years of steep rises in rent, the financial curve started to flatten as supply caught up with demand. By 2021, the growth in rents had slowed to just 0.8 percent. At the same time, the French capital had succeeded in making 25 percent of all housing accessible to people living on lower incomes. It then raised its target to 40 percent by 2035. That will take a lot of renovation and repurposing of old buildings, beyond venerable department stores. Aging hotels, offices, even parkades could be converted into housing. Ian Brossat is the city's deputy mayor and housing commissioner. He's also a national spokesperson for the French Communist Party. "Do we want to make Paris a city that would be a citadel reserved for the privileged? Or do we want to make Paris a city that allows the people who run it to actually live there? That's a choice we must make. Of course, it has a cost."

The Île-de-France region, which includes Paris and surrounding suburbs and towns, is home to 12.2 million people. Construction in the region had slowed considerably since the 1970s, and between 1994 and 2014 was averaging 43,000 new housing units every year. In 2017 more than 98,000 new homes were built, one-third of which were social housing units. By comparison, New York City permitted only 20,000 new housing units that year, and London only 19,000. So how did the French do it? How did they double housing construction in an old, densely populated metropolis where city planners in 2011 were described as "morose, arguing that construction can only fall further behind in the coming years"? The short answer is that French governments decided they had to work together to do something about it.

The Parisian turnaround wasn't the result of one single change or measure. Yonah Freemark, of the Urban Studies and Planning Department at the Massachusetts Institute of Technology, attributes the change to four complementary government policies implemented by various levels of government. Together, he writes, they offer "a model for other regions looking to identify appropriate policies to spur construction." The first policy was a concerted effort to build more public housing—a lot more. The second was for all levels of government and public agencies to make public land available for new housing construction, along with new business hubs and metro and train stations. The third key change was a series of financial and regulatory incentives that coaxed more developers to build even more units. And the final change Freemark identifies was the decision by the national and regional governments to essentially take control away from municipalities by imposing new construction quotas and enforcing them.

It's important to note that Freemark rejects any suggestion that what happened in Paris and the rest of Île-de-France was simply a reflection of outside economic conditions. He notes that the pace of construction doubled in Île-de-France while it remained flat in the rest of France, and in other comparable international cities like London and New York. "The increase can't be explained by outside factors, but was a direct result of government policies."

The first policy, as mentioned, was a renewed concentration on building more publicly funded social housing. That's nothing new in France. For the three decades following the Second World War, the country built hundreds of thousands of new homes, usually in outer suburbs, and often in giant *grands ensembles*—the brutalist concrete towers that were meant to serve as avenues towards more prosperous housing for new arrivals and disadvantaged racialized communities but instead ended up being dead ends. The economic slowdown of the 1970s brought the building boom to an end, and the often isolated towers became ghettoized.

By 2015, more than a million public housing units remained in Île-de-France, and national, regional, and municipal governments decided hundreds of thousands more were needed. The governments turbocharged new construction by reducing the Value Added Tax on new public housing projects, waiving property taxes for developers, and reimbursing local governments for the lost revenue.

They also made low-interest loans readily available from the national public investment bank, the Caisse des Dépôts. That was the carrot. The French government also gave itself a giant stick. It required all local governments in the region to build more affordable social housing until it composed at least 30 percent of their total housing stock by 2030. Every community with more than 1,500 people was told it must increase its share of social housing to 25 percent by the year 2025—or else.

The second measure was to free up more land for new home construction by identifying publicly held properties. Government-owned land was used for not only housing construction but also economic development through the construction of new metro stations and business hub areas. For example, the SNCF railway built 8,000 units on seven sites previously used for railway infrastructure.

The third component was the raft of financial and regulatory changes, including the previously mentioned financing of more public housing and the waiving of property taxes. It included narrower measures, such as reduced taxes on the construction of "intermediary" housing—housing for people who earn too much to qualify for subsidies but could not afford to pay full market rates. It also included property tax exemption and financial incentives for builders to include social housing units. The French government introduced changes to the National Building Code—adjusting height restrictions in some cases, eliminating minimum sizes in others—which reduced construction costs for many projects.

Finally, the French government established quotas for new home construction, which it imposed on local governments. It tracked the data carefully and imposed strict fines on municipalities that didn't keep up. According to French officials whom Freemark interviewed for his study, "this threat encouraged cities to accelerate social-housing projects."

One of the many remarkable aspects of the French building boom is that it was achieved primarily through infill. The pace of new construction sped up noticeably more quickly in Paris and its inner suburbs than it did in the outer suburbs. It's one thing to ramp up new home construction by paving over farmland, another thing entirely to build hundreds of thousands of new units in countless urban nooks and crannies. Following the National Assembly's 2010 law that required the construction of 70,000 new housing units a year in Île-de-France, the region itself passed a law in 2013 that protected the greenbelt that circles much of the Paris region. Yonah Freemark concludes that the "effort to spur construction was thus not primarily predicated on the bulldozing of natural and agricultural land."

The Parisian housing renaissance was changing life for many renters, and new arrivals noticed. Patty Rowe moved from London to Paris. She works in marketing, and had planned to stay only one year in the French capital when she first arrived. Her initial impressions only reinforced that. She found the long-term rental market very competitive—a "flat-hunting horror"—with dozens of people lined up outside shoebox apartments, clutching rental applications and hoping for the best. But Patty eventually found a decent rental, where she lived during the pandemic. The rent was low enough that she could afford to buy a one-bedroom apartment for €350,000 on the Canal Saint-Martin, a trendy area popular with young people along the 4.5-kilometre waterway that connects the northeast of Paris to the Seine. The area boasts low rents and lots of restaurants. "I've got a dozen bars on my doorstep," Patty says, "and I feel like the area is on the up." In her new apartment, Patty says she "can't imagine leaving now. I think I can have a much higher living standard here than in London."

The quantity of new housing is crucial, but the quality of the housing is also important and affects people's day-to-day lives. In the suburb of Romainville, 65-year-old retiree Daniel Henry moved into a new three-bedroom condominium apartment that cost the same as a two-bedroom apartment. He could do so thanks to a new program called "real solidarity lease." The principal is relatively simple. Henry bought the apartment but not the land. Instead, he has a 99-year lease on the land, and pays a modest monthly fee to the non-profit organization that owns the land. In turn, the non-profit pays less tax to the government that incentivized the program. The end result is that the apartment costs roughly 30 percent less than it would in a traditional purchase arrangement. Instead of saving the money, Daniel decided to buy a bigger apartment for himself, his wife, and their son. He loves the four-storey building, which features an old and familiar feature of Paris, the grey zinc roof. Daniel likes the modest size of the building and the fact that it's walking distance to nice shops and a new metro line. The apartment itself is a corner unit that offers a nice double exposure, with windows shaded by bright-orange awnings.

Architect Jean-Baptiste Marie, the executive director of the non-profit group l'Europe des Projets Architecturaux et Urbains, agrees supply is important. But he says it's "essential to also work on the quality of supply so that people settle more permanently into their homes and that there are fewer moves." He believes modern, comfortable homes that stay warm in the winter and cool in the summer, and offer an outdoor space such as a balcony or loggia, are crucial.

That's exactly the approach architects Anne Lacaton and Jean-Philippe Vassal took with an old apartment tower called Bois-le-Prêtre. Built between 1959 and 1962 as a public housing project, the sixteen-storey tower had ninety-six uninspiring apartments near the boulevard Périphérique, the busy freeway that circles Paris. Half a century after it was built, the tower was showing its age and looked a likely candidate for demolition. But Lacaton and Vassal reimagined it instead. They designed a self-supporting structure around the outside of the building that allowed the addition of closable terraces and balconies, and effectively enlarged the living space of each apartment. The change also opened up magnificent views of the City of Light that were barely visible in many corners of the original utilitarian design. The renovation used prefabricated elements that let the building's residents stay in their homes while the renovation was finished. Anne Lacaton says there are too many demolitions of existing buildings in Paris. She and Jean-Philippe Vassal have a motto they apply to all projects: "never demolish, never subtract, remove or replace: always add, transform, utilize." The Bois-le-Prêtre project was praised in Paris and beyond as "a model for the housing of tomorrow."

There is no requirement that new housing projects are developed in old buildings, and demolitions still happen across Paris. However, other architects have followed the lead of Lacaton and Vassal in repurposing old buildings to include new housing. The former Ministry of Defence headquarters, old gendarmerie barracks, a parkade, vacant office buildings, and many other structures have been redeveloped, including many in wealthier neighbourhoods.

If things have noticeably improved in Paris, it doesn't mean housing isn't still a struggle. More than 250,000 people remain on wait-lists to move into affordable public housing units, with the average wait time at seven years, and an average of 10,000 Parisians have left the city every year over the last decade. The competition for private rentals is fierce, and the long lineups that former Londoner Patty Rowe described are still common. But the trend in Paris seems to be headed in the right direction, as new construction continues. Yonah Freemark believes the trend could be copied in other big cities. "Île-de-France suggests that limited construction in countries throughout the West is hardly an immutable condition."

5

RENTERS IN A DANGEROUS TIME

Ottawa

LYING IN BED, looking up at the canoe hanging from the bedroom ceiling, Erin Hobson knew it was time to move. If the canoe wasn't convincing enough, there was also the television standing on a shelf under the canoe, and the bike hanging on the bedroom wall. And then there was the bedroom closet, which Erin and her spouse call their "garage" because it's packed so full of camping equipment, fishing gear, and Christmas decorations. Erin's bedroom isn't messy—far from it. It's neat and tidy and makes the most of limited space. But space is undeniably limited in the couple's one-bedroom-plus-den apartment. The bright unit is located in Centretown, a desirable neighbourhood that stretches across much of downtown Ottawa, the Rideau Canal, and Parliament Hill. While the beautifully maintained Victorian homes, leafy streets, and good restaurants that surround them are appealing, Erin decided the apartment was too small. "We just need a bigger spot."

The couple started looking for a new place to rent at the end of 2020. Specifically, they wanted a two-bedroom home with outdoor space and a parking spot. In their late thirties with full-time jobs, they had what they thought was a good budget—between $1,500 and $3,000 a month. But it was difficult to find a place that met their basic requirements. As their rental search dragged on longer, the list of possible rentals got shorter. The Ottawa market had more than three hundred two-bedroom apartments available in the summer of 2021. A year later that number had been more than halved. Rents kept rising, and by the end of the year they'd gone up 14 percent, with the average two-bedroom rental apartment costing more than $2,300 a month. That's still a lot cheaper than Vancouver's monthly average of more than $3,500 and Toronto's $3,200. But that's of little comfort to Ottawa renters searching for a new home.

As the months dragged on, Erin and her spouse found three separate rentals they liked. They applied for each one, and in each case they lost out to someone who offered to pay the landlord more. Erin still wanted more space, but as she contemplated paying even more for a bigger rental, she wondered what sacrifices she might have to make as a result. Would she and her spouse have to give up on their dream of buying a home because they could no longer set money aside for a down payment? Should they stop putting money into RRSPs? And what about student loans? "It's more disheartening than anything," Erin laments. "Do we just suck it up and pay the higher rent by sacrificing another part of our life?"

Erin isn't the only renter to feel a sense of financial injustice because of high housing costs. Renters are at an inherent disadvantage in Canada, according to Andy Yan, at Simon Fraser University's City Lab. They lack the financial backstops that homeowners enjoy, he says, such as the value of the home itself and generous lines of credit. Homeowners also enjoy a capital gains tax exemption when they sell their primary residence. "Canada needs to be a renter society," he says, "but our finance system isn't geared for it." He thinks the federal government could make a serious start at helping renters by allowing them to build lines of credit. "Someone who can pay their rent on time for twenty years is a pretty good bet, and yet they're considered a credit risk." Andy Yan thinks the federal government should make changes to finance laws to address that situation. In the meantime, renters in the national capital and across the country continue to struggle with rising rents and fewer rental homes available.

In the town of Russell, a half-hour drive southeast of Ottawa, life has long been more affordable than in Canada's big cities. *Moneysense* magazine ranked the town the third-best place to live in Canada in 2018 thanks to good schools, a low crime rate, and housing affordability. That was one of the main draws for Cindy McMurray when she moved to Russell from Ottawa in late 2020. A senior living on a fixed disability benefit, Cindy lived in a large two-bedroom apartment in the city that cost a relatively affordable $1,100 a month. But there was a reason for that—"cockroaches, cockroaches, and bedbugs." Cindy's daughter wanted to see her mother in a nicer, more affordable place. When she discovered a nearly brand-new seniors' rental apartment in Russell, she thought she'd found the perfect location. The building was clean and new, and the rent for Cindy would be only $997 a month. By the time she moved in a few months later, and agreed to spend extra on a storage locker, it was up to $1,167—an amount she called "doable but tight." The real shock for Cindy and many of her neighbours came in 2022, when a new company bought the building. Cindy presumed the rent would not go up more than 2.5 percent, the maximum annual increase set by Ontario's government for the following year. What they didn't know was that the province had brought in a law in 2018 that exempted new rental units from rent control measures if they were first occupied after November 1 of that year. So, a few weeks after her building was sold, Cindy's new landlord sent her a letter informing her the rent would rise more than $200 a month, to $1,400. That may not sound like much to young working couples who already pay more, but to a single senior living on a fixed income, it was a serious blow. "I wanted to throw up," Cindy recalls. "I cried for a week. I got frozen, trying to think of how to move forward. What do I do? Where do I go?"

Many of Cindy's neighbours were equally upset, facing similar rent increases of up to 25 percent. In a letter to tenants, the new owner, Hartford Properties, acknowledged the rent increases "may be larger than expected," before explaining that inflation, increased expenses, and average market rents led to the increase. The company claimed the higher rents were still below current market rates, and gave renters several months to either leave or come up with the additional money. Cindy didn't know what to do. She kept her car but stopped driving, to save money on gas, and looked for other little cuts she could make to her monthly budget. Then she remembered an affordable housing project wait-list that she'd put her name on three years earlier. At the time, she'd been number forty on the list. Three years later, she was number thirty. So she put her name on other wait-lists, checking each one before she did to make sure the building was subject to rent control, "where they're not brand-new buildings and the rent will just go up with the cost of living."

While Cindy was hoping to find a more affordable apartment, she faced another problem in the fact that rent controls apply only to existing leases, not to new tenancies. In Ontario and many other provinces, landlords are restricted to limited annual rent increases while a tenant lives in an apartment, but when the old tenant leaves, there is no legislative restriction on how much the rent can rise for the new tenant. As a result, new tenants in Ottawa paid 17 percent more for a two-bedroom apartment in 2022 than new tenants paid the year before.

Vacancy—or the lack of vacancy—is also a growing challenge for renters. In 2022, the CMHC Rental Market Report showed that the national vacancy rate had dropped to 1.9 percent—the lowest it's been since 2001. That declining vacancy happened despite thousands of new units being built. In fact, rental construction saw its highest rate of increase since 2013. It seems counterintuitive that rents would rise so sharply while construction was booming. But CMHC identified three key reasons for the discrepancy. The first was that the rising cost of home ownership was ending the dreams of many would-be homebuyers and forcing them to stay in the rental market. The second reason was higher immigration, which led to a significant rise in the number of people looking for a place to live. Finally, thousands of students returned to campus after the first two years of the COVID-19 pandemic, putting pressure on rental markets in communities with multiple post-secondary institutions, like Ottawa. "Rental affordability continues to pose a significant challenge across the country," the report concluded, "especially for the lowest 20% of income earners."

Affordability is certainly a challenge for serving members of the Canadian Armed Forces. Junior members of the Canadian Forces Intelligence Command—CFINTCOM in military speak— have tried to avoid moving to the National Capital Region (NCR) altogether. "We recognize how expensive the NCR is, especially for our junior members, so we're trying not to post them here," Chief Warrant Officer Necole Belanger said during a military town hall meeting that was posted on YouTube. She told the gathering that CFINTCOM was reassessing whether staff members could do the same work from other locations, like Winnipeg or Gagetown, New Brunswick. Many members of the military also wanted an increase to the Post Living Differential, which was designed to offset the added costs of living in more expensive cities. That modest financial top-up had been frozen since 2009, when the average rent of a two-bedroom apartment in Ottawa was around $1,000. When the new Canadian Forces Housing Differential was introduced in the summer of 2023, the average rent in the NCR had more than doubled. The new policy was geared to help lower-ranking members and was expanded to include more cities like Ottawa that were previously considered ineligible. But the change also cut off more than 7,700 Armed Forces personnel who would no longer qualify. Military leaders insisted the new system is more equitable, and pointed out that many soldiers, sailors, and other serving members live on military bases in barracks and officer housing. But like the rest of Canada's housing supply, that's in short supply too. The Chief of the Defence Staff, General Wayne Eyre, estimated the military needs 4,000 to 6,000 additional housing units. And while Ottawa was one of the most expensive cities, Eyre said "the number one issue that comes up as I travel around the country is cost of living and the challenges our people are facing in terms of finding afford-able accommodations."

As finding affordable housing becomes more challenging, it is also more likely that people desperate for affordable housing will come into conflict with each other. Elsie Kalu found that out the hard way. The financial adviser and mother of a child living with autism spectrum disorder decided to leave Gatineau, Quebec, and move across the river to Ottawa to access what she believed would be better health care for her daughter. She bought a townhouse in the Ottawa suburb of Orléans, but when the time came to move in, she came up against a long-time tenant who wasn't willing to move out. Elsie bought the townhouse without viewing it in person—a common practice during the days of pandemic lockdown—through a real estate wholesaler. After signing the purchase agreement, she discovered that the tenant and a roommate had no plans to leave the home. Elsie says they refused to let her inside and closed the garage door abruptly, hitting both her and her daughter on the head. She also says they refused to pay rent to her. Elsie served the tenant with a formal eviction notice and notices of non-payment. Still they wouldn't budge. That left Elsie paying rent and utility bills on the home she couldn't leave, plus the mortgage payments, condo fees, and property taxes on the townhouse she couldn't occupy. To add insult to injury, Elsie said her mortgage costs were higher than they should have been because the tenants refused to allow a property appraiser into the home, which prevented her from getting a mortgage from the bank and led her to turn to a private lender offering loans at higher interest rates. Added all up, Elsie's monthly housing bills totalled more than $5,000. "I'm just sinking," she admitted. "Financially, it's wrecked me."

Elsie's situation went from bad to worse when she lost her job as a financial adviser, four months after purchasing the townhouse, because she failed a credit score that was a condition of employment. She said her credit score dropped as a direct result of the extra loans and credit card debt she was amassing because her tenants refused to leave. Elsie tried to take the tenant to the Landlord and Tenant Board of Ontario, but she met more delays. Eventually, the tenant's legal representative informed Elsie's lawyer that they would not be able to appear before the board until April 2023, a full year after Elsie bought the property. The board finally granted an eviction order, telling the tenants they had to leave by the end of July 2023. Elsie's lawyer, Matt Marshall, described the time that his client was kept out of her new house as "sixteen months of Ms. Kalu being forced by the province to act as a provider of public housing."

Varun Sriskanda, a director with the Small Ownership Landlords of Ontario, says Elsie and her daughter were penalized for doing nothing wrong. "They did everything by the book, and now [she] end[s] up at the Landlord Tenant Board trying to prove [she has] the right to move inside the house." He says the province's top priority should be to eliminate the often long waits for disputes to be considered by the Landlord and Tenant Board. Some disputes languish for up to a year, he says, and some tenants take advantage of that fact by not paying rent while they wait. If the board guaranteed that all disputes would be heard within thirty days of being filed, he believes fewer tenants would default on their rents. But a lawyer representing the tenant in Elsie's townhouse insisted his client had the right to occupy the premises until the matter was decided by the Landlord and Tenant Board. "Everyone knows how inflation has caused rents to skyrocket," he wrote. "Affordability is a huge problem. Moving onto the street is not an option." And yet moving onto the street was a very real fear for Elsie Kalu, just a few months after she purchased a home in an effort to help her daughter better deal with a serious disability.

Elsie couldn't make one of her mortgage payments. Then she was evicted from the rental home where she was still living. She says she called three shelters to reach out for help. One put her on a two-year wait-list. The other two said they couldn't help until she was homeless. "My daughter can't end up on the streets."

The fear of ending up on the streets leads some renters to stay in woefully inadequate housing. In one of Ottawa's most desperate rental complexes, that decision may even have cost some renters their lives. In a rundown row of old brick rooming houses in the Sandy Hill neighbourhood, four men died in squalid conditions between the summer of 2020 and January 2022. The 108-room Osgoode Chambers complex was "appalling, dark, filthy and infested with insects," according to the sister of one of the men who died there. Housing advocates say it was also infested with rats.

The steps in front of one of the Osgoode Chambers rooming houses, in visible disrepair.

Alexander William Faulkner—"Sandy Bill" to his friends—was 57 when he died. In his obituary, Alex's brothers and sisters described their youngest sibling as "an outdoorsman at heart," and "a solitary man in an urban landscape" who was known to adopt and feed stray animals. He had lived with schizophrenia for many years and relied on assistance from the Ontario Disability Support Program, which paid his $500 monthly rent. It wasn't clear how Alex died, but the deplorable conditions in Osgoode Chambers didn't help. The coroner reported his body was found in "an advanced state of decomposition" due in part to the "insects and rodents that infested the building."

Robert Gagnon died the following winter. The 59-year-old grandfather was originally from Timmins, according to a brief obituary written in French and English. *"Robert avait un grand coeur, il aimait aider les autres"* (Robert had a big heart, he loved helping others). The obituary made no mention of how he died.

James Grzesik died seven months later. The 63-year-old was a former Canada Post employee whose varied interests ranged from ancient coins to astronomy, gemology to politics. Housing advocate Josh Hawley, with the Herongate Tenant Coalition, was a friend to James Grzesik and a few other residents of Osgoode Chambers. "James was dealing with bedbugs too," he says. "They were driving him nuts." Josh went back to James's room several months after his friend died, and found it looking much as it had when James was alive, cluttered with empty cans of bug spray and roach spray. The bug spray is toxic and is kept behind locked glass at the local Canadian Tire store. Instructions on the can say any room that's been sprayed should be left empty for at least four hours. But James and many other residents were spraying constantly because they were so desperate to be rid of the bugs.

Bill Weaver, 77 years old, died four months after James Grzesik. He had lived in the complex since 1978, in various suites. His last room was in the house known to residents as "D Block," considered the worst because of the filthy conditions and infestation inside. The irony that a man who had worked many years as a cleaner would have to live in such squalor was not lost on his friends. Bill lived in a room on the main floor, where the shared bathroom was not only filthy but out of order. So he had to climb the stairs every time he wanted to go to the bathroom. That would be a chore for many 77-year-olds, but Bill had COPD, which made every step extremely difficult.

The Osgoode Chambers complex was sold to Smart Living Properties in March 2020, a few months before the first of those four deaths. In a statement to the *Ottawa Citizen*, the company stressed that the buildings were already in disrepair when it bought them, and that it was trying to refurbish all the units. "The company offered tenants a generous relocation package which vastly exceeded what the law requires." It said it helped displaced tenants find new accommodation, and that the refurbished units would continue to be "much-needed affordable residential units."

Josh Hawley doesn't know what caused the deaths of the four men inside Osgoode Chambers, though he suspects one may have been caused by suicide. But he insists the appalling conditions in the buildings are a direct result of intentional neglect by a series of what he calls "slum lords" who refused to put the bare minimum into buildings that made them significant profits over the decades. Josh knows one elderly woman who rented a room there for many years and relied on Old Age Security to pay the $500 monthly rent. Despite having a cat, she was bitten by rats in her bed almost every night. The Herongate Tenant Coalition hired a building inspector—a former city bylaw officer—to examine the property. "He was shocked and appalled at just how bad the conditions were," Josh recalls.

A handful of residents still lived in Osgoode Chambers after the four deaths, despite receiving eviction notices. The landlord claimed tenants were offered generous compensation—up to $20,000 in one case. But Josh says they didn't want to leave until they could find new homes—an extremely difficult task given Ottawa's rental market. Josh worried about the elderly woman with a cat, who stayed in her room despite being tormented by rats. "She'll be sleeping on the streets if she's evicted." She appealed the eviction notice, while renovations continued on the rooms left vacant in Osgoode Chambers, but the court eventually rejected her appeal and she was forced to move out. A lawyer for the landlord said the newly renovated rooms would likely be rented out for about $1,000 a month—double what was charged before the renovations.

While Josh worries about evicted renters, he feels a sliver of hope that more renters are starting to realize they'll have to work together to protect themselves in a brutal housing market. "I do think tenants are organizing more and more, and realizing the only way things will change is if we address this power dynamic head-on."

In 2020 councillor Catherine McKenney brought a motion to Ottawa city council that declared a housing and homelessness emergency. It passed unanimously. But the crisis has grown much worse since then. Catherine ran for mayor two years later, pledging to eliminate chronic homelessness, and came in second behind entrepreneur and broadcaster Mark Sutcliffe, who said he would "keep the dream of home ownership alive for young people" and add a thousand community units a year.

For now, though, many in Ottawa are left in limbo. Some are stuck searching for a more affordable apartment. Three hundred families live in motels, cooking for their children in microwaves, if they cook at all. Others endure the misery of a rented room in a rooming house, hoping they don't end up sleeping on the streets. "When they are evicted so that these places are renovated, it is a sentence to homelessness," Catherine McKenney says. "There is nowhere else for them to go. They are on the streets or in shelters, likely for the rest of their lives. That is the face of our housing crisis."

6

A CO-OPERATIVE APPROACH

Berlin

LIKE A LOT OF PEOPLE in Berlin's Kreuzberg district, Carlo Wahrmann appreciates the unconventional things in life. Many of his long-time friends were house squatters, living for free in vacant homes—a badge of honour in Berlin's anti-establishment culture. Carlo and his wife taught massage therapy in an alternative health centre in a squatted factory. The couple wanted to move into the factory with their two daughters in the 1990s, but there wasn't enough space. They later found a social housing apartment and raised the two girls there. Carlo and his wife eventually separated, though they stayed in daily contact and he supported her through several years of living with cancer before she died. In the meantime, his girls grew up and started families of their own, and Carlo held on to his dream of living in a shared housing community in the bohemian heart of the German capital.

In 2007, a group of hundreds of like-minded people formed a housing co-operative in Berlin with the goal of building an environmentally friendly community on a former rail yard, called Möckernkiez. Co-ops are essentially non-profit companies that buy or build multi-home dwellings and then rent them back to their members at an affordable rent for as long as they want to live there. Tenants often pay rents that are much lower than they would be in comparable private buildings. Carlo heard about Möckernkiez while members were still planning their housing project, and he joined two years later. He says he was lucky that he could afford to join. The entry fee of €48,000 was just shy of the €50,000 inheritance his father had left him.

While the housing co-op made plans, rents across Berlin continued to climb. Once relatively affordable, the German capital was getting more expensive every year. Now on his own, Carlo decided his apartment was too big and too expensive. He wondered how long he would have to wait to move into a newly built home in Möckernkiez.

Things didn't look good for the ambitious development in 2014. Building 471 apartments in fourteen separate buildings wasn't going to be cheap, and construction had to be stopped in the autumn of that year because the co-op essentially ran out of money. The shells of four buildings stood incomplete, makeshift tarpaulins covering what windows had been installed. The construction cranes were dismantled and the co-op members wondered when, or even if, their new homes would be finished. The banks that were financing the €130 million project asked for a general contractor to oversee the construction and a consortium of different builders was hired. The excavators didn't return until 2016, and when they did, the plans called for a little less green space and a few more fees. But the project was back on track, and construction didn't stop until new residents moved into Möckernkiez in 2018.

Carlo was one of the first to move in, on a chilly February day. Scaffolding still surrounded some of the buildings, as plasterers and window installers worked on finishing touches. New residents, bundled in winter clothing, held a modest but cheerful gathering outside one of the building's entrances. They bought fresh-baked pretzels and quiche along with bottles of champagne, which did double duty pinning down the blue-check tablecloths. Smiling residents raised paper cups of bubbly to mark the occasion as a hand-painted banner fluttered in the wind: *Herzlich Willkomen im Möckernkiez!* ("Welcome to Möckernkiez!") The combination of cold weather and anticipation drove most people inside before long.

Carlo moved into a modest one-bedroom apartment with a good-sized living room, a kitchen, and a balcony. In total, his building has thirty-six apartments that house several single people and families with as many as three children. There's plenty of storage in the basement, with individual storage units and space for more than a hundred bicycles. And the building has elevators so all residents can easily get to any one of the five floors—a nice feature for Carlo, who is now a grandfather in his seventies. The building also has a giant common terrace on the roof, where residents hold parties in the summer to watch the sun set over the Gleisdreieck park next door. But Carlo, and all the roughly one thousand residents, get more than just their building. There's a shared workshop for people wanting to repair things, a café, and a large room called a forum to host larger gatherings such as movie nights and yoga classes. There are also large shared green spaces between buildings, racks for a thousand bicycles, and car-free roads that allow children to play without having to watch out for traffic. "Our kids can run and play free on the whole project. Their parents don't have to worry about traffic." When the weather is nice, café tables are set up outside. People bring beer and wine, and often dinner. Concerts and outdoor theatre performances are common. All the activities are open to everyone, and all are free. Even the coffee and cakes in the café are free—at least, members are invited to pay what they want. For Carlo, "the whole social life in Möckernkiez is special and totally different to the place I lived before."

Co-op living at Möckernkiez in Berlin includes a number of shared activities, like outdoor meals in summer.

But Möckernkiez isn't for everyone. Most poor Berliners couldn't afford the down payment even if the co-op's buildings weren't already full. Still, it is attainable for many Berliners who have the money to join, and the monthly rents are reasonable. Carlo Wahrmann pays €790 every month for his rent and his heating, thanks to his pension, and his monthly bills won't go up for ten years. The co-op can make that promise thanks to good financial planning, and because it generates its own heating from an array of solar panels on the buildings' roofs and a biogas plant that provide heat and electricity for all fourteen buildings. As people across Germany watched their utility costs skyrocket following Russia's invasion of Ukraine, it was a huge relief not to have to worry about bills.

Apart from generating their own energy, residents of Möckernkiez also benefit from the fact that all its buildings were designed to meet Passive House building standards, which means they use about 90 percent less heating and cooling than conventional buildings. Carlo says he usually keeps his radiator off, even in the winter, and is quite comfortable behind his apartment's triple-pane windows. Not only do the windows keep the place warm, he says they also keep it quiet. "It's the calmest apartment I've ever lived in."

Some of the hype about Möckernkiez has centred around its car-free status. While it's true that the central square, plaza, and paths are off limits to all vehicles other than garbage trucks and emergency vehicles, there are parking spaces reserved for some residents. But not many. Although a thousand people live in Möckernkiez, the development has only a small underground parkade, with about one parking space for every five apartments. Most people either walk to local shops or ride their bikes. Many residents own or share larger cargo bikes, and take advantage of the fact that all the doors and elevators in the buildings are big enough to allow residents to wheel the cargo bikes straight to their front doors. The development is also close to U-Bahn and S-Bahn trains, and many residents either take taxis or belong to a car co-op. Of the people who do own their cars, many say they use them rarely. One woman even admitted that when her car was towed from a nearby street, it took her three weeks to notice.

Möckernkiez has received a lot of attention since it opened, from interested visitors who wonder if a similar co-operative housing development might work in their own home city or country. But it's far from the only co-op in the city. The German capital is home to more than a hundred different co-ops, with more than 200,000 separate apartments between them. In total, co-ops compose about 12 percent of the city's rental housing stock. Some of them are huge, with a few dozen including more than 3,000 apartments; one of them has more than 11,000 units. While hundreds of new co-op apartments open every year across the city, the idea is nothing new in Berlin. Some date back to the 1800s, including one aptly named the "1892" housing co-op. The Bismarck government encouraged the formation of housing co-ops as a way to improve the living conditions of workers and make revolution less likely. There was another boom in co-op construction following the First World War, then again after the Second World War, especially in East Berlin in the 1950s and 1960s. Many angry East Germans rioted in 1953 out of frustration at the poor quality of the homes the Communist authorities were building. More than seven hundred housing co-ops were formed in response, providing homes for more than 70,000 people. Most of the co-ops were tied to specific workplaces, giving co-op residents something closer to direct control of their living conditions than they had under national Communist housing agencies. Most Berlin co-ops have two paid directors and a volunteer board made up of residents, who are elected. The boards manage the co-op and encourage residents to participate in the ongoing management of the buildings.

While Möckernkiez isn't cheap, many co-ops are very affordable. In the centre of the city, about five hundred metres from the former Berlin Wall, an American expat named Santitas lives in a small co-op building of fourteen units. It was built in 2006 and has kept rents nearly frozen since then. Santitas estimates her modest one-bedroom would rent for triple what she pays the co-op if it were owned by a private company. She loves the fact that the rent has hardly risen since she moved there in 2016. And while many would assume low rents lead to a lot of deferred maintenance and a run-down building, she says the opposite is true—the occupants all volunteer to keep up with maintenance and preserve the building in good condition. Apart from affordability, Santitas loves the sense of community she feels in her building. "The people who live here have a co-op mindset and they really help one another out."

Of course, co-ops aren't for everyone. Many co-operative housing networks make a point of sharing some key questions people should ask themselves before deciding to join. What balance between privacy and community do I need to be happy? Am I willing and able to accept disagreements with my close neighbours? How will I feel when I'm not allowed to do some things I want to do? The answers to these questions lead many people to conclude they'd rather live alone. But millions of Germans love housing co-operatives, and that love extends well beyond the capital. Across Germany, about 5 percent of the country's housing stock, and 10 percent of all rental housing units, are owned by co-ops. In total, more than 5 million Germans live in more than 2.2 million co-op units. That's nearly double the share of the country's housing market taken up by public housing. In Canada, only a quarter of a million people live in co-op housing, slightly more than 0.5 percent of the total population.

Housing co-operatives work well in German cities, but they're also popular in smaller towns and rural settings. About twelve kilometres outside the spa town of Aachen, near Germany's border with Belgium and the Netherlands, eight families joined together to form a co-op of their own in 1985. The families decided they didn't like living in apartments in the city. So they formed the co-op, bought land, and designed a complex of eight joined houses with one common community house, called a Gemeinschaftshaus. One of the members was an architect and took the lead on the design. But all eight families weighed in, and most worked on some components of the construction. Nearly thirty years after moving into their new homes, most members are still there. And some of their now-grown children came together to form a new co-operative of their own, to build themselves homes on a nearby farm.

Andreas Mense, an economist at the Institute for Employment Research in Nuremberg, says co-ops are a cornerstone of the German housing market. He says the significant presence of co-ops sets Germany, as well as Austria and Switzerland, aside from most other developed countries. And while Germany, like many other developed countries, has struggled with rising house prices, its large stock of co-op housing has acted as a sort of buffer against surging prices. "Because their members try to keep rents low. But on the other hand they invest in their buildings and try to keep them nice. And so taking the two things together, I think that's a win-win for the people who live in these units."

Many Germans who don't live in housing co-ops feel they're losing out on housing. Like Canada, the country has struggled to keep up with the demand for new housing, at least in bigger cities. Construction boomed during the 1990s, following the reunification of East and West. A sense of optimism about the country's future fuelled a building boom that peaked with the construction of more than 600,000 new homes in 1994. Now the country struggles to build half that every year. Housing professor Michael Voigtländer says housing is abundant in many rural areas, but it's increasingly scarce and expensive in cities like Munich, Hamburg, and Berlin. He says Germany has also faced similar pressures to Canada due to population growth. That's a relatively new dynamic in Germany. Between 2000 and 2010 the country's population remained relatively flat and some Germans even thought it might shrink. Like Japan, house prices were much more affordable than in many other developed countries. But between 2011 and 2019, net migration into Germany topped 3.6 million people, and Voigtländer says new construction failed to keep up. German house prices and rents have gone up faster than incomes since 2012, especially in cities. "Germany is facing many of the same pressures that other developed countries face," he says. "We see all the big cities increasing in population as we lose jobs in industry, but we gain people working in the service industry." On top of that, more people are living alone these days. That trend is creating even more demand for apartments in Berlin, as it is in many cities worldwide.

But while house prices have risen sharply in Germany, they've arguably had less of an impact than rising prices in Canada, due in part to the high proportion of Germans who rent. Germany has been called a nation of renters because slightly more than half the population rents—the highest proportion in the European Union. As a result, German rent controls have acted as a financial buffer for millions of people. But as many Canadian renters know all too well, rent control only goes so far. When tenants leave, landlords often raise rents significantly, either to meet rising borrowing costs or to maximize profit. Tenant organizations also say some German property companies are so big they can subtly get around some rent controls because they manage so much of the market. For instance, where local regulations prohibit rents from being more than 10 percent above the local average, property companies that own thousands of apartments can directly elevate that average by raising their rents the maximum amount permissible at every opportunity. If that sounds like an unlikely scenario, it's worth looking at just how big some German property companies have grown.

The biggest landlord in Berlin, Deutsche Wohnen, owned more than 113,000 apartments in 2021. Among its many buildings is the famous Hufeisensiedlung (Horseshoe Estate), which was originally built by the city in the 1920s. The property is listed as a UNESCO World Heritage Site, and for good reason. The bright, open building surrounds a large, park-like garden and provided working-class Berliners with modern homes at a time when many residents were much more accustomed to cramped, cold hovels. The Horseshoe Estate was designed by the famed architect and urban planner Bruno Taut, and it still retains much of its original charm. It is cited by many as a perfect example of how good public housing can be. But it is no longer publicly owned. Deutsche Wohnen bought a majority share in the Horseshoe Estate several years ago, when the debt-ridden city was selling off public housing. As rents continued to rise and new supply failed to keep up with demand, more and more Berliners clamoured for drastic action on housing.

In a 2021 referendum Berlin voters were asked if they approved of the expropriation of rental buildings from property companies that owned 3,000 or more individual suites. Advocates of the plan claimed large companies have what amounts to a monopoly, and as a result can raise prices higher than they would if there were more competitors in the market. There's considerable debate around this claim, and the expropriation wouldn't affect all Berlin rentals. But nearly one in six of the 1.5 million rental apartments in the city would have been nationalized under the plan.

More than 57 percent of voters said yes. It was a strong endorsement of a radical plan that made real estate investors across Europe more than a little nervous. At least, it would have been a radical plan if it had been carried out. But the initiative was non-binding, so nothing happened immediately. Mayor Franziska Giffey, a member of the centre-left Social Democratic Party, had campaigned against the expropriations. The mayor dragged her feet while many Berliners, including many in her party, urged the city to follow through on the referendum results. Instead of immediate action, though, Mayor Giffey and others said they were studying the legality of expropriation, and reiterated the need to build more rental housing in Germany. Some German leaders hoped to emulate the building boom they saw transforming Paris. But Berlin seemed to be missing some of the French capital's secret ingredients, and the plan to build 200,000 more homes in the German capital in a decade is woefully behind schedule.

While renters paid more and more with every passing year, and took to the streets demanding drastic systemic change, most co-op residents could take comfort in a more stable living arrangement. But Carolin Schröder cautions against seeing housing co-ops as a cure-all. An urban development and governance researcher at Technische Universität Berlin, she studies co-operatives for a living, and lives in a housing co-op herself. She appreciates the sense of stability and solidarity they can create, but she says they have limitations too. One of them is the cost of land, which is becoming prohibitively expensive in many cities. "If there's no affordable land, there's no affordable housing." She says new co-ops in big cities are becoming more expensive, with some of them being the exclusive domain of the upper middle class. She also worries that if governments are too sympathetic to housing co-operatives—which, she points out, are still private entities—they may give co-ops public land that would be better used for truly affordable public housing. Still, Carolin Schröder says housing co-ops have many benefits, including playing a valuable role in local climate action. She says environmental values are top of mind for many new housing co-operatives, especially smaller ones started by young Germans. Some bigger co-ops prioritize the environment too, like a large Hanover co-operative that switched to smart thermostats to lower members' heating bills and their collective carbon footprint, and organized classes for elderly residents who found the new thermostats difficult to use. And then there's Möckernkiez with its solar panels, Passive House design, and biogas heating plant. While the actions of a few hundred people alone won't change the fate of 8 billion people on planet Earth, Carolin Schröder says housing co-ops can spur similar actions in the wider community.

Carlo Wahrmann regularly shows visitors around Möckernkiez. They come from other parts of Berlin, across Germany, and overseas to have a look. Carlo says one of the things that strikes visitors is how what looks like just another housing development seems more like a real community when they walk into the central plaza. Though it's in the middle of one of Europe's largest cities, Carlo says Möckernkiez feels more like a village. Maybe that's because he spends so much time volunteering and working with his neighbours. One night he'll be meeting with refugee support groups, the next day he's offering credit counselling to neighbours. Carlo is also responsible for the co-op's central copy machine and the printers. "Sometimes it's not easy to leave this place," he offers. "You always meet somebody who wants to talk to you!"

7

HOMELESS

Duncan, British Columbia

THE SNOW STARTED FALLING five days before Christmas. That's nothing remarkable in most parts of Canada. But in Duncan and other coastal towns on Vancouver Island, snow spells trouble. Heavy, wet flakes started piling up just as the temperature began to drop. It fell below freezing but felt like minus six with the wind chill. Again, not a major event in most of Canada, but in the damp coastal air, with no shelter for warmth, the weather could prove deadly. On the night of December 20, 2022, it did.

Gina Dias and her "hubby" Josh Derrah were living on the streets of Duncan, and struggling with addiction. But Gina said they dreamed of getting clean and getting off the streets. They were an odd couple in some people's eyes. Gina was 48. Josh—JD to his friends—was 28. But they loved each other and had gone through a lot together. Two years earlier, the couple had survived a fire in a fourth-floor apartment by jumping out the window to safety. Gina didn't want to make the leap, but Josh had convinced her, and the jump very likely saved her life. Two years later, with the snow falling and the wind howling, Gina missed her chance to save his.

All she did was go inside for a cup of coffee and a bit of warmth. She left Josh out in the A&W parking lot, confident she'd see him again shortly. When she came back outside a few hours later, she found him lying still on the freezing pavement without a blanket. Gina called for help, and when paramedics arrived soon after, they told her the bad news. JD was dead. "I just wish I'd stayed with him," she said, sobbing, a few days later. "If it wasn't for him, I wouldn't be here, and now I'm here without him."

The BC Coroners Service said it would investigate Josh's death but couldn't immediately say what caused it. He may have been another victim of BC's poisonous drug supply, which claimed nearly 2,300 lives in 2022 (the eighth year of the province's toxic drug public health emergency). Or maybe he just froze to death.

Adrian Sylvester—a member of the Cowichan Tribes, the largest single First Nations band in British Columbia, with more than five thousand members—suspects Josh died from the cold. Adrian is now housed, and has spent the last twenty-five years cycling around the streets of Duncan helping those who aren't. "That week, I was out there, I literally had to lay down with four or five people to warm them up. They were just shivering away so bad on the cement."

The city of Duncan had hoped to open a cold weather emergency shelter on the night Josh died, but couldn't do so in the end because of a wave of unspecified illness among the people who would have staffed the centre overnight, just as the Omicron subvariant of COVID-19 was peaking across much of Canada. Adrian couldn't help but wonder if Josh would have survived if the shelter had been open. "When I see or hear of people dying on the streets because there's no warming centres, it really hurts because I was on the streets myself." An emergency overnight shelter was opened the night after Josh died in the A&W parking lot. The city had scrambled to find more volunteers, and managed to open the shelter with a limited capacity of thirty people that night.

Duncan's mayor, Michelle Staples, says the small city of only five thousand people faces a number of challenges trying to support a growing homeless population. Staffing is an issue, obviously. But she says the lack of a permanent location for a shelter is probably the biggest. People simply don't want an emergency shelter for the homeless in their neighbourhood. "There will always be a percentage of people who need supports that are different from the majority of people," she says. "You add the types of street drugs and the affordability crisis and you're ending up with more and more people falling through the cracks."

Stacy Middlemiss sees all the people who fall through Duncan's cracks, including Gina Dias and Josh Derrah, and she sees them from a number of different vantage points. Stacy is an elected municipal councillor, a psychiatric nurse, and an outreach worker who's interacted directly with people on the streets for years. She believes she knows every single homeless person in Duncan directly, including several she's revived from drug overdoses on multiple occasions. Stacy has devoted years of her life to helping the homeless, and she knows others in her community who have too. Still, she sees the crisis of homelessness getting worse. "It blows my mind! Every day it seems like there are new faces. People are losing their houses, and I just don't see how we're going to catch up."

As rents soared in recent years, more people moved into recreational vehicles. Carolyn Lawson moved into a 35-foot fifth wheel in a nice campsite and RV park overlooking the Cowichan River. The retired logger and trucker lived there for five years, paying a monthly rent of $497. "I really thought this would be my last home until the day I died. I was just so happy." That happiness ended abruptly one summer day in 2022, shortly after the campground and RV park were sold to a new owner. Carolyn noticed that her next-door neighbours were packing up their RV and getting ready to leave. When she asked why, she was told the monthly rent had more than doubled, to $1,200 a month. RV owners in British Columbia have some protections: they can't be evicted without sufficient notice and their landlords are supposed to follow annual rent increase caps. But when a campground or RV park is sold, the new owner is allowed to set new rents.

Carolyn received no notice of the change. But she knew in an instant that she would have to find a new home, because her monthly Canada Pension Plan and Old Age Security payments added up to just $900. "I just cry myself to sleep some nights, and when a new day comes, I don't want to get out of bed . . . It's just absolutely heartbreaking for me that I have to leave, and heartbreaking that the city has nowhere to go."

Apart from her 35-foot fifth wheel, Carolyn also owned a pickup truck and a small camper that sits on the back of the truck. She planned to move into the camper and find a new place to park it. But that was becoming more difficult in and around Duncan as more people moved into recreational vehicles. Most of the other residents of the fifteen riverside RV pads had to leave as well. There were another thirty-five RV sites, and many more campsites. In total, more than 150 people had been living at the campground and RV park. Many suddenly found themselves looking for a new place to live, and they were far from alone.

Shauna Hall and her husband found themselves homeless after losing their rental apartment. They couch surfed for a few months and scanned rental ads constantly. But with small houses renting for $2,500 a month, they gave up on living in a traditional home. "After a few months," Hall reflects, "we were like, well now what are we going to do?"

The couple owned a recreational vehicle, so Shauna placed an online ad seeking a pad for an RV instead. Their budget—$1,500 a month. They were optimistic they'd find a place to park their rolling home.

But as more people moved into small homes on wheels, more people in permanent homes started to complain. Local bylaws prohibit people living in vehicles, and the bylaws are a complaints-driven process. So bylaw officers started handing out tickets to people living in cars, vans, and campers. Carolyn Lawson was frustrated that so many people like her spent much of their time avoiding bylaw officers, while not being able to find anyone at any level of government to offer help. "There's really no resources out there that care, there is no support system for people like me."

In response, people like Keith Simmonds stepped into the void. Simmonds was a minister at the Duncan United Church, a fifteen-minute walk away from the A&W parking lot where Josh Derrah died. In walking around downtown Duncan, and driving around the greater North Cowichan area, Keith got to know many of the people living in vehicles. "We see people and talk to them all the time for whom it's a reality in their life. In fact, it's a step up for many of the people who are homeless or who are trying to live in tents or underneath the eaves of buildings."

Many of the people who are fortunate enough to have a vehicle have been injured and are relying on disability benefits of around $1,300 a month to make ends meet. In a town where two-bedroom apartments are renting for $1,800 or more, and single-family homes start at $2,300 a month, where else would they go? "It's obscene, frankly," Keith says. "I don't know why people wouldn't rent-strike and just refuse to move. I don't know what other option people have. Maybe the province would act then."

While some ministers tend to stick to matters spiritual, the Reverend Keith Simmonds is more than willing to talk politics. A former trade unionist and political organizer, Keith sees homelessness as both a spiritual and a political crisis. "The reason we're in a housing crisis," he offers, "is because the federal and provincial governments walked away from housing and said, 'It's all the private sector's: you're on your own now.'" While he reserves his most pointed criticism for the higher levels of government, and believes municipal governments are "just stuck," Keith believes both Duncan and its next-door neighbour North Cowichan could do more to help. Along with other local housing advocates, he urged the city to focus less on enforcing bylaws and more on providing solutions. They suggested the municipality could provide more sani-dump sites, as well as supervised sites for people to park their RVs. They also suggested the provincial government could build new RV parks, and even supply new RVs, in a community where some old trailers were sold for as little as $3,500 but many more were listed for ten times that amount. Keith and other housing advocates acknowledge that the presence of public RV parks could in fact end up being a magnet that draws other RV dwellers to the area to take advantage of the free services. But, they insist, something has to be done, even if it's only a stopgap. "Individual communities can work really hard and house as many people as they can," he says, "and of course next week there will just be more people. If you don't have a provincial or a national housing strategy, then we're always going to be screwed."

What really bothers Keith is what he sees as the hypocrisy of federal and provincial governments. "I'm just appalled! We live in a province that can house fifty thousand people when a city is threatened by forest fire, but we can't figure out how to deal with people who are homeless and who are living in RVs. We seem to be able to turn our backs on those folks."

It's not hard to find people who agree with that sentiment. Carolina Ibarra is the CEO of Pacifica Housing, a charity that provides affordable housing and support services for more than 2,500 people on southern Vancouver Island. She sees people experiencing homelessness and people on the verge of it every day, and says, "Modern mass homelessness had its roots when the federal government withdrew from affordable housing investment in the 1980s and '90s." So she welcomes the federal government's 2023 update to the National Housing Strategy. The $82 billion strategy includes specific targets of cutting chronic homelessness by 50 percent, removing 530,000 families from housing need, renovating and modernizing 300,000 homes, and building 160,000 new homes. That's a significant increase from the original pledge to build 100,000 new homes, when the NHS was introduced in 2017. But five years after the initial plan was introduced, it was already well behind its original targets, according to Canada's auditor general. Carolina Ibarra says the strategy won't be nearly as effective as it needs to be if the government doesn't do a much better job of keeping track of how many people need truly affordable housing. "We need better high-level analysis. On the ground we have a good picture. But people who receive supplements still can't afford the units that are up for rent, so high-level analysis would help us set housing targets so we know exactly how many deeply affordable units need to be built."

Another barrier, according to Carolina, is the lack of long-term funding for non-profits like Pacifica Housing, which often have to reapply for funding year after year. Without more stable funding and better tracking of exactly how many publicly subsidized affordable units should be built, Carolina expects to see more people ending up homeless for economic reasons, instead of addiction and mental health struggles. "What we're seeing is people who are homeless for the first time because they can't pay their bills. Whereas before they may have [been able to] . . . with inflation they just can't make ends meet. We find [this] in our own work with single mothers who all of a sudden can't afford food and rent, and they're now on suicide watch." Carolina says this is a key point that's often missed in discussions around housing—that even if a person becomes homeless for simple economic reasons, that homelessness itself can push the person into mental illness. "So that is severe and that actually develops a lot of mental health issues in people, that level of stress. Issues of mental health and addiction often stem from poverty. So that's just being exacerbated [by] the current situation."

Overall, Carolina says there just isn't enough housing to go around. That's apparent in the high prices and the lack of space for anyone to go. When older buildings need to be redeveloped, it's often seniors who are most affected, as they're more likely to live in older buildings, "but there is nowhere affordable for them to go. So the problem is not the redevelopment, it's the shortage of housing stock at an affordable level." Carolina believes the solution is a major increase in the construction of deeply affordable housing units across Canada, and because land costs are now so high she thinks it should be paid for by the federal and provincial governments. "They can't be left to the private sector or non-profits to build, because we simply can't afford to do so."

Both the provincial and federal governments have already promised to build thousands of units of affordable social housing. Economist Marc Lee, at the Canadian Centre for Policy Alternatives, says both governments have failed to live up to their promises. He notes the BC NDP government, when it was elected in 2017, promised to build 114,000 affordable housing units over a decade. Six years later, they'd built or started only one-fifth of their goal. Similarly, the federal Liberal government's National Housing Strategy is well off the mark. But Marc Lee says both levels of government could still make major investments in direct public support for housing construction, offer grants to non-profit housing providers, and donate public land for housing. He says both levels of government could also make a meaningful improvement on both affordability and home-lessness if they commit to the construction of 25,000 new units of affordable housing every year in British Columbia. "To fix this broken market at its source, we need to greatly expand the non-profit development and delivery of non-market housing."

In the meantime, people will continue to sleep on cardboard under stairs, in tents pitched in parks, inside dying cars, or maybe, if they're lucky, in a camper or larger RV. They will continue to struggle in towns and cities across Canada. Keith Simmonds finds it difficult to watch. "It also affects us in being on the streets in Duncan and seeing that we've reduced ourselves to this, to a community that accepts that people can live unhoused and marginally housed in RVs and we're still the community that says, 'If you're unfortunate enough to find yourself in that situation, could you go someplace else? Because there's no room for you here.' And I think that really affects us on a deeper level, on a spiritual level, on a sense of who we are, that living beings are of the least value in our society. That affects everyone in a way that's hard to quantify, but goes deeply into our sense of self-worth and who we are as humans."

There have been efforts to help. A temporary complex of 34 small shipping container homes, called the Village, was set up in 2022 on an unused lot that was owned by BC Housing, the provincial Crown corporation that builds subsidized housing. Residents swapped sleeping on the streets for clean rooms with simple furnish-ings and shared washroom and storage facilities. At around the same time, the 52-unit Sq'umul' Shelh Lelum' supportive housing complex opened its doors, a ten-minute walk away from the Village. And a similar 48-unit building was opened the following year.

While Duncan, North Cowichan, and the Cowichan Tribes have all built new housing and added new supports for people trying to get off the streets, it's still not enough. Keith says that despite significant effort from many, they add up to a piecemeal approach. "Duncan provides housing for two hundred people, but there's still a thousand people unhoused in Victoria and they hear maybe there's some hope for them in Duncan, so they go to Duncan."

Stacy Middlemiss welcomes the addition of more subsidized housing in and around Duncan, but she says the community still needs a lot more support staff to help people with serious addiction and mental health struggles. And she says it will need more affordable housing units with a wider range of different living arrangements. "You can't just move someone into an apartment. There have to be different levels of support."

8

HOUSING FIRST

Helsinki

PASI HIETANEN STARTED DRINKING at the age of 12. When he was a teenager, his two alcoholic parents were deemed unfit and he was sent to live in foster care, where he started using cannabis and amphetamines. Pasi grew up and moved out into a home of his own. He got married and held down a variety of jobs—delivery driver, roofer, sprinkler installer. While he struggled after his first divorce, he managed to hold things together. It wasn't until after his second divorce, at age 33, that Pasi went into a tailspin. He started using intravenous drugs and reconnected with old friends who had become severely addicted to street drugs. Before long he was using daily, and eventually lost access to his young daughter. When he could no longer afford to pay for the growing quantity of drugs his addiction demanded, he turned to petty crime and bottle collecting, and finally found himself homeless in Helsinki.

Finland's capital is home to more than a million people, in the city and surrounding suburbs. Standing at the tip of a peninsula that juts out into the Gulf of Finland, Helsinki is known to many Scandinavians as the Daughter of the Baltic. For four years, Pasi Hietanen was a son of her streets.

When he wasn't trying to score drugs or scrape up the money to pay for them, Pasi would look after lesser priorities, such as finding food or keeping warm. Helsinki can get extremely cold in the winter, with temperatures occasionally dipping down into the minus thirties. For people living on the streets it can be difficult to find a place to stay warm. One of Pasi's favourite locations was one of the green public washrooms that are a common sight in Helsinki. If only for a few hours, he could lock himself away and find a small moment of peace and quiet in the middle of the night. Not that the damp, slatted floors were comfortable. Far from it. But with some thick cardboard and a locked door, he could drift off to sleep for a few hours. Occasionally Pasi would run into someone who said he owed them money, coming out of the green washroom just as he was going in. That was one of the biggest risks of life on the streets—that he'd get beaten up, or even stabbed. Once, when he was vomiting and peeing blood, he called emergency and asked for an ambulance but was told he'd have to be patient. After a bit of begging and pleading over the phone, paramedics were finally dispatched. He passed out in the ambulance and woke up two weeks later in the hospital, told he was suffering from two open stomach ulcers, pneumonia, and blood poisoning.

The other big risk of life on the streets, not surprisingly, was that he'd overdose. "I have been declared clinically dead eight times due to overdose," he insists in Finnish. But Pasi did not die on the streets. Instead, he was given a second chance. And it started with a simple decision, based on a simple philosophy that's been adopted across Finland—that before anything else, a person living on the streets needs a home to call their own. Yes, many other supports are needed.

Treatment for addiction and for mental and physical health can all be crucial. But before any of those can be addressed—the Finnish thinking goes—housing must come first.

Finland didn't invent the Housing First model. Sam Tsemberis, a Canadian psychologist at Columbia University in New York, is often credited with developing the idea and demonstrating its potential for success in the 1990s. It challenged the notion that people struggling with serious addiction and mental illness couldn't be housed until those underlying issues were addressed. The Housing First model flipped that assumption on its head, and said real healing couldn't happen until a person had a safe space to call home.

Pasi started spending time at a day centre for people struggling with substance abuse and mental health problems, where he could warm up and find something to eat. While he was there, he met social workers who told him they could find him an apartment. And even though Pasi was still struggling with addiction, debt, and all the other demons that kept him on the streets, that's exactly what they did. They found Pasi an apartment in a building called Ruusulankatu 10. The seven-storey concrete building comprises ninety-one apartments. It's modern, safe, and secure. It is not cozy. Not even close. The corridors are finished in institutional tones, with wipeable surfaces and no adornments other than the considerable felt marker graffiti on the two stainless steel elevators. But what it lacks in luxury it makes up for in stability.

Ruusulankatu 10 allows residents to use drugs, and is equipped for some of the problems that go along with that. Social workers and security staff keep watch, clean syringes and needles are available, and a poster in the lobby reminds residents that HIV testing is available in the building Monday to Thursday from 8 a.m. to 2 p.m. Residents are also taught basic life skills that many have missed along the way: cooking, cleaning, and looking after their finances.

There is no time limit; residents can stay for years. A few choose to leave, and a few more are evicted for behaving violently. But the vast majority stay. Pasi says having his own apartment in a safe building "revolutionized" his life. "Frankly," he told Finnish broadcaster MTV, "I wouldn't be here telling you my story without this apartment and the social workers."

Like many countries, Finland has been grappling with homelessness for a long time. In 1883, a shuttered theatre was converted into a makeshift shelter. The Helsinki Guest House—Helsingin Vieraskoti—let homeless Finns sleep in the old theatre seats. Known to locals as the Chapel of the Wretched, it offered better accommodation than sleeping outside in a deep freeze. The country's first dedicated shelter opened a decade later in Helsinki. The Salvation Army moved to Finland fifteen years after that, offering shelter to men in exchange for work in a woodyard attached to the shelter. Helsinki's shelters were overwhelmed at the end of the Second World War, when parts of Finland were ceded to the Soviet Union and more than 400,000 Finns were displaced. The country established a public housing agency in 1949, but homelessness was never eliminated. It reached a crisis point in 1967, the fiftieth anniversary of Finnish independence, when 950 prisoners were pardoned and released in honour of the anniversary. Most of the released prisoners had nowhere to go, and ended up homeless. At the same time, the Helsinki shelter that housed alcoholics closed its doors. The end result was that as many as fifty homeless people froze to death. In response, an overnight emergency shelter was opened that was often filled with more than a thousand people a night. In the decades that followed, more Finns called for an end to homelessness, and the national government made it an official priority.

"We decided to make the housing unconditional," says Juha Kaakinen, the CEO of Finland's housing non-profit Y-Foundation, "to say, 'Look, you don't need to solve your problems before you get a home.' Instead, a home should be the secure foundation that makes it easier to solve your problems."

Around the world, various housing agencies and communities have adopted the Housing First strategy, including Medicine Hat, Alberta. But Finland became the first country to take on the approach at the national level, and it seems to be working. While it's notoriously difficult to take an accurate census of homeless people— do you simply count people sleeping on sidewalks, or those couch surfing as well, and how many people have you missed?—national estimates put the number of single homeless people in Finland at about 20,000 in the mid-1980s. By 2021, that number had dropped below 4,000. The sight of people sleeping rough, on the streets or in parks, has been almost entirely eliminated in Helsinki. Only one overnight shelter remains in the Finnish capital. Others, like the 250-bed Salvation Army shelter, have been transformed into buildings of separate apartments, staffed with support workers around the clock.

The Y-Foundation was well situated to take advantage of the Housing First policy when it was adopted in Finland. The housing non-profit had already been buying rental apartment buildings for a few decades, whenever they came up for sale on the private market. But more was needed. The Finnish government paid in excess of €250 million to buy and build new apartments, and hire hundreds of support workers who were indispensable in helping the hardest-to-house residents live in their apartments. Between 1985 and 2016, the number of supported housing units soared from 127 to 1,309. Independent rentals went from 65 to 2,433 during that period. Meanwhile, the overnight shelter spaces plummeted from 2,121 down to 52.

So, is it worth it? That's a difficult one to answer. The people who have been housed will almost certainly say yes. So will their families.

And so will many of the people who have grown so tired of and troubled by seeing people sleeping on the streets. But what about from a strictly economic point of view? Does the money spent on buying and building public housing, and paying support staff to work around the clock, offset the costs of just leaving homeless people out on the streets? There is considerable evidence to suggest that it does. The Y-Foundation claims that moving one chronically homeless person into stable housing saves the government around €15,000 a year in social costs.

Housing First has been studied in other countries too. Angela Ly, with the Quebec Ministry of Health, and Eric Latimer, a psychiatry professor at McGill University, reviewed several studies that looked at the cost-benefit of Housing First in various countries. They concluded that costs in shelters and emergency departments decreased with Housing First, but found that costs to the justice system and hospitalizations were more ambiguous. However, they cautioned against simply looking for an economic rationale. "Such an approach can hardly be justified," they wrote, "as few health care innovations that governments agree to fund do so (for example, new cancer drugs); often, they generate no cost offset at all. Rather, they are judged to yield sufficient benefit to merit their cost."

The merit of Housing First is clear to the many people who have been housed because of it. Their lives aren't measured in euros or dollars, but are told in stories about their new homes. One of those stories features a 44-year-old former social worker who broke up with his girlfriend and wound up living in a hillside park in a tent. He cooked on a small barbecue and washed every day in a nearby boat terminal. "The best spot in Helsinki, my friends called it." Well, that was in the summer. Things got a lot more difficult in the winter. He dragged an old mattress into the tent and covered it with a tarp. When it was too cold, he'd make his way to those green public toilets and lock himself inside for a few hours of partial warmth. But on very cold nights he'd have to squeeze inside with as many as five other people. Moving into an apartment has been a huge improvement. For one thing, he stopped drinking. "You can't get sober when you're homeless—no one can." He also started to enjoy nature and personal relationships in healthier ways. Instead of camping in parks, he now goes for long hikes in the summer. And if he has an argument with his new girlfriend, he can simply go back to his apartment. "It's easy to leave when I have keys of my own in my pocket."

Another Housing First success story involves an American entrepreneur who moved to Finland after the 2008 financial crisis. He set up a business in his father's home country, rented an expensive apartment, and bought a luxury car. Things went well for a year, until business dried up. "So the business went down and I got evicted from my apartment because of circumstances that were just out of my control. It felt like a nightmare, so surreal. I had to move my things to my employee's house and go live in a hostel." When his secretary told him about the Y-Foundation—the non-profit housing provider that is now the fourth-largest landlord in Finland—he applied for housing, and moved in less than two months later. A back injury limited his ability to do manual labour. But his ground-floor apartment, coupled with the shared sauna in the building, helped him recover and start formulating a business plan for an American-style pizza parlour. "Having this apartment has provided me the ability to return to normal life and start planning the future again."

Finland's supported housing buildings are full of stories like these. In the Helsinki suburb of Espoo, a three-floor apartment building called Väinölä stands in a park-like setting beside a lake, with a barbecue area out back and a path down to the beach. Unlike Ruusulankatu 10, where Pasi Hietanen lives, Väinölä was not designed to house people with complex addiction and mental health needs. Many of the residents moved to Väinölä after several years of living in buildings that offered greater support, like a recovering alcoholic in his late fifties who spent five years in buildings with more intense supports. He stopped drinking eventually, and now helps fellow residents of Väinölä in their recovery. The man has lived on a disability pension for more than a decade, which pays for his small studio apartment and his other costs. "I want to stay and live in Väinölä. I don't have any urge to leave." New residents tour the building before moving in, and must sit through an interview as well. They're asked if they would be willing to do some of the basic chores that are a requirement of living there, like shovelling snow. Neighbours recognize the bright safety vests that all Väinölä residents wear while working on the property, and see daily reminders that the residents care about where they live.

Still, not everyone wants to stay. Some residents want an even more independent life, especially those who have never struggled with addiction. After all, homelessness affects people who led stable lives for decades. Sometimes it's a simple thing that leaves them homeless, like the 58-year-old asthmatic woman who lived in Espoo. When the building where she rented an apartment underwent a major renovation, she gave notice that she was leaving because all the dust made breathing so difficult. She spent the summer living with friends and looking for a new apartment. But she couldn't find one she could afford, and before she knew it, she was officially homeless. "That made everything feel uncertain," she wrote. "I felt like I was a second-class citizen, a reject. I started blaming myself and wondered if I could have done something differently." She was officially home-less for eight months before moving into Väinölä. Though grateful for the safety it provided, she was excited to move into a more inde-pendent building that offered more privacy. "An apartment means security—now I have a home to return to."

For many renters in other countries, security is the last thing they feel. But Finland has continued to put more people into stable housing while so many other countries have struggled. The national government's goal is to end homelessness by 2027. The city of Helsinki set an even more ambitious target of 2025. Juha Kahila, the head of international affairs at the Y-Foundation, says that's possible because both the country and the capital city continue to increase supply. "Every year we build more social housing, and every year 25 percent of that new housing must be affordable housing. So, frankly speaking, it's not some kind of utopia. It's actually doable."

That doesn't mean there aren't challenges. Juha used to be a support worker with homeless youth, and he knows first-hand that some people are just exceptionally difficult to house. He acknowledges not everyone manages to stay in housing. But he says the Y-Foundation has succeeded in keeping almost everyone indoors by offering a wide range of housing options, including small buildings with extra staffing and round-the-clock support for people with the highest needs. He points to one building that houses only seven people. They all have serious challenges, so those seven individuals are supervised by fourteen support staff. That may seem an inefficient use of resources, but Juha says that's the extreme, and that on average it costs less to house people than to pay for them to move through shelters, hospitals, and courtrooms indefinitely. He points to a study in Belgium that calculated the city of Brussels pays an average of €40,000 a year per homeless person. Apart from the cost of supporting people with significant needs, Juha says there is one other big challenge to the Housing First model: complacency. "When you visit Helsinki, you don't see people sleeping outside in sleeping bags anymore, so of course some people ask, 'Why are we even spending this money anymore?'"

There are also challenges for the people who've left a life on the street. Pasi Hietanen is grateful for the roof over his head and the support he receives in his new home. But living in a building with active drug users creates significant hurdles for someone trying to stay clean. He still gets knocks on his door, day and night, from people looking to score drugs. While that's a challenge, Pasi says it can also act as motivation "to get a new apartment of your own."

9

THE AIRBNB EFFECT

Montreal

JEAN-FRANÇOIS RAYMOND WASN'T EXPECTING an eviction notice in the last few days of 2022. He'd lived in his spacious apartment in Montreal's east end neighbourhood of Hochelaga-Maisonneuve for twenty-two years. It was home, in the truest sense of the word. "It was the place that I raised my kid," he said. "There are plenty of memories." But somewhere along the line, as Jean-François and his partner raised their child and lived their lives, the local borough established rules in an effort to limit short-term tourist accommodations like Airbnb. That was back in 2016, when the Mercier–Hochelaga-Maisonneuve borough council was under growing pressure to clamp down on the boom in short-term rental suites. So the elected officials drew up a set of what they hoped would be relatively simple rules that prohibited—at least on paper—apartments being operated as short-term vacation rentals in most areas. However, the council permitted vacation rentals "in areas where there are businesses and buildings with three or more dwellings."

Unfortunately for Jean-François, that included his three-storey building on Ontario Street. The busy thoroughfare is lined with an array of shops, cafés, and restaurants. "A thriving urban village with a friendly, small-town feel," according to Tourisme Montréal. Jean-François was shocked to learn his building was eligible for short-term rentals, and that the landlord would evict him for that purpose. "I am very angry because we're not leaving for his old mother or his child going to school. He's going to change us for a hotel, an Airbnb, for tourism."

Jean-François was upset about losing his home, and worried about his neighbour, a 68-year-old man who had lived there for more than half a century. The man is a senior and didn't want his name published because he feared it might make it harder for him to find a new place to live. It's hard to blame him for being unfamiliar with the rental market—he'd moved into that apartment with his parents when he was just 14 and had been there ever since. "It shocked me," he said. "After 54 years in the same place it will be difficult to move, especially at my age. It's demoralizing." Like Jean-François and his partner, the elderly man was given six months' notice. They had until July 2023 to find a new place. Not an easy task, given that he was paying only $685 for what's known in Montreal as a 6½ but would be described in many other cities as a three-bedroom apartment.

Jean-François's rent was $910 a month—nearly $400 more than he paid when he moved in, but a great deal less than most new rents in 2023. The price of the average two-bedroom rental apartment advertised in Montreal had ballooned to $1,800, with an average one-bedroom costing $1,470. Sure, Montreal rents are still significantly lower than in Toronto and Vancouver, but wages are lower in Montreal too, and rents were rising much faster than wages. Those rises were also more pronounced in certain areas, like Mercier–Hochelaga-Maisonneuve. Similar-sized apartments to those rented by Jean-François and his neighbour were listed the previous summer for $2,500 a month for long-term rentals. Short-term rentals could bring in even more money for the landlord.

Despite the law and the profit motive working against him, Jean-François wasn't willing to give up without a fight. He called local reporters to share the story, and unfurled a large improvised banner across the front of the building. A stark message was painted in red and black on a large white sheet: ÉVICTIONS EN COURS POUR UN FUTUR AIRBNB (Evictions under way for a future Airbnb). A pair of skull-and-crossbones symbols was added for good measure. But the publicity would only go so far. What Jean-François really needed was the law to back him up. He took the landlord to Quebec's Tribunal administratif du logement (administrative housing tribunal), asking for compensation from the landlord in recognition of all the years he and his elderly neighbour had spent in the building. The owners turned down interview requests, but the eviction notice clearly stated they planned to convert the apartments into short-term tourist rental suites.

Housing advocates urged councillors to change local rules to prevent the eviction of tenants by landlords intent on switching to short-term rentals. If nothing else, they argued, the borough could restrict conversions to apartments where a tenant has already decided to leave, or if the suite is in a new building. But the mayor of Mercier–Hochelaga-Maisonneuve said his hands were tied by provincial laws that restricted municipal bans to residential areas. "If it was up to me I would ban rentals for more than 30 days a year on Airbnb throughout the territory," Pierre Lessard-Blais lamented. "Someone who rents out their home for a week during their vacation is fine. But when it's more than 30 days a year, it becomes a business that prevents a family from having access to housing in a residential area." City politicians had already asked the Quebec government to change the law to ban evictions caused by short-term rental conversions. But when Jean-François and his neighbour received their eviction notices, there were no such bans in place.

It's not hard to imagine why landlords might want to convert old apartments in Hochelaga-Maisonneuve into Airbnbs or other short-term vacation rentals. The francophone neighbourhood was historically industrial and working-class—not the stuff of tourist brochures. But like a lot of Montreal's old neighbourhoods, its authentic character appeals to a lot of visitors. In the years since Jean-François moved into his modest apartment, other working-class neighbourhoods such as Verdun, Mile End, and St-Henri have gentrified. Once affordable areas with modest dépanneurs and shops, these neighbourhoods now boast chic cafés, microbreweries, and trendy restaurants. As new people and new styles moved in, prices went up. And as those neighbourhoods gentrified, surrounding areas like Hochelaga-Maisonneuve faced similar pressures. From a tourism perspective, the change in the neighbourhood is a good thing. Tourisme Montréal certainly thinks so: "From recycled factories to beautiful churches to striking institutional buildings, the borough's architectural landscape tells a tale of transformation and evolution . . . there's always something new to discover, with a wealth of new restaurants, cafés, local artisans, designers and socially-responsible boutiques ever-adding to the neighbourhood's allure."

It's a matter of opinion, or perspective, whether any given neighbourhood is more appealing once it gentrifies. What's less debatable is the general rule that neighbourhoods get more expensive for the people who live there as they gentrify. New rentals in Hochelaga-Maisonneuve are now several times higher than Jean-François and his neighbour can afford. But landlords could make even more money by cashing in on the demand for nightly vacation rentals, especially in the summer, when Ontario Street and Ste-Catherine Street East host outdoor festivals. The streets are closed to traffic, so patios and sidewalks fill up and visitors pour in. A quick scan of Airbnb shows two-bedroom apartments on Ontario Street going for anywhere from $265 to $460 a night in July. Single rooms were cheaper, at closer to $100. But an apartment like Jean-François's could fetch more than $10,000 a month in the summer, if it was renovated.

Of course, Airbnbs are in demand for a reason. Bruno Berumen, visiting Montreal from Guadalajara, Mexico, put it succinctly: "I'm staying in an Airbnb because I think it's cheaper than hotels, and also you have the facilities to take your food in the house and cook. Basically, that's why I prefer Airbnb to the hotels." The boom in Airbnb and other short-term rental websites has changed cities and towns around the world, with many Montreal residents among the millions of travellers staying in charming abodes on their overseas trips. For some Montreal renters, like Félix Blanche, there's an uneasy suspicion that the same platforms that helped them have a great vacation are also making their life back home a lot more difficult. "I've been to Europe last year, and it was great over there. But in this neighbourhood, as somebody who's trying to look for an apartment, who did for a few months, it was pretty rough probably because of Airbnb. I think it didn't really help the task, and made it much more difficult for me and my roommates."

For its part, Airbnb says the "home-sharing" service it provides amounts to a "significant boost to the Quebec economy." In 2018 it claimed that Airbnb visitors spent $475 million in Montreal—more than in both Toronto and Vancouver. Airbnb's director of public policy in Canada, Alex Dagg, said, "Airbnb guests visit stores, coffee shops, and restaurants in the neighbourhoods where they're staying—which supports local businesses and helps create jobs in the community." Of course, the same could be said of hotel visitors. But Airbnb points to a survey it commissioned that suggests "75 percent of Airbnb guests are more likely to travel to Montreal again because of Airbnb's offerings." It's difficult to say if that's true and, if so, whether it's worth the impact on local rents.

Cities around the world have debated the effects of short-term rentals on the affordability of housing. But in many cases it's been difficult to find enough data, from both companies and governments, to make an accurate assessment. That's started to change in recent years. Professor David Wachsmuth, at McGill University, is the Canada Research Chair in Urban Governance, and led a study on the impact of short-term rentals in Canada. He concluded the relatively new revenue source for landlords across Canada has been a major cause of housing financialization, where housing is treated as a commodity, or vehicle for profit and investment, rather than a social good. He also found most short-term rentals are owned by big companies rather than private individuals, and that financial incentives placed significant pressure on housing as more long-term rentals were converted to short-term. Wachsmuth's study found 31,000 homes were taken out of Canada's long-term housing market as a direct result of short-term rentals. The impact was higher in neighbourhoods with good transit, amenities, and easy access to city centres, like Hochelaga-Maisonneuve. Across Montreal, Wachsmuth estimates 6,000 homes were taken out of the rental market to be converted into vacation suites. "Removing this chunk of short-term rental apartments off the market makes it substantially harder to find a rental apartment in Montreal."

Jean-François Raymond loved Hochelaga-Maisonneuve. But as he started to look for other rentals, he realized his modest carpenter's income was no longer enough to afford the neighbourhood he'd called home for decades. "It will be very, very hard to find somewhere on Montreal Island, so we'll probably move off the Island like everybody else because it's too expensive."

Short-term rentals are a long-term concern in many cities, but the worry is especially pronounced in Montreal because the city has so many renters. In fact, Montreal has the highest share of renter-occupied housing of any large or mid-sized North American city. More than 63 percent of Montreal housing units were rented, according to the 2016 census. The city was known for many years as a renters' paradise because of low rents and high vacancy rates, thanks to an abundance of low-rise rental housing. But the seeds of change were sown in the 1990s, when the federal government stopped building social housing and legalized real estate investment trusts (REITs), a model of pooled real estate ownership developed in the United States. REITs have been a popular choice for Canadian investors, big and small, and have purchased thousands of rental buildings across the country, with the purpose of maximizing profits for investors. In many cases that meant renovating old buildings to charge much higher rents. For many long-time renters, it led to renoviction—an eviction that's carried out to renovate a rental unit.

Rents in Montreal started to rise in the 2010s, even though construction of new purpose-built rental units remained healthy. The city added 13,500 purpose-built apartments between 2016 and 2020, but new rental buildings are exempt from rent control laws for five years after construction. In 2019, just before the outbreak of the COVID-19 pandemic, Montreal's rents rose 4.2 percent, the largest average increase in twenty years. That's higher than the annual rate of increase that's allowed by Quebec law, where rent control is supposed to apply to the rental unit rather than the tenant. But a 2023 study into the financialization of rental housing in Montreal found that didn't always work: "In practice there is no way to ensure that rents are not raised illegally when a new tenant arrives. There is no registry to consult, the outgoing tenant does not always communicate the previous rent to the future tenant, and not everyone has the courage to speak up against their landlord's violations." Cloé St-Hilaire and her co-authors found the high demand for rentals stifled many tenant objections to rent increases "because tenants fear they will lose their homes and be unable to find a replacement." That's not surprising, given that Montreal's vacancy rate had dropped to an all-time low of 1.6 percent in 2019. It all adds up to a rough ride for renters.

Meanwhile, the city of Montreal was trying new measures to protect affordable rentals. In 2022 it legislated a sixty-day right of first refusal that allows the city to step in on the sale of any rental property and match the offer on the table. The new law allowed the city to buy seventy-eight rooming houses that housed hundreds of low-income residents. That's good news for those renters. But across the city, many are still struggling with rising rents and evictions.

Guillaume Dostaler, a tenants' rights coordinator with the group Entraide logement Hochelaga-Maisonneuve, sees it every day. He tries to help tenants who've been evicted to make way for short-term rental conversions, and counsels new immigrants who are too timid to speak out against illegal rent increases. But he doesn't think things will get better for Montreal renters unless the provincial government creates a comprehensive new registry of all rental units. Without that, he says, apartments will continue to be converted into short-term rentals, and landlords will jack up rents illegally between tenants. When asked if he expects the provincial government to do that, Guillaume scoffs. *"Pas du tout,"* he says. Not at all.

Many renters wonder whether their political leaders really understand their plight. When Quebec premier François Legault and his wife put their 8,000-square-foot Victorian mansion in downtown Montreal up for sale in 2021, the listing price was just under $5 million. During the provincial election campaign the following year, Legault disclosed he'd moved into a condominium with a declared value of $3.2 million. Legault had come under fire during the pandemic from the opposition Québec solidaire (QS) party for suggesting Montreal renters could find an apartment for as little as $500 a month. "It depends on the size of the apartment, but I would say it can start at maybe $500 to $600 a month, and it can go up to $1,000 a month pretty quickly," he said. QS's Manon Massé invited the premier "to meet people who've been kicked out, by eviction, of their apartment, and talk with them, and maybe ask questions such as: How much? What is the impact of the rent of your apartment on your family budget? How much money stays in your pocket to pay the bills, to pay for food?" The premier bristled at the suggestion he was out of touch with the working classes, whom he considered his people, saying his comments were misconstrued, and that he only meant a student sharing a larger apartment could expect to pay so little. Legault also went on to win the 2022 election, with no obligation to create a rental registry.

Even if Quebec does create a registry, there's reason to wonder if it would really work. After all, the provincial government enacted wide-ranging restrictions on short-term rentals when the Liberals were in power in 2015. Hosts had to register their short-term rental unit with Revenu Québec or face fines. No fines were handed out the first year the law was in effect. None. A few years later, Legault's CAQ government made the rules more stringent; short-term landlords had to buy a registration number and display it on their listings. But critics say these rules have had little effect. "I think Quebec has the best system in the whole country on paper," David Wachsmuth of McGill University says, "but it has not put in any effort to make sure that anybody follows those rules." Hopefully, that will just take more time. The city of Montreal allows boroughs, like Mercier–Hochelaga-Maisonneuve, to choose areas where short-term rentals are restricted to thirty days a year. And Revenu Québec reported handing out more than nine hundred fines to short-term rental hosts in 2021. Still, that's probably a drop in the Airbnb bucket. The independent activist group Inside Airbnb found 12,500 Airbnb listings in Montreal in December 2021, and claimed more than 95 percent of them were unlicensed.

Stories of unlicensed vacation rentals causing problems for neighbours spread across Montreal in both official languages. A frat house atmosphere is described in some buildings, with people vomiting out of windows at 3 a.m. and raves that last until 11 a.m. Jammed elevators and wrecked laundry rooms are among the bitter memories, along with one memorable evening when a drunk woman yelled out a window, "We love you, Montreal!" The neighbours did not reciprocate. Of course, bad behaviour has been around a lot longer than Airbnb, and many who have stayed in short-term rentals have followed the rules and done their best to respect the neighbours. But many neighbours complain they don't like the arrangement, and would rather see the surrounding apartments occupied by permanent residents.

Despite the inconvenience and rising rents, many tenants won't complain. Rebecca Bain has seen that first-hand. A musician in her fifties, with a master's degree in medieval music from Switzerland's Schola Cantorum Basiliensis, she's seen the benefits that affordable rents and stable housing give to a community. "Montreal was a haven for artists," she says wistfully, remembering a time when most of the apartments in her working-class neighbourhood were truly affordable for the vast majority of people. She's called St-Henri home for more than twenty years, but has seen it change rapidly of late. "Montreal's character is changing, and my neighbourhood is completely changed." Like Hochelaga-Maisonneuve, the southwest borough where St-Henri is located has become much more expensive in the last decade. She's watched as the post office and local dépanneurs closed their doors and were replaced with expensive restaurants, and noticed fewer families with young children on the streets. She understands that young professionals and other people moving into the neighbourhood also need a place to live, but she wonders where the people who have lived in St-Henri for decades will go when they get evicted. "The elderly people live on a fixed income. There's literally nowhere else for them to go. They will not find anywhere else."

Again, Rebecca has seen this first-hand. When the sixplex she lived in was sold to a Montreal property company, she and all the other tenants in the building received eviction notices. The building was going to be renovated, they were told, despite having been refurbished just a few years earlier. Rebecca believes the new owners just wanted to make them fancier so they could charge more money. First they got formal letters, then the phone calls started. A woman who refused to identify herself called Rebecca repeatedly. Eventually, she told Rebecca her name was Cindy and that she was talking to her from a room full of lawyers. "But she was rude to me, so I hung up." Rebecca then went to her local tenants' rights group, and learned the same company had bought several buildings in the neighbourhood and had handed eviction notices to more than forty renters. Rebecca says they all received similarly intimidating phone calls. Eventually, all of the five other residents of Rebecca's building agreed to leave. But she refused. "I know my rights." Along with dozens of other tenants, she fought the landlord and was allowed to stay, paying roughly $900 a month for her 4½ (small two-bedroom apartment). She lived through all the renovations of the other units, and befriended the workers, hoping they wouldn't harass her (they didn't). And when the new tenants moved into her building, they all ended up paying much, much more. "So everyone else in my building now pays twice what I pay, and every time a new tenant comes in, they add another two hundred on . . . It's only supposed to be a very small percentage more."

Without a rent registry, there are few complaints and little oversight. And renters are often relieved just to find somewhere they can afford, even if it does gobble up a large portion of their income. Rebecca isn't holding her breath that things will change, and she wonders if too many people are more concerned with their own personal gain than the overall well-being of their communities. "Housing is a right and I feel somehow it's become a privilege," she laments. "It shouldn't be a luxury to have a decent place to live."

10

A LONG-TERM STRATEGY
ON SHORT-TERM RENTALS

Santa Monica, California

WHEN SCOTT SHATFORD WAS laid off from his six-figure corporate job in 2013, he decided to take a vacation. He booked himself a one-way plane ticket to Bangkok, not knowing when he'd come home to California. Before he left, he wondered what he should do with his swanky Santa Monica apartment. He briefly thought about packing up all his stuff and putting it in storage. Maybe he could find someone to sublet the place. But then one of his neighbours suggested he list the apartment on a relatively new website called Airbnb. The company was started in 2008 in San Francisco when a pair of enterprising roommates came up with the idea of renting out an air mattress in their apartment to people who couldn't find a hotel room in the city. By the fall of 2012, the company was a tech darling worth more than a billion. Scott had heard of Airbnb, but he'd never given it much thought until now. The need to pay his $3,000 monthly rent focused his attention, though, so he decided he'd give it a try.

He took a few photos of the apartment on his iPhone, created a listing on the Airbnb website, and agreed to loan a friend free use of his SUV if the friend would manage his apartment while he was gone. "Within a week I was flying over the Pacific, nervous that I had just opened the doors of my home to a bunch of lunatics."

Scott was relieved to find out his first guests were a retired couple from Wisconsin, who were so friendly they started sending him travel advice based on their own trip to Thailand the previous year. Scott's Airbnb anxiety eased, and he decided to let more guests come and go. A series of visitors stayed in his apartment while he was seeing new sights in Southeast Asia. It took three weeks and six bookings for Scott to earn enough to pay his rent. He stayed on holiday for almost four months, and as both the bookings and money added up, he started to think of other possibilities.

When he returned to Santa Monica, Scott moved into his girlfriend's cramped one-bedroom apartment and started some number crunching. He was still in his early thirties, and decided he could live like a student again in the interest of pursuing a new business venture. He cut back on some non-essential utilities and raised some of his nightly rates. Before long, he was bringing in more than $6,500 every month from his apartment, and starting to think bigger. He then rented a luxury penthouse apartment for $3,695 a month. He spent nearly $7,000 to furnish the place, then listed it on Airbnb. The penthouse was booked almost immediately, and started paying for itself quickly. Within a few months Scott was making an extra $3,500 a month from the penthouse, over and above all his costs. But he didn't stop there. In the months that followed, he signed more leases and eventually had five separate Airbnb listings in five separate rental apartments. By 2014, without owning any property, he was pulling in more than $300,000 a year—a profit margin of around 60 percent. And all that for roughly four hours of work every week.

Scott calculated his new endeavour paid him an hourly wage of about $425. "I've made all of my money without owning much of anything," he boasted in an e-book he wrote called *The Airbnb Expert's Playbook: Secrets to Making Six-Figures as a Rentalpreneur.* "I sign long-term leases on properties for the sole purpose of renting them on a short-term basis. In the financial world they call this arbitrary opportunity—taking advantage of differing prices for the same commodity."

Practically speaking, Scott's arbitrage opportunity had taken five long-term rental apartments out of the local housing pool and turned them into de facto hotels. But his operation was much smaller than some. Scott started consulting for other Airbnb hosts, many of whom were operating between twenty-five and fifty vacation listings. Others had more than a hundred.

While Scott Shatford and other "rentalpreneurs" signed leases across Santa Monica, other residents were getting worried about what that would do to local housing supply. The scenic coastal city, west of downtown Los Angeles, already had some of the highest rents in the United States. Housing advocates warned rents would only go higher if more apartments were taken out of the rental market, and local politicians were inclined to believe them. When Santa Monica city councillors met in the spring of 2015, they discussed growing concerns around the rise of vacation rentals, which were defined locally as whole homes that could be rented out for less than thirty days. Council members voted unanimously in favour of new rules to ban vacation rentals of whole homes but allow people to rent out single rooms, if they purchased a business licence from the city and paid a 14 percent hotel tax. The legislators were trying to allow for the important distinction between people who needed a bit of financial help with their rent or mortgage payments and those who were looking to make an easy profit through those arbitrary opportunities, as Scott called them. The Home-Sharing Ordinance spelled out exactly what would define home-sharing in Santa Monica—that the primary resident remain "on-site during the visitor's stay." By contrast, vacation rentals were defined as any rental less than thirty days where a guest "enjoys the exclusive private use of the unit." City officials said there were 1,700 vacation rentals in Santa Monica at the time. They estimated the new ordinance would return more than 1,300 of those back to the long-term rental market.

Airbnb argued its "home-sharing" service was used primarily by normal people trying to make ends meet. A 2014 report from New York's Attorney General cast doubt on that. It found 37 percent of all host revenue in New York City was collected by just 6 percent of Airbnb hosts. The company suggested it was the victim of an orchestrated lobbying campaign by the hotel industry, which by that point was more than a little concerned about the financial threat that short-term home rentals posed to their bottom line. "We know that the hotel industry is out there running a full-fledged campaign," a company spokesperson said.

While other cities looked at legislation to restrict vacation rentals, Airbnb levelled specific criticism at Santa Monica. "The proposal fails to provide clear, fair rules for home sharing," the company said in a statement. "We will continue to highlight the importance of fair rules with leaders in Santa Monica and throughout Southern California." Santa Monica is home to about ninety thousand people—a relatively small drop in the Greater Los Angeles bucket of more than 18 million. But the city established a full-time task force dedicated to enforcing its new vacation rental ordinance. The small team included two enforcement officers and an analyst.

Scott Shatford continued his lucrative business, in spite of the new city ordinance, keeping all five Airbnb listings active. "The money's too good," he told one reporter. But city officials received a complaint from one of the guests who stayed in one of his apartments. She was surprised to learn she was staying in a short-term rental that was illegal, and said she was uncomfortable with the arrangement. City officials decided to investigate, and as part of that investigation they made a reservation in one of his apartments. The four-night stay cost them $1,200 but provided them with a rental agreement that would eventually be used as evidence in court. Before that, however, the city sent him citations, informing him that his Airbnb listings were illegal and he should stop. Scott said he didn't receive those citations because they were mailed directly to his vacation properties, where he wasn't in the habit of checking the mail regularly. He wasn't convinced he would face any consequences, but prosecutors proved him wrong, charging him with eight misdemeanour counts of operating a business without a licence and failing to comply with citations. He pleaded no contest and was placed on probation for two years. He also agreed to pay a $3,500 fine. "Even with the $3,500 fine, that's what one of my properties makes in a month."

But Scott Shatford wouldn't be making that money anymore. He agreed to one other important provision as part of his plea deal with the city prosecutor: he would stop renting properties in Santa Monica. Despite the outcome, Scott Shatford was unapologetic. "The city came after me to make me their little poster child and be able to promote me as their first victory. It's pretty silly." City officials didn't use the term "poster child," but they were quick to point to Scott Shatford as a cautionary tale for other Airbnb landlords. "The city views its rental prohibition quite seriously," deputy city attorney Yibin Shen said, "and it takes enforcement of these laws quite seriously." And the Los Angeles press gave the story considerable coverage: "Santa Monica Convicts Its First Airbnb Host Under Tough Home-sharing Laws," was the headline in the *Los Angeles*

Times. The popular local blog *LAist* declared "Santa Monica Busts Its First Airbnb 'Rentalpreneur.'"

Scott Shatford had lived in Santa Monica for thirteen years. But in 2016 he decided he'd had enough. A few weeks after making headlines, he moved to Denver, where he hoped to focus his attention on his other business venture—a vacation rental analytics company called AirDNA that claimed it could help homeowners "Airbnb like a pro."

But Airbnb wasn't about to leave town. The company teamed up with another short-term vacation rental site, HomeAway, to take the city of Santa Monica to court. The companies claimed the city's ordinance was in violation of the Communications Decency Act—a federal law that protects online platforms from liability when publishing third-party content—because it forced them to monitor and potentially remove what home renters put on its site. But a district court judge rejected the companies' argument and ruled that the ordinance simply required the companies to ensure listings came from people with registered properties, and a panel of three appeal court judges upheld that ruling.

The companies weren't the only ones to take the city of Santa Monica to court. Local resident Arlene Rosenblatt sued, claiming the ordinance was an unconstitutional infringement on commerce. She'd been renting out her home for $350 a night when she and her husband left town. She said her home was more affordable than the "ultra-luxurious, highly occupied and pricey hotels in the city." She argued the city passed the ordinance in an attempt to stop a decline in the revenue it collected from the 14 percent hotel tax, and that it was an illegal attempt to regulate interstate commerce because the overwhelming majority of visitors were from outside California. A panel of three judges on the US Ninth Circuit of Appeals rejected her arguments and ruled out the possibility of a class action suit.

Despite winning in court, the city of Santa Monica was struggling to keep up with the heavy burden of monitoring the huge demand for vacation rentals. Kevin McKeown, who served two separate terms as mayor of Santa Monica while the city was grappling with the Home-Sharing Ordinance, said enforcement was the city's biggest challenge. Not only did it have to monitor and fine illegal vacation listings, but city officials were kept busy with legal listings. "Wherever you have regulations, you'll have people who exploit the loopholes," he said.

By 2019 there were only 351 registered home-shares in the city, most of which were listed on Airbnb. But some of those proved more challenging than others. A beautiful Spanish-style house in the North of Montana neighbourhood caused an uproar among neighbours who complained it was a "quasi hostel." The 2,786-square-foot house had four bedrooms, three bathrooms, and a converted garage. It was sold in the spring of that year for nearly $2.9 million. The new owner listed it on Airbnb just a few months later, with individual bunk beds going for $49 a night. The listing claimed a "maximum of 36 people in total can stay at the same time combining all rooms." The new owner appeared to have taken one of Scott Shatford's key pieces of advice to heart: "more heads in beds." City officials confirmed to local media that the owner of the home had purchased a home-sharing licence from the city, and appeared to be taking advantage of a loophole in the Home-Sharing Ordinance that required the host to live in the house and restrict stays to thirty days but did not limit the number of guests. The only obvious limit was the local fire code, which fire officials said would allow only fourteen paying guests in that house. Neighbours complained on social media and directly to city staff. They described litter, fleets of e-scooters and e-bikes, and noise at all hours. "It's worse than a hotel," neighbour Paula Kayton complained, "it's just an absolute mess." Others complained the city wasn't enforcing its Home-Sharing Ordinance, with one person writing, "it appears that your 'enforcement' policy is quite timid." One elected council member countered that the city had prosecuted three other landlords. But the incident proved that the problems associated with short-term rentals wouldn't simply disappear with one law.

City officials were learning the hard way that effective regulations on short-term vacation rentals would require significant oversight, and a fair bit of tweaking. After years of defending its laws in court, the city finally came to an agreement with Airbnb in December 2019. Officials said the agreement would "dramatically reduce" the number of illegal listings in Santa Monica because it required Airbnb to include a city licence number on every listing. It would limit the number of listings to two per residence—a measure specifically aimed at preventing the creation of de facto hostels with multiple bunk beds rented out to multiple strangers at a time. Airbnb also agreed to collect two dollars to go to the city's coffers for every night booked—a modest fee, and one the company collects in some other cities, but one that Santa Monica officials hoped would pay for the construction of affordable housing. The company agreed to provide the city with regular reports to help with its compliance and enforcement efforts. Former mayor Kevin McKeown called the agreement with Airbnb a win for affordable housing, saying, "We can now better protect real permanent homes, especially our affordable rent-controlled apartments, from being used as de facto hotel rooms, displacing our neighbors."

Santa Monica got to work building hundreds of affordable apartments and funding the construction through its Housing Trust Fund. Several new mid-rise apartment buildings went up, with units ranging from studios to three bedrooms, and all reserved for people with lower incomes. Each building had its own specific stipulations:

some were reserved for seniors; others for people making between 30 percent and 50 percent of the local median income. For a single person in 2022, that would have meant an annual income between $25,000 and $41,000. A family of four could earn between $35,000 and $59,000. The new residents could enjoy comfortable new apartments that were built to a high standard, as well as the security of knowing rents would not increase more than a few percent a year. The apartments were snapped up as soon as they were built—proving both their popularity and the acute need for affordable housing in Santa Monica. It convinced many city officials that they would need to continue to build more affordable apartments, but also provide other, more immediate forms of support.

Santa Monica started a pilot project to give local seniors extra money to help them pay their rent. To be eligible, the seniors needed to be 65 or older and have lived in a rent-controlled apartment in Santa Monica for twenty years, and to have an income of less than $39,450 for a single person or $45,050 for a couple. The monthly cash topped up seniors' after-rent income to $700 for singles and $1,225 for couples. For a 70-year-old renter named Kaye, the extra money was the difference between being housed and being homeless. "If it weren't for the city of Santa Monica helping me, I would probably by now have been evicted and on the street." A quick glance at Kaye gave no indication she was struggling. Dressed in a red skirt and top, with matching lipstick and an elegant scarf, she looked comfortable, even prosperous. But her social security cheques brought in only a thousand dollars a month, and that left Kaye with almost nothing after paying the rent. "If I didn't have money to eat after paying my monthly bills, I just didn't eat." But the monthly cheques from the city made a huge difference and stopped her regular trips to the food banks. The city of Santa Monica deemed the pilot project a success and expanded it to support hundreds more people. But while the city helped more seniors with rent assistance, it found itself in a rental apartment version of Whac-A-Mole, where the construction of a new apartment building, or the development of a new financial assistance program, was followed by yet another challenge for the Home-Sharing Ordinance.

In 2020 the tenants' rights group SMRR (Santa Monicans for Renters' Rights) claimed a growing number of landlords were renting out fully furnished apartments. The group said these apartments were "corporate rentals" and were being used as temporary lodging for people who were visiting Santa Monica. City council members responded with a new ordinance that required new units to be rented unfurnished for at least a year. SMRR hailed the move as an "additional layer of protection for existing tenancies and rental housing units against permanent loss and misuse." But Santa Monica remains a popular destination with tourists looking for the long beaches and vibrant cityscapes they associate with Southern California. Kevin McKeown says it's inevitable that the demand for tourist accommodation will continue to strain the local housing supply for years to come. "It's just an endless chase!"

Meanwhile, Scott Shatford is still chasing the short-term rental dream. After he moved to Denver, he turned his attention to his analytics company AirDNA, which helps tens of thousands of short-term vacation rental hosts. The company offers specific advice on pricing and marketing, and other important information on how to maximize profits for existing rentals and, maybe more importantly, which specific communities could be the next tourist hot spots. "We're really pushing everybody into Joshua Tree, or some places in Tennessee, or Destin, Florida, where there are appreciation rates that far exceed anywhere else . . . and homes get more expensive in those markets pretty quickly." He describes the process as taking a home and turning it into a hotel. "It's like, 'Okay, cool, what can I actually make to live on this property as a real commercial property?' And that's the interesting thing we see happening—people are actually paying premiums, bidding up, getting into bidding wars for properties that have predictable revenue or have revenue streams that are going to be pretty substantial." It remains to be seen which new hot spots will also see substantial concerns being raised by renters and housing advocates. Scott Shatford believes demand will keep growing, and says, "The only thing that puts a damper on short-term rentals is regulation."

Former mayor Kevin McKeown agrees that regulation will be the main way to keep vacation rentals in check, but he sees regulation from a very different perspective. He thinks capitalism and housing "work against each other in a community like ours," and he believes the long-term solution is to somehow separate home ownership from wealth. For now, though, he says the city of Santa Monica will have to remain vigilant and take a long-term approach on short-term vacation rentals. "The price of success will be eternal vigilance, and the willingness to sometimes lead constituents in what they think they want, not follow them."

IN SHORT SUPPLY

St-Boniface, Quebec

DIANE LONGPRÉ STARTED LOOKING for a new place to live almost six months before she had to move. As a writer, editor, and publishing house coordinator she understood the value of being organized and not leaving things to the last minute. So she started her house hunt in January, just a month after separating from her partner. She needed a home or apartment with enough space for herself and her four daughters, who ranged in age from two to 14. Diane thought she had enough time to find a new rental that she could afford. "But I found nothing," she recalls. "I searched and searched. I made so many phone calls!" There weren't many homes for rent in the Mauricie region, where she and her daughters lived. But Diane wanted to stay in the area so the kids could remain at the same schools and daycares, and so it wouldn't be too far to drive back and forth to their two fathers' homes.

As Quebec's annual July 1 *jour du déménagement* (moving day) approached, Diane scoured listings in several small towns between Shawinigan and Trois-Rivières. Moving day is the remarkable tradition that sees thousands of people across the province move into new homes at the same time. Many years, more than 100,000 households move on one chaotic day. The custom dates back centuries to a time when French colonial rulers banned leases from expiring before the spring snow melt. For many years, the law dictated that leases would begin on May 1 and end on April 30. In 1973, the Quebec Liberal government pushed the date back to July 1 so children wouldn't have to move schools before the summer. It also helped that it fell on a public holiday so most people would already have the day off. Lease agreements can now be signed with any dates that both landlord and renter agree to, but most leases in the province still begin on July 1 and end on June 30.

In her search, Diane found a few suites with three bedrooms. But when landlords heard she had four children, they told her their listings would be better suited to couples, or single renters. "Single mothers are not popular with landlords! But I just wanted to settle down with my family and start a new life in a new home."

As July 1 got closer, the stress grew worse, and Diane found herself constantly distracted by the simple question, Where will we live? *"J'étais tellement stressé,"* she recalls. (I was so stressed.) Sick with worry, Diane found herself awake many nights. In the daytime, she was irritable and impatient with her kids. She kept scouring new listings, and calling landlords as soon as new rentals appeared. She offered signed proof of her employment and income, and managed to view a few units in person. Diane found a large house for rent in St-Élie, and was sure it was big enough, but the landlord told her he didn't want more than four people living there. "I'm not moving in with five roommates to party all the time. I want to settle down with my children, that's all!" Diane found another three-bedroom rental listed at $1,600 a month that looked promising. But once again she was told she had too many kids.

Diane wasn't alone. Other families across the Mauricie region were in a similar predicament. Affordable housing had been getting harder and harder to find, and in the summer of 2022 local housing advocates and officials feared they'd have more homeless families looking for emergency shelters. The city of Trois-Rivières had an existing agreement with local hotels to temporarily house tenants after July 1. But it was an uneasy arrangement, as Quebec's moving day falls right at the start of the busy summer tourist season. Hotels that would otherwise provide emergency accommodation might be fully booked. Some of the families who moved into temporary hotel accommodation might qualify for subsidized public housing, but Diane's middle-class income disqualified her. Financial thresholds that were determined a few years earlier, it seemed, hadn't kept up with current market costs. She continued to search and apply for new rentals, but when the beginning of June rolled around, she still had nowhere to go.

Fortunately for Diane, the father of her older two daughters let her move into his house in St-Boniface. The modest single-family home was surrounded by a big green lawn with a trampoline and plenty of space for kids to burn off youthful energy. But it was a temporary solution. And the stress of not knowing where or when she'd find a permanent home was showing on Diane's face as she continued house hunting while staying at her ex-spouse's home. Smartly dressed, with a short haircut, a nose ring, and fashionable glasses, Diane was still professional and organized, but the worry was visible on her face as she carried her youngest daughter on her hip and wondered when, or even if, she would find a new home of her own.

Karyne Cloutier found herself with similar questions. Like Diane, Karyne was a single mother of four. And also like Diane, she had an extremely difficult time finding a place to rent. While Diane was looking in small towns, Karyne was looking in Montreal, but the struggle was similar and also stretched on for six months without success. "I'm so exhausted, I feel like crying," she said. "Everyone is refusing me or completely ignoring me as soon as I mention that I have four young children." Finding an apartment for five is difficult at the best of times, but Karyne eventually found a 5½ with a basement and a backyard advertised for $1,600 a month. She jumped into action as soon as she saw the ad, messaging the landlord on Kijiji to ask if it was still available.

"Oui, c'est disponible pour le 1 octobre," the landlord replied. (Yes, it's available on October 1.)

"Vous acceptez les enfants dans l'immeuble?" Karyne asked. (Do you accept children in the building?)

"Combien d'enfants?" the landlord asked. (How many children?)

Karyne replied— *"Quatre"*—and held her breath, waiting for the text reply.

"Malheureusement on cherche une famille avec 2 enfants ou moins," the landlord wrote back, dashing Karyne's hopes again. (Unfortunately we are looking for a family with two children or fewer.)

It isn't legal for a landlord to refuse a tenant because they have children, according to the non-profit legal advice organization Éducaloi, which says Quebec's Charter of Human Rights and Freedoms explicitly prohibits that type of discrimination. But when landlords can pick and choose between multiple prospective tenants, it's difficult for desperate renters to complain about the practice, let alone stop it.

With no home to call her own, Karyne and her four young children stayed with her mother at her home in the Montreal borough of LaSalle. Karyne was studying at Champlain College to become a hospital orderly. She was collecting social assistance cheques and hoping for a brighter future, eventually, in an apartment of her own.

But while she did, she worried about her young children—a six-year-old, a five-year-old, and three-year-old twins—as well as the stress that living with them was putting on her aging mother.

Across Quebec, more families faced similar stresses. A 2022 Léger survey of Quebecers, for the Observatoire des tout-petits, found the rising cost of living and the shortage of housing put extra pressure on parents and affected the development of their children as the families cut spending on activities, clothing, and even food. Parents who were renters suffered most, with 60 percent saying they had less money to spend. In single-parent households that number rose to 75 percent. More than half of all renting parents feared not being able to pay their bills.

In 2021, the Pan-Canadian Women's Housing & Homelessness Survey found 28 percent of women-led single-parent households are in "core housing need," a bureaucratic term that refers to people who live in accommodation that is deemed either inadequate or unsuitable, or where more than 30 percent of before-tax income is needed to pay rent. In other words, people in core housing need are in dire need of better, more affordable housing. The high rate for women in this category was almost double the equivalent for families where the sole parent is a man, at 16 percent of before-tax income. The survey found "experiencing a breakup was the primary reason that women and gender diverse people lost their most recent housing," with 47 percent reporting that experience. This suggests that housing for this group is deeply dependent upon maintaining a personal relationship with someone who earns more money. "[I]n order to remain housed many women and gender diverse people have to remain in a romantic and/or sexual relationship of some kind."

An hour east of Montreal, in Quebec's Eastern Townships, Marilène Bédard found herself looking for a new home after she split from her spouse. The couple separated in the spring of 2022, leaving her little more than a month to find a new home for herself and her two teenaged children to move into on July 1. The average rent advertised on Kijiji in Granby, where she lives, had gone up an astounding 55 percent from 2021 to 2022. That left Marilène struggling to find a three-bedroom apartment she could afford. All she found were a few listings between $1,500 and $2,000, and even those were hard to come by. By the end of June she'd only found one apartment that she might move into, but it wasn't going to be available for another five months. As a result she had to take turns living in her ex-partner's house with their kids. When her ex was staying with the kids, Marilène stayed with her parents.

While single mothers like Marilène Bédard, Karyne Cloutier, and Diane Longpré rely on family for help, others are not so lucky. Sylvie Bonin, with the Association coopérative d'économie familiale de l'Estrie, an advocacy group for low-income consumers, sees some women who are stuck in toxic relationships because they can't afford to leave and find a new home. She's been watching the more subtle, often invisible effects as rising rents have spilled out of Montreal into smaller towns across Quebec. "The alarm bells have been sounding for years." With July 1 looming and more renters across Quebec scrambling to find new homes, she spent much of her time urging the Quebec government to create a provincial emergency fund for renters who end up homeless when their lease expires.

In the meantime, many smaller cities and towns across Quebec decided to provide their own emergency funds. In Cowansville—population twelve thousand—the town did exactly that for the first time in 2022. The modest fund of $5,000 came out of the municipal budget and was intended to "pay costs associated with temporary housing and storage." The town also asked Quebec's Ministry of Municipal Affairs for more financial assistance. Mayor Sylvie Beauregard said a rash of renovictions had brought the situation in her hometown to a crisis point. "People have been taking lump sums of cash to leave their apartment, and then finding nothing else was available." Little more than a week before July 1 moving day, she said as many as thirty families in the town would have to move into emergency housing. Over the next few days a handful of families found apartments, but by early July twenty-three families were still without a home in Cowansville.

The social housing advocacy group FRAPRU (Front d'action populaire en réaménagement urbain) estimated that more than a hundred families were in similar straits in other smaller Quebec cities and towns, and they pointed at the remarkably low vacancy rates in those towns as proof. An annual CMHC survey, conducted a few months earlier, showed that thirty Quebec municipalities had a vacancy rate below 1 percent, with a rock-bottom rate of just 0.2 percent in Drummondville. Things got so bad in that city of eighty thousand people that the local shelters were "at maximum capacity," according to Mayor Stéphanie Lacoste. So Ensoleilvent, a non-profit group that helps the homeless, accepted an unusual offer of twenty tiny homeless shelters from a private donor. Each of the basic wood structures has a door, a bed, a mattress, a desk, and little else. The move was criticized as a stopgap by some housing advocates, who pointed out that sheds are no replacement for real homes. But Mayor Lacoste said they were preferable to people sleeping outside on a freezing February night. "The need is immediate."

The fear of becoming homeless has a significant impact on rental markets because many renters stay in unsuitable or even unsafe apartments out of fear they'll never find an affordable home again. Mario Mercier, with the tenants' rights group Association des locataires de Sherbrooke, says, "If you stay in your house, your rent increase is usually not that high, but if you go somewhere else, it will go way up. It's in your interest to stay where you are unless there's a danger to your health." As more people stay where they are, it gets considerably more difficult for new arrivals to find a safe and affordable place to rent. Many of the people Mario helps are immigrants who've recently arrived in Canada, who often "have more kids, three or four, so they need bigger homes." Mario has watched the shortage of affordable housing get worse over the last two decades. He's noticed more invisible homelessness, where people are couch surfing, living in vehicles, or hiding in parks and wooded areas. And he's seen the housing crisis affect several different demographics.

In addition to the immigrant families, Mario sees a lot of post-secondary students who can't find a place to live. Sherbrooke (which includes the borough of Lennoxville) has multiple post-secondary institutions, with more than forty thousand students among them. Post-secondary students make up more than 10 percent of Sherbrooke's population—the highest concentration in Quebec. And while many students still receive accommodation in university dorm rooms, others struggle to find a safe place to live. When 17-year-old Bianca Beaulne was accepted into the nursing program at Champlain College Lennoxville in 2022, her mother, Jessica Brown, assumed there would be a dorm room available for her. But one of the dorm buildings was closed for renovation, and the waiting list for student accommodation had more than a hundred people on it. The family was told there was no way Bianca would get a bed in residence. So Jessica, who works as a real estate agent, got to work looking for a rental apartment off-campus. She was shocked by how difficult it was to find anything. "Honestly, it was a lot easier to find an apartment in downtown Montreal, even with a housing crisis."

Universities are trying to offer more housing. The following year, Bishop's University in Lennoxville opened a new residence with space for ninety-three students. But the shortage of student housing in Quebec has been building for decades. There are roughly

250,000 student renters in the province. The students' housing advocacy group Unité de travail pour l'implantation de logement étudiant (UTILE) says that kind of new student housing construction is needed all over Quebec, and in much greater amounts. Laurent Levesque, UTILE's executive director, says, "We can clearly talk about a shortage of student housing in Quebec, even an accumulated deficit because it's been several decades since we've built a substantial amount of student housing." Laurent says students are struggling across Quebec, in big cities and small towns alike. He says one of the most difficult markets is the capital, Quebec City. When fall classes started at Université Laval in 2022, more than two hundred people were listed on the student housing wait-list. But even when students find somewhere to live, rising rents make devoting time to their studies more difficult, according to Akpelozim Lokoun, a student coordinator at the university. "More working time, more time worrying about paying the rent, is less time actually studying."

Mario Mercier worries things will get worse before they get better. He sees more affordable rentals being renovated and sold, either to higher-income residents or to people who want to rent out the renovated properties as short-term vacation rentals. In the meantime, he thinks municipalities should create rental registries to keep track of all rental units and their prices, so rents can't be raised beyond the legal rates in between tenancies. In the long term, he's hoping for a revolt in public opinion that pushes higher levels of government to build a lot more public housing for people who can't afford to pay market rents.

For now, many renters will stay where they are, even if their homes or relationships are unhealthy. Others will find themselves thrust into an unforgiving rental market with far too much demand and not nearly enough supply. Some of them will end up staying in emergency accommodation, others will end up squeezing in with extended family members, and a few might get lucky. That's what happened to Diane Longpré. A couple of months after moving in temporarily with her ex-spouse, she received an offer she couldn't refuse from a close friend. The friend would buy a house that Diane and her daughters could live in. The friend paid the down payment on the home and Diane agreed to pay the monthly mortgage payments as rent. She says the house is a perfect fit for her family. It's spacious, with plenty of room for her kids and even space for Diane to work at home. It's also located close to her daughters' schools and daycares. Diane calls the house and her friend's down payment a giant gift, *"un gros cadeau!"* But she knows a lot of renters, especially single women, aren't so lucky. "Many families have the same problem as I had," she laments.

Now that she's settled into a stable new home, Diane is better able to concentrate on her work and on being a good mother to her children. Thinking back on the months of stress when she didn't know where they were going to live, she marvels at the effect that stress had on the rest of her life. "How do I manage to be a good, balanced mother with my children when I don't know where I'm going to stay? If you don't have housing, how do you emancipate yourself? Housing is the basis of a stable life."

SUBSIDIES FOR (ALMOST) EVERYONE

Singapore

WHEN THE BIG DAY finally arrived, Liz and Ben were ready. The young married couple arrived at the new apartment building and got into the new elevator—hand bars still wrapped in protective plastic and Styrofoam—to go up to the seventh floor. They got out of the elevator and walked to their new front door, locked shut behind the kind of metal bar security gates that are common in Singapore. Liz stood ready with a bag full of housewarming supplies in one hand and her phone in the other to make a video recording of the big moment. Ben opened a new red folder bursting with eighteen keys grouped evenly on multiple yellow key rings. After a bit of trial and error he found the right keys to unlock the security gate and finally the front door. And for the first time, the couple walked into their new flat. Their home.

The brand-new three-bedroom apartment was completely empty. The kitchen appliances hadn't even arrived yet. But Liz and Ben had another first priority—to bless their new home. Liz reached into her bag and pulled out a ripe pineapple and handed it to Ben, who crouched low and swung his arm back as if bowling, before rolling the pineapple across the living room floor to bless their new home with "abundance and prosperity." Liz then opened a small bag of dry rice and went from room to room, scattering small handfuls to "keep good energy and protect against bad energy." They moved from the compact living room to the empty kitchen, past the second bathroom and into each of the two single bedrooms, before walking into the larger primary bedroom and its ensuite bathroom. Finally, Liz brought out a pair of ripe oranges for good luck and happiness.

The furniture and appliances would soon follow Liz and Ben into their new home. They had chosen all of it. After all, they planned on being there for a long time to come. The young couple, both from working-class Singapore families, had just bought their new home. Or, to be more precise, they had just leased a brand-new apartment for ninety-nine years. The kind of "fee simple" (or freehold) land ownership that's common in Canada and other countries is rare in Singapore. But couples like Liz and Ben are not. In fact, roughly 90 percent of people in Singapore are "homeowners," under this modified Singapore lease model. And roughly 80 percent of the people in this small island nation-state lease homes that were built by the government-owned Housing and Development Board. HDB flats, as they're known, are ubiquitous and span a wide range of sizes and styles. That includes a popular "3Gen" flat, which has two single bedrooms for children plus a primary bedroom with ensuite for their parents and a secondary bedroom with ensuite for their grand parents. The smallest, most affordable one-bedroom flats are attainable by the vast majority of people in Singapore, largely through government subsidies, while much larger and fancier luxury condominiums are as exclusive as they sound. As a result, there is little to no stigma about living in "public housing" in Singapore.

Liz and Ben paid a little more than 511,000 Singaporean dollars (almost the same in Canadian dollars) for their three-bedroom apartment. They had both been working as financial auditors, and were able to save up to pay a 10 percent deposit in 2017, before construction started. They didn't move into their new home until five years later. In the meantime, they rented and saved more money to pay for their new home. When they finally moved in, they needed a loan of just under $200,000. That worked out to a modest $900 monthly mortgage payment. They would need to pay the remaining shortfall of $263,000 as well, either in cash or out of a savings fund that both Liz and Ben had been contributing to, called the Central Provident Fund (CPF).

The CPF is a compulsory savings and pension plan for all working Singaporeans and permanent residents. Singapore law requires them to contribute 20 percent of their wages to the CPF. Their employers are obliged to kick in another 17 percent. In exchange, the worker can choose what they spend the money on, provided it falls into one of a few categories. The most common use of CPF funds is to purchase a home. More than half of Singaporeans do so, and most of those use the funds to buy HDB flats. Some take the money with them when they move to another country. Others wait until they turn 55, at which point they're allowed to withdraw money for whatever they choose. Others never spend any of it, and pass it along in their inheritance instead. Through this forced financial savings program, Singapore has given most of its citizens a helping hand in finding homes. Make no mistake, Singapore is not cheap. A 2022 comparison of 92 housing markets around the world placed the city state 53rd, roughly middle of the pack, and noted the pandemic had made housing significantly less affordable. Still, housing remains attainable, if not exactly affordable, for most residents.

Singapore is one of the world's leading financial centres that has flourished as an international hub of banking and trade, and yet from a practical point of view it has removed most housing from the free market. While housing is far from cheap in Singapore, it is still based on the ability of most people to pay. Ownership rules help by keeping prices lower than they would be in a market where speculators could drive prices up quickly. People in Singapore can own only one public flat at a time, and while foreigners are not banned entirely from buying, they are effectively discouraged from investing in Singapore real estate through a high stamp duty, which is a tax the buyer pays on the purchase of a property. These measures aren't accidents—they are specific choices that were made in an effort to ensure housing would remain first and foremost a place to live, not an investment. There is still a financial incentive and reward to homeowners, however, and one that doesn't exist in public rental housing models where residents have no financial interest in maintaining or improving a property: leaseholders in Singapore are allowed to sell if they follow a strict set of rules. They must live in a flat for five years before they can sell. They can also bequeath the flat, and whatever remains of its lease, after they die. Seniors are also encouraged to sell their flats in order to downsize into a smaller unit, and thanks to those "3Gen" flats mentioned earlier, many elderly people can sell their flats and move in with their children and grandchildren. The government remains the true owner of the land, but the resident still has an asset, if a more modest one than many Canadian homeowners have come to expect.

As Liz and Ben got settled into their new home, they had some numbers to crunch. How much money should come from savings versus their CPF accounts? They also had another financial choice that many young Canadians would be envious to consider: they could rent out just one of their two spare bedrooms for anywhere between $2,000 and $3,000 a month, double to triple their monthly mortgage costs. Not all rents in Singapore are so high, but the couple's new flat was located in the highly desirable and central Bidadari neighbourhood, just an eight-minute walk from the nearest Mass Rapid Transit (MRT) train station. The highly efficient (and air-conditioned) mass transit system whisks more than 3 million people around Singapore every day, and living near one of its stations is a significant criterion for many people. The neighbourhood also features a grocery store, a mall, and several schools. That's common in Singapore. More than 1 million public flats are scattered across twenty-four "new towns." Each town is home to between 100,000 and 200,000 people, and has all those amenities, as well as hospitals and fitness facilities.

With more than 5 million people living on a relatively small island, it goes without saying that most Singaporeans don't have a backyard. High-rises are the norm. The newly built neighbourhood that Liz and Ben chose comprises thirteen different buildings, the tallest of which is sixteen storeys. City planners try to place tall buildings next to shorter ones, to keep common areas as light as possible. They also pride themselves on keeping as much green space as possible in such a dense urban environment. Flat blocks include gardens and parks at ground level, and significant communal space as well. Most buildings have what's called a "void deck" that can be reserved by residents for various types of group gatherings, such as Chinese funeral wakes or Malay weddings.

Singapore's housing market wasn't always so meticulously arranged. The population grew rapidly in the first half of the twentieth century, while Singapore was still a British colony, ballooning from around 250,000 in 1907 to nearly a million by the end of the Second World War. The Japanese occupation of Singapore, and the destruction of thousands of homes during the war, increased crowding. Thousands of homes were rebuilt in a haphazard manner during and after the war, which led to poor living conditions for many residents and crowded conditions for most. Things hadn't improved much by the time Singapore gained independence from British rule in 1959. A report for the newly independent government described the "unhygienic slums and crowded squatter settlements" that were common across Singapore. But the new prime minister rose to power with housing as one of his top priorities. "My primary preoccupation was to give every citizen a stake in the country and its future," Lee Kuan Yew wrote later. "I wanted a home-owning society . . . I believed this sense of ownership was vital for our new society which had no deep roots in a common historical experience." Lee disbanded the Singapore Investment Trust, which the British had created in the 1920s to address the problem of overcrowding. In its place he created the Housing and Development Board, and gave it both considerable freedom to build and a personal assurance that the money to do so would be provided. The HDB was exempt from many of the building restrictions that applied to private developers, and allowed to operate without many of the required permits from other government departments. It went to work building apartment buildings— flat blocks, as they're known in Singapore. Early buildings were practical in the extreme, offering mostly single-room flats with the most basic amenities. But every new block of flats let the local authorities tear down an unwanted squatters' camp, as the campers moved up into the new buildings.

In 1961 a giant fire tore through a squatters' camp and prompted the government to pass a more aggressive law that allowed them to acquire any land that had been cleared by fire or natural disaster. Throughout the 1960s the HDB acquired more land and built tens of thousands of new homes. In 1964 it founded its Home Ownership for the People Scheme, which encouraged almost everyone in the country to save money to buy themselves a home. By the middle of the decade, hundreds of thousands of people had moved into the new flats. Some complained it wasn't natural to live so high above the ground, or that they couldn't budget for the utility bills. Others were grateful to have a safe home with clean water. Meanwhile, Singapore's government kept building. New laws were enacted that allowed it to appropriate even more land if it was deemed in the public interest. Disgruntled landowners were powerless to object to the loss of their land or the financial compensation, which they considered insufficient, because the government had all the power. The Singapore government eventually ran out of land, so it started reclaiming shallow seabeds, turning them into usable land. Today, roughly one-fifth of Singapore is reclaimed land. By 2005 the government owned 90 percent of the land in Singapore, double what it had owned when it achieved independence.

Economists, urban planners, frustrated renters, and many others around the world have looked at Singapore's housing situation with envy. But Singapore's "Housing Miracle," as it's been called, doesn't seem all that miraculous to some. And before other countries adopt its measures, they should consider carefully whom the Singapore model leaves out. Strong government controls can work well in achieving larger goals, but on small scales, in individual lives, they can have unintended consequences. Singapore has strict ethnic quotas that in 2016 capped the Chinese community's presence in any given neighbourhood at 84 percent, the Malays at 22 percent, and Indians and other communities at 12 percent. At the same time, those groups made up 74 percent, 13 percent, and 12 percent of the population. The quotas had been introduced many years earlier in an attempt to reduce ethnic segregation and ensure members of different communities would know and interact with each other. (Similarly, Singapore planners will put small flats next to larger flats, to encourage the mixing of different family types and socio-economic classes.) But the flip side of quotas is that people can be prohibited from buying homes in areas where a quota is full, simply because of their ethnicity. And then there's the question of sexuality.

Singapore's generous housing subsidies favour married couples, who can receive up to $80,000 towards the purchase of a home. In Singapore, a married couple means one man and one woman. Lesbian, gay, bisexual, transgender, and queer couples are not eligible—at least, not as couples from the age of 25. They can apply for more modest subsidies, as individuals, at the age of 35. Singapore decriminalized sex between men in 2022 but stopped short of expanding the definition of marriage beyond heterosexual relationships, and even amended the constitution to block marriage equality. The discrepancy is apparent within some families. Andee Chua managed to buy a one-bedroom condo on the private market when he was 29. "The down payment was difficult. I used up all my savings and my parents had to step in to help." For around the same price, his sister bought a spacious three-bedroom apartment with her husband and their two children. Subsidies for families with young children may be justifiable, but of course non-straight couples can have children too, while many straight couples have no children. Adrianna Tan is married. But because she married another woman, and that marriage isn't recognized in Singapore, she's not eligible for many of Singapore's generous subsidies. "The barriers to entry are high simply because we are not heterosexual."

Jove Nazatul knows that all too well. A queer, trans, non-binary person of colour, Jove grew up in Singapore but now lives in Victoria, BC. Despite being in a common-law relationship, Jove would not be eligible for any of the generous home purchase incentives offered to young straight couples back home. "My relationship with Singapore is more complex because of my gender identity and my sexuality." While Jove has no plans to move back to Singapore—"I don't want to live in a country where I'm treated as a second-class citizen"—they think Singapore has valuable housing lessons for countries like Canada. "I think Singapore has gotten to where Singapore has gotten to with caveats."

Despite the inequality and social controls, Jove thinks Singapore has done many things right on housing. First of all, it's built upwards. High-rises don't give people as much space as single-family homes, especially outside, but they do allow the construction of a lot more housing in any given city. Second, Jove says Singapore has mastered good public transportation. Like Tokyo, Singapore has an excellent train system. More than 3 million people funnel through more than 140 MRT stations every day. There are dozens more Light Rapid Transit (LRT) stations and thousands of buses. Jove also thinks Singapore's mandatory CPF payments play a huge role in housing by helping so many people save up a down payment for their first home. As a tradesperson, artist, and activist, Jove understands that the inability to save up a big enough down payment is a huge barrier for many young Canadians. The CPF savings help many young Singaporeans, but Jove believes they should help everyone equally.

While young, straight, married Singaporeans have the housing welcome mat laid out for them, young singles have to work much harder. And just because they don't have children to support, it doesn't necessarily mean they don't have dependants. A single 24-year-old named Lisa needed a new flat for herself and her 54-year-old mother, who is not a Singapore citizen and therefore not eligible for many housing subsidies. Lisa knew she needed to be 35 to apply for an HDB flat, or else marry a man, but she decided she couldn't wait for either of those possibilities. So she started to look for a way that she could afford a home for herself and her mother. They had been living for many years with Lisa's aunt, ever since financial difficulties forced the family to sell their two-bedroom HDB flat when

Lisa was twelve. The family of four moved into the single spare bedroom in her aunt's flat. It was crowded, but at least it was financially secure. Lisa's father used the money from selling his flat to pay off his sister's mortgage.

Things were tolerable for many years, but when Lisa was in university, her father died without leaving a will or any kind of clear instructions about his $70,000 in CPF savings. The money was transferred to a public trustee, who then sent it to a sharia court because Lisa's father was Muslim. Sharia law spells out specific percentages of an inheritance that should be left behind to a widow, daughter, and son. The court split the inheritance into twenty-four shares—fourteen for Lisa's brother, seven for her, and only three for her mother. Lisa's brother could not receive the money until he turned 21, which left the family with only $30,000. They also learned they had no equity from their father's co-ownership of their aunt's flat because it had been set up as a joint tenancy arrangement, which left Lisa's aunt as the sole owner.

Apart from the legal and financial questions, there was the practical inconvenience of having three adults sleeping in the same bedroom. Lisa's brother started to sleep on the couch, then moved in with another relative. And Lisa decided she needed to find a home of her own for herself and her mother. She soon learned she was ineligible for many loans because she wasn't married and because her mother was neither a citizen nor a permanent resident. A two-bedroom flat would have cost more than $300,000, so they had to settle for a one-bedroom instead. At the age of 24, with a monthly salary of $3,000, she found a small flat for $256,000, and signed on for a 25-year mortgage. "I only did it because I had no other choice that was acceptable to me." When compared with young people in Toronto, Vancouver, or Victoria, Lisa's situation seems secure and relatively affordable. When compared with young married

Singaporeans who would have received much more financial assistance, it seems unfair.

Jove Nazatul sees significant barriers on both sides of the world. In Singapore, it's sexual orientation and gender identity; in Victoria, it's the extreme shortage of affordable housing. Both make it more difficult to afford the purchase of a first home. But it's also worth noting the stark difference in homelessness between the two far-flung cities. In Greater Victoria, recent counts have estimated 1,500 people are unhoused. Singapore, with roughly thirteen times the population, had just 530. Still, Jove says there's no question about where to live. "As a trans non-binary person, Victoria is the place to be." Jove jokes they found the farthest country from Singapore and moved there. For all its faults, though, the highly controlled city state has lessons to offer Canada on housing. "I think there's that middle ground that we need to find."

13

AN ESSENTIAL PROBLEM

Toronto

TORONTO IS EXPENSIVE. That's no secret. But Nicola Montgomery wasn't prepared for just how expensive Canada's largest city would be when she agreed to move there in 2021. A registered nurse in Calgary, Nicola had managed to buy a three-bedroom, three-bathroom house of her own just a few years earlier. It cost $390,000. But when she fell in love, she sold her house and moved into an apartment with her new partner. Then she got pregnant and gave birth to a baby boy. At around the same time, her partner was offered a good job in Toronto, and the couple decided to pack their things and move east. "We ended up doing the flight with a cat and a one-month-old baby!"

The flight wasn't the only uncomfortable part of the move. Nicola and her young family were moving to a three-bedroom apartment they'd never seen, in Mississauga. The giant Toronto suburb is a city in its own right, and ranks as Canada's seventh-largest municipality by population. While it's cheaper than Toronto, Mississauga is still an expensive place to live. Nicola had started searching for rentals while she was still in Calgary, and committed to the apartment before they left. "We rented it online and over the phone, and we never saw it."

At $2,200 a month, the apartment was affordable by Mississauga standards. But Nicola soon discovered the reason for that. "It's not nice," she says bluntly. "It's very rundown. We don't have in-suite laundry. The fire alarms go off three or four times a month randomly, so there are a lot of safety concerns. Plus, we have mice in our apartment, and we keep trying to get rid of them, but we have no idea where they're coming from, which makes you feel really dirty. So every day we're scouring Facebook Marketplace trying to find places to rent, but they're all going so quickly."

Nicola didn't bother looking at houses for sale. Despite having owned her own home in Calgary, she knew she couldn't afford a house in the Greater Toronto Area. They were just too expensive. Between 2008 and 2018, housing costs jumped 115 percent while the median income went up only 25 percent. Prices went even higher during the pandemic, and spiked just as Nicola was moving in with the mice in Mississauga. Prices finally started to come down a year after she arrived, but when she looked at a few listings, she realized they were still far too expensive, and unappealing as well. "Even then, you're looking at a house that might be $900,000, but it's super rundown, full of mould, or just horrible. And you just basically have to gut it and start over."

Nicola accepted that not everyone can live in a detached house, and she did her best to adjust her expectations. But she felt an acute disappointment watching a new condo tower start to rise near her rental apartment building, and realizing its small one-bedroom condos were selling for more than $600,000. Even with prices softening, and even with her partner's salary, she concluded she'd never find a home in Toronto that was both affordable and big enough for her family.

If purchasing a property was out, the rental market didn't look much better. While rising interest rates drove home prices down, they had the opposite effect on many rents—pushing new listings higher, as would-be buyers were forced to abandon dreams of home ownership, and landlords with variable rate mortgages recouped higher monthly payments through higher rents.

Not only were rents high, but they seemed to be rising right in front of Nicola's eyes. She applied for several apartments, only to lose out to other renters who offered more. "All the rentals are going into bidding wars," she recalls with a sigh. "We were interested in this one house, and we weren't willing to go any higher than their price of $2,900, and it got bidded out at $3,500. Those people who got the house decided they were willing to go that high, so of course the landlord gave it to them."

Nicola Montgomery is not alone—not even close. All across the Greater Toronto Area, middle-class renters are scrambling to find accommodation they can afford. A report by the Toronto Board of Trade and WoodGreen, one of the largest providers of affordable housing in the city, concluded, "the supply of housing has not kept up with population growth, job creation or changing housing needs and preferences." At least, affordable housing has not kept up with population growth. Toronto has added more high-end condos and houses, while the city spent billions on the maintenance of existing social housing units with wait-lists that only got longer. While the problem is widespread, the report noted it is especially acute in crucial public sectors like health care, education, and social services, all of which rely on large workforces of people being paid modest middle-income salaries that haven't kept up with the rise in housing costs.

Of course, the people most affected by a lack of affordable shelter are the roughly ten thousand people in Toronto who are homeless, of whom about 90 percent sleep in the city's emergency shelters. A lack of affordable housing is one of the key contributors to homelessness—along with addiction, mental health issues, and past trauma—as was discussed in previous chapters. While homeless people undoubtedly have it worse, we shouldn't dismiss the housing woes of nurses, teachers, and other crucial workers as minor, middle-class problems. Not only are they disruptive to thousands of those workers and their families, but they're starting to have a disproportionate impact on some of the most vulnerable people in society. "Without urgent action on housing or additional funding in these sectors," the Board of Trade–Woodgreen report concluded, "the ultimate impact of the affordability crisis will be reduced service levels that will particularly harm the elderly and other vulnerable members of our society."

The end result in Toronto is an undersupply of essential workers that never quite catches up with demand. As a registered nurse with several years' experience working in hospitals, Nicola Montgomery was in high demand. When her maternity leave came to an end, she was hired on a two-year contract at St. Joseph's Hospital, near High Park in west Toronto. Having had no luck looking for rentals in Mississauga, she wondered briefly if she might be able to afford a smaller rental near the hospital, and at least benefit from a shorter commute. Ultimately, nothing in the expensive area was affordable. The cheapest rental she found was a one-bedroom apartment listed at $3,900 a month. Single houses were going for up to $9,900 a month. As a result Nicola stayed in her Mississauga apartment, paying $2,200 a month and wishing she were somewhere else. "We're desperate to get out of here."

While she wants to move, Nicola tries to keep a positive attitude about life in general. "You just have to say, '*C'est la vie*, this is it,' and

embrace it. When you move, you move, and it's a new adventure."
Besides, she knows not everyone is as fortunate as she is. She's talked
to cleaners and other hospital workers who have gruelling commutes
on two transit systems every day. The comparison makes her feel
lucky that at least she owns a car and can drive to work. Still, Nicola
spends more time driving than she would like. That's a common problem for nurses in Toronto, according to the president of the Ontario
Nurses' Association, Cathryn Hoy, who says long commutes are more
difficult for nurses than for many other professions because of twelve-
hour work shifts. "A lot of people say, 'Oh, they can go live somewhere
else,' but their hours aren't conducive to living outside the city."

Long commutes are a well-documented detriment to employees'
quality of life. Apart from exhaustion, people with long commutes
tend to have higher cholesterol, blood pressure, depression, and
anxiety. Their workplaces and colleagues suffer too, because of more
frequent absences. Researchers at the University of Cambridge,
RAND Europe, and Mercer estimated that employees who commute
more than an hour each way lose the equivalent of seven workdays a
year because of absenteeism, fatigue, and lateness. The 2016 census
found almost 16 percent of workers in the Greater Toronto Area
commuted more than one hour each way.

On a good day, with absolutely no traffic, the drive from Nicola's
apartment in Mississauga to St. Joseph's Hospital takes twenty-two
minutes. But with traffic, it can take as long as an hour. And then
there's the drive to her son's daycare. In good traffic, it's a half-hour
in the opposite direction. Add it all up and Nicola spends a few hours
behind the wheel every day. Despite her positive attitude, she admits
life in Toronto is frustrating. "It is tough because I owned this beautiful home in Alberta, and now this. Your average family should be
able to afford a house if they have education and stable work, but
that's just not the case here."

While Nicola continues to struggle with the costs of housing, the hospital where she works continues to struggle as well, and many others along with it. The list of challenges facing our public health care system is long, but a shortage of nurses is surely at or near the top. A 2022 Statistics Canada survey of health workers found nurses were the most likely to want to change professions; 24.4 percent of them said they intended to leave within three years. Burnout during the COVID-19 pandemic and relatively low pay are obvious problems. And in Nicola's experience, so is the high cost of housing. The hospital signed her to a two-year contract and enrolled her in a training course so she could upgrade her skills and work in the operating room. With thoughts of housing never far from her mind, she asked the other young nurses if she was the only one struggling. "They all said, 'No, it's Toronto! None of us can afford to buy a house here.' And that was a room full of nurses."

Kim Le faced a similar challenge. A registered nurse at St. Michael's Hospital in downtown Toronto, she went on maternity leave when her first child was born. At the time, Kim and her husband were on the hunt for a house, and were prepared to offer up to $850,000. With such a seemingly generous budget, they were hopeful they could find a home for their young family in Toronto. But as prices soared, it became clear that a combined household income of $150,000 a year just wasn't enough. They were forced to look farther and farther afield for a house they could afford. They looked in Oshawa and Courtice, sixty and seventy kilometres away from the hospital respectively. They finally found a house they could afford in Barrie. The three-bedroom home was close to a public school and a park, but it was a long way from Kim's workplace of ten years—a commute of between one and one and a half hours. Kim decided it was simply too far away for a young mother working twelve-hour shifts. She resigned her position, and St. Michael's lost another essential worker.

Some Ontario communities have tried to lure more new nurses with cash incentives. The Community Commitment Program for Nurses offers $25,000 to nurses who commit to working two years in a community with serious health challenges. It wasn't offered in Mississauga, but even if it was, Nicola Montgomery isn't sure it would help buy a house. "I mean, $25,000 wouldn't even cover my rent for a year."

Offering extra cash to make up for rising costs isn't a new idea. In recent years, various Toronto employers have offered wage premiums. The Toronto Board of Trade estimates senior managers in the GTA earn 68 percent more than their counterparts in other parts of Ontario. But the bonus is much more modest for most essential workers. Nurses in Toronto earn a premium of only 2.9 percent. By comparison, health care managers make 11.4 percent more than their counterparts in other Ontario cities. The almost non-existent premium for nurses, physiotherapists, and other health care professionals is largely the result of the collective bargaining process and contracts that mostly eliminate regional salary differences. Whatever the reason, it's left many of Toronto's essential workers farther and farther behind.

Nicola says she and many other young Toronto nurses who want a better standard of living face a stark choice. They can either leave, or they can find other work that will make them more money, "because the pay rate for nurses never changes, while the cost of living keeps going up." As a result, many of the nurses she knows have found side hustles. A lot of them find work in plastic surgeons' offices, giving Botox injections or refiller injections, because the pay is considerably better than what they make in hospitals.

Nicola is thinking of joining them. She could do Botox injections, part-time, and have more money for rent at the end of every month. For now, though, she's determined to continue nursing. "I love it too much. I enjoy taking care of people and helping them, and trying to make their day better. It would be hard to let that go." She's also considering another side hustle that some Toronto nurses pursue—real estate. "A lot of the nurses I know actually work part-time, and they do real estate on the side, just to make ends meet." Nicola is aware of the irony of high housing costs pushing people out of essential work only to end up selling houses. But she's equally aware of the high local rents and house prices.

While some essential workers pivot to non-essential work, others try their best to accept their circumstances and hope things might change one day. Deborah Buchanan-Walford teaches English at the Emery Adult Learning Centre in Toronto's Humbermede neighbourhood, but she lives in Brampton, a 45-minute drive away if traffic is good. Deborah lives in a rented house with her parents, her partner, and her young son. "There is nowhere in Toronto that I can think about affording to rent, much less buy." As a teacher, Deborah makes more than many essential workers, such as education assistants or hospital cleaners. She does not earn a $100,000 teacher salary that would put her on the Ontario government's annual sunshine list, but in a few years she'll reach the top of her pay scale—about $90,000. It's a healthy income in many Canadian cities. But Deborah says it isn't enough to let her live in Toronto. It's a sentiment shared by many of her colleagues who have moved out of the Greater Toronto Area altogether. One even moved to Orangeville—an hour-and-a-half drive from downtown Toronto—to buy a house. Deborah calls it a stark reality, "but it's also one I have reconciled with. I'll just do what I can until hopefully something changes."

While nurses and teachers struggle, the housing crisis is even harder on lower-paid health care workers and other essential workers—that large group of workers the Board of Trade report calls "the invisible backbone of our city." Care aides, education assistants, cleaners, dental assistants, daycare workers, pharmacy staff, and others make considerably less than nurses but still have to live in the same city. It might even be argued that many of them have a more difficult time with housing than people who make less. An analysis by the Toronto Region Board of Trade's Economic Blueprint Institute estimated there may be as many as ninety thousand essential workers in this unenviable economic window—earning between $40,000 and $60,000 a year. That's too much to apply for social housing, but too little to afford a decent place to live in the city.

The housing crisis in general, and the effect it's having on essential workers in particular, is a growing priority for both business groups and social agencies. In 2021 the Toronto Board of Trade and WoodGreen Housing issued another report on housing that predicted Toronto will follow San Francisco and New York "as places where only a select class of professionals can afford to live" if urgent action isn't taken. The report notes that in 2018 the city's population grew ten times more than the number of rental units built, housing prices grew four times faster than income, and rents for new listings rose twice as much as average income.

The report urges governments to take specific measures that target essential workers and make it possible for them to afford homes they want to live in that are located in the communities they serve. Without specific measures for essential workers, they predict, many more will either leave or switch professions entirely.

Nicola Montgomery and her family are staying in Toronto for now. She and her partner both have decent jobs, but the disconnect between their pay and the cost of housing in Toronto has made them wonder whether staying in the city is worth it. "I don't think we have a long-term goal to stay here. Two years and we'll be out. We're just going to try to save as much money as possible, and then maybe head over to Ottawa or the Kingston area, or maybe a different province altogether. We've even talked about going back to Alberta just so we could buy a house again."

If Nicola leaves Toronto, she won't be alone. Despite decades of rapid expansion, Toronto's growth rate started to slow significantly in the years leading up to the pandemic, and actually declined from 2020 to 2021—the only major Canadian city to see its population drop that year. While the pandemic precipitated many sudden departures, the trend had been building for a long time, and was somewhat hidden from public view because Canada's largest city receives the lion's share of international immigrants every year, and as a result its population kept going up. At the same time, however, young families were leaving in droves. In 2019, Mike Moffatt from the Ivey Business School at Western University analyzed the demographics of who was coming and who was going. "The two biggest cohorts of leavers aren't retired people at all," he wrote, "they're people in their 30s, along with kids under the age of 5." The reason, he said, is "blindingly obvious." Families are being priced out. "Between housing and daycare costs, young families simply can't make a go of it in Toronto."

While those who leave Toronto busy themselves in their new homes and new jobs, some who stay are left in a kind of limbo, according to Nicola Montgomery. "It absolutely made me think, 'What's the point of making friends, and investing a lot of time and effort into something, if we're just going to leave?'" She describes the experience as isolating, and says it's taken a toll on her mental health. "It's so nice to be able to settle down and nest in and create a life, but we can't really do that here."

14

KEY WORKER HOUSING

London

EMILY FITCH WAS STILL in her twenties when she moved to England. A native of Calgary, Fitch made a home for herself in the East End of London and found a job as a primary school teacher in a poor neighbourhood. The area wasn't pretty per se, and she lived in a shared house with several other young renters, but she lived life to the fullest for three or four years.

Things changed in 2006, when she became pregnant. She was single at the time and living with roommates, but it soon became apparent the living arrangement wouldn't last. "They said, 'You can't stay here.'" But on her modest teacher's salary, Emily couldn't afford to rent a one-bedroom apartment by herself. She quickly found herself in a difficult dilemma: either leave London and the teaching job she loved, or end up homeless.

Emily didn't want to leave London, so she started looking for other options. She soon found a new program for essential workers in Britain who were struggling with the high costs of housing. It was called key worker housing and the idea was relatively simple: people who worked in essential jobs—nurses, firefighters, police officers, teachers, paramedics, care aides, and others—could obtain government help to find and pay for housing. There were a few different models. One offered subsidies to help key workers buy a portion of a home, in a shared ownership arrangement between the key worker and the government or a non-profit housing agency. Another offered key workers a rent-to-buy arrangement. The simplest was a program that set aside new homes to rent at an affordable price.

Emily applied for the latter, and though she found the application process rather confusing, she was soon put on a wait-list. Because she was a teacher, pregnant, and close to being homeless, Emily was offered a new two-bedroom flat less than two months after she applied. She was on a brief trip back to Canada to visit family when she received the offer, and quickly recognized it for the good luck that it was. She said yes immediately and took the flat, sight unseen.

The new concrete building wasn't especially attractive. Neither was the street. But it was safe, secure, and extremely affordable. As an eligible key worker in a building designated for key workers, Emily paid £450 in monthly rent for her two-bedroom flat. A similar flat at market rates would have cost three times that. "It's what kept me in London. Otherwise I would have left—there's no way I would have stayed in London without that key worker flat."

Emily was still pregnant when she moved into her new home in 2006. It was brand new and spotless, but it was also empty. She had to spend what little money she had saved on furniture. The new apartment quickly became a home, and the new building quickly became a community, "because we were all the same sorts of people," she recalls fifteen years later. Though her neighbours came from an array of different cultures and countries, they all had two things in common: they all worked in caring professions, and all were grateful to have a safe, affordable place to call home. "This little oasis of love-liness" is how Emily describes it. A nurse lived in the flat beside her. A firefighter moved in directly below. She made fast friends and lived in the building for years. She continued working at the same school, just a ten-minute bike ride from her flat, and eventually gave birth to a second child.

With two children, Emily felt the need for more space. But she found herself single when her younger child was just three months old, and her teacher's salary wasn't enough to pay market rent for a bigger home. So she had to stay put, and what she lacked in space was made up for by community and affordability. After living in the flat for seven years, Emily became eligible to buy it from the local coun-cil at a price £20,000 lower than the market price. That worked out to £290,000, which required a down payment of £40,000—still a significant amount of money. But because she'd been paying a sig-nificantly reduced rent for seven years, she had been able to save half the down payment needed. That's no small feat, given that child care fees cost her nearly half of her take-home income for much of that time. Her mother in Canada was able to help with the rest of the down payment, and Emily was able to buy her home. "I felt so lucky. Coming from Canada, where we didn't have anything like that, it just felt so progressive."

Emily later started a new relationship, got married, and moved into a bigger house with her new partner and their blended family. Now Emily Bere, she still owns that flat in east London, and still counts several residents in that building as friends. She rents the flat out to two teachers, though rising taxes on small landlords in Britain have forced her to charge higher rents than she'd like. That's not the only thing that has made life more difficult for teachers and other key workers in Britain in recent years.

The British government cut key worker housing initiatives as part of widespread austerity measures a few years after Emily moved into her first flat. That left local councils and housing non-profits scrambling to subsidize homes for key workers, and it left countless teachers, nurses, firefighters, and other essential workers facing similar dilemmas to the one Emily faced in 2006, with no similar relief. Thinking back on her good fortune, and seeing her now-teenaged daughter dream of pursuing a career in nursing, Emily wonders if her child will be able to afford a caring profession. "I don't think she's going to have that same opportunity, at least not in London. Young people are going to have to start looking elsewhere."

Indeed, many young Britons already have, especially during the belt-tightening decade leading up to the COVID-19 pandemic. But when the importance of nurses and other health care workers was thrust into the spotlight in the early days of the lockdown, both the British government and local councils decided it was time to bring back some key worker housing initiatives.

The west London borough of Hammersmith and Fulham is one of the four most expensive residential property markets in Britain. It's home to three professional football clubs, including Chelsea FC—which was worth more than $3 billion in 2022—and headquarters to many multinational corporations. It's a lovely place for those who can afford it. But millions of Britons can't.

Catherine Brennan is a 48-year-old teacher in the borough, at West London Free School. It is largely independent from the local school authority, though it receives government funding and is free to attend as a result. But the school's employees, like many essential workers, struggle to pay for housing in Britain's expensive capital city. Catherine couldn't normally afford to live in the area; her teacher's salary simply wouldn't cut it. But when she heard about a new equity share scheme offered by the local council, the impossible suddenly seemed possible. When Catherine enrolled in that equity share plan, and a local Home Buy program, she was able to afford a one-bedroom flat in an area called White City. Put simply, Catherine bought 48 percent of the flat, and pays regular mortgage payments on her share. The borough owns the rest. The end result is that Catherine Brennan has an affordable home she wants to live in, close to her workplace, and the West London Free School still has a valued English teacher.

A ten-minute Tube ride away, more teachers and health care workers are moving into a similar new building in North Kensington. Choosing which key workers would move in was not an easy task. The local council received more than three hundred applications for just fourteen flats. Councillor Kim Taylor-Smith said the overwhelming response proves "there's a real demand for homes like this. We will use what we have learned to shape a policy that benefits many more key workers in the future, alongside our plans to build six hundred new Council-owned homes in the borough."

For now, though, many nurses and teachers there are stuck with long commutes and expensive rents in substandard homes. But for those lucky few who moved into the new building, their lives have changed for the better.

"Before this I was in a private rental and my living conditions weren't so great," says Cate Latto, a single mom and mental health professional. Now that she can walk to work and stop worrying about housing, Cate can focus more on her son and her job, helping mental health patients transfer out of the nearby St. Charles' Hospital and back into their homes. "So to move here and be able to call this my home is surreal. I can't believe it's actually real."

Physiotherapist Lydia Roderiques is feeling similarly lucky. She faced a tiring daily commute from her rental flat in the district of East Ham to Guy's Hospital and St. Thomas' Hospital in central London. A long walk followed by a crowded ride on the London Underground became a drudgery near the end of her seven-day work rotations. So when her rent went up, she started looking for a new home.

Lydia was shocked to find a brand-new apartment building offering affordable rentals in Canary Wharf, the forest of modern skyscrapers on the old West India Docks that's become the new financial centre of London. "We had never considered that we might be able to live in Canary Wharf. It's a central area with a high-quality lifestyle, and to be honest, my first impression was that it might be too good to be true."

But it was true. The new building offered 176 apartments, from studios up to three bedrooms, at discount market rents, and reserved them for households that make less than £60,000 a year. Lydia and her roommate moved into a two-bedroom apartment on the twelfth floor. Stepping out onto the balcony, she has a full view of the modern glass skyscrapers surrounding her new home, with glimpses of the River Thames in between, as well as a unique village of houseboats tied up at the nearby Blackwall Basin moorings.

"When we moved in, we were jumping up and down on the balcony as we couldn't believe we lived here. You don't really expect these kinds of apartments on an NHS (National Health Service) salary. When my dad first came to visit, he couldn't believe we were in Canary Wharf."

Apart from living in a clean and comfortable apartment, Lydia likes the neighbourhood. While Canary Wharf became famous as one of the world's financial centres, it's quickly evolving into a livable neighbourhood, with new apartments, shops, restaurants, medical clinics, and a school. Her commute is shorter—less than half an hour door to door. Lydia put the extra time in her day to good use as soon as she moved in by going back to the gym on a regular basis for fitness classes.

Affordable housing is also in short supply in London's suburbs. In the town of Ashford, near Heathrow Airport, the local borough council took a key step aimed at keeping essential health care workers in the community. In 2021, local councillors voted to replace an underused parking lot with a new housing development for key workers. The location is ideally situated near a train station and a large supermarket. But what really sold local politicians was its proximity to Ashford Hospital, just a few minutes' walk away. Like many hospitals, it struggled to retain enough staff during the pandemic. And a survey of hospital employees showed many workers—especially lower-paid workers—faced long daily commutes. The local council and hospital administrators knew that in order to have a meaningful impact, the development would need to offer more than just a handful of apartments. So the final plan included 127 homes in total, of which 105 were set aside for hospital staff and other essential service workers. The vast majority of units in the development were two-bedroom flats, but it also included eight three-bedroom family flats and five family homes.

The quantity of new housing was important in Ashford, but so was the quality. Hospital administrators made it clear the new homes would have to be appealing so staff would want to live there. With that in mind, the development included extra child play areas and more green space than was required by local regulations. Mature trees were protected around the property. And the quality of the building itself was prioritized, with the developers promising that high standards would be applied to heating and security systems, and modern amenities like electric vehicle charging stations would be included during construction. The head of the local NHS Trust, Suzanne Rankin, called the hiring and retention of health care staff one of the trust's greatest challenges. "Being able to offer those colleagues housing that is affordable is a really important element of our strategy to meeting those ongoing sustainability challenges."

The lack of affordable housing is also a concern outside the

British capital. In the town of Warrington, east of Liverpool on the banks of the River Mersey, rents are rising and homelessness is a growing concern. In 2020, the non-profit Warrington Housing Association opened its first new subsidized housing development in a decade, with ten two-bedroom flats and one three-bedroom house. The association worked closely with a local construction company to design and build the homes for key workers, in a convenient location close to the centre of town and the local hospital. Kerry Parker was delighted to move into one of the two-bedroom apartments with her son, and relieved she could afford to pay the rent on a cleaner's salary. Paul Boden also moved into the new development. The 56-year-old bus driver had worked throughout the pandemic, when millions of people stayed home to avoid getting close to others. Moving into an affordable new home with his partner of many years, also named Paul, was a huge relief. "We have both been working through the pandemic, and it has been tough for everyone, so it is great to have this move to look forward to, and it will be our forever home."

Of course, good intentions can go bad. Helping essential workers with housing, if done poorly, can actually hurt them in the long run. Vulnerable employees whose employers are also their landlords can become even more vulnerable. New immigrants may not raise concerns or ask for better pay for fear of losing their housing. They may choose to decline offers of better work for the same reason. Well-designed key worker housing programs will have clear rules laid out at the beginning, and many will allow the workers to stay in the housing after switching jobs so long as they worked for a predetermined minimum length of time. Public sector employers may be better suited to providing key worker housing programs, which are usually more regulated and monitored. Even then, though, there are potential pitfalls. For instance, employer-subsidized housing can act as a disincentive for an employee ever to save enough to buy their own home and build the long-term equity that many homeowners enjoy. I've met several retired Anglican priests, for instance, who never bought their own homes because they lived in church-owned rectories for decades. Their short-term financial relief eventually translated into a long-term lack of both financial and housing security. So while many key workers are grateful for affordable rentals, others want to buy their homes outright.

During the COVID-19 pandemic, British key workers could take advantage of a few different government assistance programs that offered help with down payments and other purchase costs. In the seaside town of Seaport, north of Liverpool, 31-year-old nurse specialist Christine McLaren was busy juggling her work life with her family life. As a single parent to three-year-old Oscar, she decided she wanted more space and more stability than was offered by the rental accommodation she'd been living in. She also wanted a garden, and a bit of room for her cat, Wayne, and dog, Elvis, to roam in. But when she looked at local house prices, she felt discouraged. "As a single parent at the time, I never thought it would be possible to get a mortgage and buy a house."

Fortunately, as a nurse, Christine was eligible for multiple benefits that helped her buy a new semi-detached three-bedroom house. The key one was called a Help to Buy Equity Loan, which let key workers pay a deposit of as little as 5 percent of the purchase price and use an interest-free government loan to pay the rest of the down payment. Christine also avoided paying the Stamp Duty Land Tax, a property purchase tax paid in England and Northern Ireland that was put on hold in 2020 because of the pandemic. Still, it wasn't easy. Christine had to work a lot of overtime to save enough for her down payment, and she received a little help from her family as well. But she says the government assistance plans were crucial—"without them none of this would be possible."

Now that Christine and Oscar—and Wayne and Elvis—are settled into their new home, she can focus her time and energy on her work and her family. "I had to remain local due to constraints with child care. But my work is close to the [housing] development, which means an easy commute, and I'm still close to home." Now time that was once spent house hunting or commuting is dedicated to enjoying long walks and blackberry picking with her son and her pets.

Despite success stories like these, there are countless key workers in Britain who continue to struggle, and by extension so do the communities that need them. Two decades after she left Canada to make a new life for herself in London, Emily Bere is still working as a teacher. She's at a new school now, with a new role as a senior teacher responsible for special education needs and inclusion. And as she's watched both students and teachers come and go over the years, Emily has grown to appreciate the extra value of having teachers live in the communities where they work—teachers who know family histories and local struggles more intimately than outsiders. But without more investments in key worker housing, she suspects teachers, nurses, and other essential employees will continue to move farther away from the urban communities that need them. Or, in many cases, they will simply choose other professions. "If you know you're going to be a nurse and live in poverty, you might not choose to become a nurse at all."

Emily counts herself fortunate now to live in a bigger house with her bigger, blended family. But thinking back to how it started in that two-bedroom key worker flat, she remains grateful for the support, and she has no doubt the government program did exactly what it was designed to do. "It did what it said on the tin," she concludes. "It allowed me to stay in London as a single mom and stay in my job as a senior teacher. I would never have been able to stay in London otherwise."

15

SQUEEZED OUT BY
SINGLE-FAMILY ZONING

_____

Victoria

THE SUN IS SHINING, the concrete trucks are pouring, and construction workers are busy framing his company's newest apartment building, but Victoria developer Luke Mari isn't smiling. Though building is booming and construction cranes are a common sight on the skyline, Luke knows the frenetic activity in British Columbia's capital city isn't enough to keep up with demand. Luke is an urban planner by training who now works for a private home building company called Aryze Developments. The company has been going gangbusters over the last few years, designing and building a wide range of new homes, including houseplexes, townhouses, and both low- and mid-rise apartment buildings. But Aryze has tried, unsuccessfully, to build many more, and that's the reason for the weary expression on Luke Mari's bearded face.

Victoria has the lowest vacancy rate in Canada, some of the highest house costs, and rents that are rising steeply. It's simply too expensive for a lot of people to think about moving here from more affordable cities. Even people with high-paying jobs, like family doctors coming out of medical school, say Victoria is just too expensive for them. In 2023, the BC government announced it would now hire civil servants in any city or town across the province that has a provincial government office, rather than insisting they move to the capital. Meanwhile, homeless camps have become a regular sight in parks and on city streets, and many renters in old buildings worry they might be next. There are several reasons for this perfect storm of housing unaffordability. The mildest climate in Canada attracts wealthy retirees, universities and colleges here bring in thousands of students, and many people who live elsewhere own vacation properties in Victoria that sit vacant most of the year. But the most obvious reason is that Victoria doesn't have enough homes to keep up with a rapidly growing population. Housing advocates blame the federal government's decision thirty years ago to stop building public housing in large quantities. Some developers scoff at this, but not Luke Mari. He grew up in Greater Victoria and lived in public housing as a child. He now sits on the board of the Greater Victoria Housing Society, a non-profit dedicated to providing affordable housing to low- and moderate-income people, which believes "safe and affordable housing is essential to a person's well-being and a foundation for success in life." But Luke also believes private companies like Aryze can build a lot of new housing if the conditions are right.

A visit to the Aryze Developments office offers a quick view of what he sees as Victoria's major problem. The old two-storey building stands in the Fairfield-Gonzales neighbourhood, a leafy expanse of single-family homes intermingling with colourful rhododendrons and shiny Teslas charging in driveways. Though it sits less than a ten-minute drive from downtown Victoria even with the

30-kph speed limit along Fairfield Road, there's little to hint that the neighbourhood is in the middle of a city that needs a lot more housing. Office blocks and high-rise apartments are allowed downtown, but neighbourhoods like Fairfield-Gonzales are dominated by single-family homes, and Luke says that is the fundamental problem. Townhouses are a rare sight in the neighbourhood. But Aryze recently finished a brand-new townhouse complex a few blocks from their office—a project that replaced two small single-family homes with 22 new townhomes—and Luke would like to build a lot more. The problem, he says, is that it simply takes too long for municipal planning departments to approve projects like that. The 22-townhomes project took five years to move from proposal to occupancy because it required rezoning. Luke says delays like that can kill a lot of otherwise viable construction projects. "We take projects and put a lot of care and attention into them, and they just die on the vine!"

Be it ever so humble, single-family zoning still dominates the housing supply in Victoria, and most Canadian cities.

Luke can point to several examples. Top of mind is a pair of six-storey rental apartment buildings the company proposed for the Vic West neighbourhood, just across the inner harbour from downtown Victoria and a ten-minute bike ride to the BC legislature. "It was a banger when we submitted it," he sighs. But not anymore. While Aryze went through the application process—something Luke says takes two to three years on average in the city of Victoria—all of the costs went up. Materials, labour, financing. All of it. The end result is that what started out as a sound economic proposition turned into a $4 million loss while the company waited to hear whether it would be approved. Luke and his colleagues managed to whittle that loss down to $2 million by removing various options, like on-site parking. Still, he says the project is a money loser. "Why are we even bothering?"

Luke points to another proposal in neighbouring Saanich—the most populous municipality on Vancouver Island—just a short stroll from the Commonwealth Pool, two shopping centres, and a major transit exchange. It included both market-rental units and afford-able units that would be subsidized by BC Housing, the provincial housing agency. But it took five years for Saanich to rezone the property, during which time costs went up so much that Luke says it wasn't financially viable anymore. "And guess how much of that building is affordable now? Zero! So who won in that scenario?" Luke says that wasn't the only development that took that long to be approved in Saanich. He reckons five years is average there.

It could be worse. Neighbouring Oak Bay took nine years before finally rejecting a four-storey, fourteen-unit condominium building, fittingly called the Quest. "You would be amazed at how many things go to city halls, multi-million-dollar decisions, hun-dreds of people potentially being housed, and you get someone who says, 'Nah, I just don't like it.' And you ask, 'Can you describe to me why you don't like it?' You get a shrug and a 'Nah, I just don't like it.' And you think, 'Okay, we'll throw half a million dollars of drawings in the garbage.'"

Despite his frustration, Luke recognizes that city staff can't control everything—the building code and new, stronger seismic provisions, for instance. No responsible planner or inspector can turn a blind eye to laws that are updated on a regular basis in an effort to make buildings safer, even if builders complain that those new requirements are pushing up costs. There is considerable debate among engineers about whether the new guidelines are too onerous, but it's not up to city staff to decide. They also have their hands tied by the provincial Local Government Act, which requires them to stick to municipal bylaws on building height and setbacks. So if a new type of housing was proposed to city staff that was taller than nine metres in height, or within four metres of the property line, it would deviate from city rules and therefore need to go before city council for approval. This is a common problem in Victoria because the city has far more variety in lot sizes than most cities. It also has almost no back lanes that would make it easier to add smaller housing options— carriage houses, garden suites, and so on. In short, city staff lack the authority to allow case-by-case modifications to make a project work. This means city staff need more discretion to approve new and inno-vative housing forms in traditional single-family neighbourhoods.

It should be noted that the city of Victoria has approved multiple rental apartment buildings in the downtown core and on major arterial roads in recent years, both private and public. If the city's population was static, the addition of those units would likely lead to a serious improvement in both affordability and availability of rental housing. But the population of Victoria, like that of many Canadian cities, keeps rising, and the new construction that's been approved so far simply isn't enough. That would be a problem at any time, but it's been all the more so in the early 2020s because of rapidly rising costs.

Just before the pandemic, Aryze paid roughly $185 per square foot in construction costs. Four years later, that had more than doubled. By 2023, it cost them at least $400 per square foot for townhomes. In bigger rental apartment buildings, larger shared spaces like common rooms and parkades brought the average construction cost per square foot of rentable living space to more than $700. "So your thousand-square-foot, three-bedroom condo is $750,000, and that's just the cost. There's no developer profit at that price."

Independent housing analyst Leo Spalteholz is sympathetic to Luke's frustrations. Leo is a professional engineer who worked in industry for ten years before taking a job at the University of Victoria. Along the way he picked up a side expertise in real estate. "I was thinking about buying a house back in 2008, and then, because I'm nuts, that turned into thousands of hours of research!" Leo started poring over data with the precision one would expect of an engineer. He eventually became frustrated that he couldn't access all the data that's available to real estate agents, so he took a few courses and obtained a real estate licence, not to sell houses but to gain access to all the data so he could buy one. "At first I thought it was a bubble," he admits of Victoria's rapidly rising prices. He presumed they had simply risen too high, and that a market correction would bring them back to where they should be. But apart from a few relatively small setbacks, Victoria house prices have gone up and up and up, to the point where most first-time buyers can no longer afford them. "The expectation that you'll get a single-family home is gone," he says, "and it isn't coming back." Like many business and construction associations, Leo says there simply isn't enough supply to meet housing demand. At first he dismissed that explanation as a "self-serving argument" from those who stood to benefit. But over the years he's come to believe it's correct.

So what's needed to fix that imbalance between supply and demand? "Municipal zoning reform and federal money." Leo believes single-family zoning and other onerous municipal guidelines simply make it too difficult to build as many new homes as a city like Victoria needs, as quickly as it needs them. He points to numerous examples, including a proposal to replace a single-family home with a sixplex. Because it was forty centimetres taller than a mansion that would only need a building permit to proceed, the sixplex had to go before a public hearing and a vote by city council. After several hours of back and forth, councillors approved the project by a vote of six to three.

Leo also thinks the federal government has been missing in action on housing. Not only did it cut most of what it spent on public affordable housing projects in the 1980s and 1990s, it missed many opportunities to incentivize the construction of hundreds of thousands of rental units through the use of tax incentives, like waiving the GST on construction and operating costs. The net result has been not enough rental housing. "In the last thirty years Canada has grown by 10 million people but added only about 355,000 purpose-built rentals."

Luke Mari agrees the federal government should have done more to incentivize the construction of rental housing. He says almost every affordable housing project on Vancouver Island and in Vancouver is being financed through the Canada Mortgage and Housing Corporation because traditional lenders can no longer justify the projects financially, and he wonders why it didn't freeze interest rates on loans for all affordable housing projects a few years ago. "That's the most surprising thing to me about this whole inflationary period. Why didn't the federal government create an interest rate hold for projects that met certain affordable housing criteria?"

Home builders were hit hard by rapidly rising interest rates in 2022, just as many mortgage holders were. The triple whammy of higher borrowing, labour, and material costs all served to make new housing even more expensive, at a time when house and land prices were already soaring. And there are other rising costs that make new housing more expensive, such as the BC Energy Step Code that requires greater energy efficiency in new construction. In addition, some new buildings have to include heat pumps instead of natural gas heating because they lower a building's carbon footprint. There's also a new seismic code every five years that's meant to strengthen all new buildings before the next big earthquake hits the British Columbia coast. There are deconstruction requirements that are meant to salvage and recycle building materials rather than send them to the landfill. But wait, there's more! Community amenity obligations, tenant assistance funds, inclusionary housing contributions, not to mention all the permitting fees—they all have a purpose, but they all add to the cost of building new homes as well. "We should be incentivizing [new construction] instead of taxing it out of existence."

The scale and pace of all the price acceleration in Victoria has been such that the economics of building affordable housing may have shot past the kinds of missing-middle housing—fourplexes and townhomes—that so many young buyers in the city were desperate to see built. Luke says Aryze is "going straight from single-family homes to four-storey apartments because land prices are just too high." The timing was ironic, because it happened just as the city of Victoria was debating a new policy to allow the construction of multiple units on existing single-family lots. Victoria was a leader on this, replacing single-family zoning with multi-unit zoning three months before Toronto city council voted to do something similar. After months of debate, public hearings, and a civic election, Victoria councillors voted to pass the Missing Middle Housing Initiative in January 2023. The initiative allowed the construction of six-unit homes on most city lots, and townhomes of up to twelve units on some corner lots. The city's mayor and housing advocates hoped it would increase the supply of affordable housing. Critics claimed it would simply allow the construction of million-dollar townhomes. But three months after the policy was introduced, there had been no applications at all.

Luke Mari tried to make it work. He looked at the city's maximum building heights and minimum setbacks, and calculated they couldn't build a houseplex on a lot that could be profitable for the company at a price that would sell on the local market. He also looked at corner lots that could accommodate townhomes, but found only a handful across the city that were big enough to meet the fine print of city requirements. In the end, he concluded the new Missing Middle Housing policy, as written on paper, just didn't work. "Every step we take forward, we take five steps back," Luke sighs. "It's like, 'Okay, we're going to allow townhouses,' but then we under-densify them in the policy so they can't even work." Even with free land, he says, building rental housing in Victoria is only economically viable for private companies that will rent at market rates.

All this has left him feeling pretty pessimistic about the future of Victoria as a livable city for a wide range of people. "We're slowly going to descend into a resort municipality," he predicts. He suspects Metro Vancouver will be somewhat more livable, even though the average house price there is still higher than in Victoria. That's because Metro Vancouver has better transit and more suburbs with housing that is at least attainable to middle-class buyers. Someone in Pitt Meadows, for instance, could buy a new three-bedroom townhouse for $750,000 and ride the 75-minute West Coast Express train into downtown Vancouver to work. Luke thinks that kind of arrangement would be much harder to find in Victoria and the twelve other municipalities that make up the Capital Regional District and its roughly 450,000 residents. He thinks Victoria will increasingly be home to well-off people who have either family money or a lucrative income from somewhere else, alongside a dwindling population of service workers struggling to afford to stay in the community. "I don't think we're ever going to get out of it, because we are not remotely close to accepting the level of density required to accomplish the needs of the city. We're just not even scratching the surface."

Leo Spalteholz agrees and thinks the problem lies in the fact that the first solutions rest with municipalities, which are often not disposed to implement them. "It's so political that it can't be solved by someone who is so close to the direct voter." He believes many mayors and councillors don't want to introduce greater density to neighbourhoods because of local opposition to change. "Right or wrong, people perceive the impact of a townhouse going up next to them very acutely, but they don't feel the shortage of housing across the city to the same degree, especially if they spend most of their time in their comfortable neighbourhood." He points to citizen surveys that have shown a variety of top issues for people over the age of 40 but only one overwhelming concern as top of mind for younger demographics: "Housing, housing, housing!" He keeps an email from a former student as a reminder of how serious the situation has become. "After graduation," the student wrote, "I got the best possible engineering job I could have wished for. However, committing to a career in structural engineering seems like absolute financial suicide these days." Hearing young engineers complain that they can't afford housing has convinced Leo of one thing—"We need to fix the housing crisis."

While developers wait for zoning reform at the municipal level and financial help from the federal government, they're always keeping an eye out for future possibilities. Cities like Paris have demonstrated that more space can usually be found within existing urban boundaries, in department stores, old barracks, vacant office buildings, and bare land. Luke Mari sees similar potential almost everywhere he looks. The municipally owned Cedar Hill Golf Course in Saanich, for instance. The eighteen-hole "working man's course" has rolling green hills, beautiful mountain views, and a whole lot of land in the middle of Greater Victoria. The course has faced financial hardship in the past, and Luke thinks it should be reinvented as a home for twenty thousand people. "You could line that whole golf course with six-storey apartments! I've done it in a sketch-up. Ten thousand units and you're touching less than 2 percent of the land base of the golf course. The rest would be a gorgeous central park. That's the power of six-storey buildings."

The other power Luke thinks local governments should use is the power of taxation. He notes that British Columbians pay some of the lowest property taxes in Canada, when compared with property values. He suggests the Capital Regional District could implement a housing levy, similar to gas taxes that fund transit projects, to fund the construction of more affordable housing. "We have low taxation and high expectations, but when you look at the countries that are building mass public housing, their taxes are all much higher than ours." However, Luke doesn't expect to see significant tax increases, or to build towers around golf courses, any time soon. He thinks many of these changes will take a generation. "I think we're just at the beginning of a tidal wave of reforms," he says. "But will we ever catch up?"

Housing advocates in Victoria, Vancouver, and Toronto will likely have to wait a few years to find out if "missing-middle" zoning changes will help their cities. In the meantime, it's worth looking south to a city that's a few years farther down the rezoning road.

16

INFILLS FOR AFFORDABILITY

Portland, Oregon

ERIC THOMPSON BUILT a good life for himself by building good homes for families in Portland, Oregon. While every house was different, the model for most projects was roughly the same—buy a small, old, single-family home in an established neighbourhood, tear it down, then build something much bigger and much nicer in its place. The new houses were roughly three thousand square feet and built to a high standard, with fine-quality finishes and nice appliances. Most people in Portland couldn't afford these houses, which typically sold for well over $1 million. But demand was strong and Eric's company, Oregon Homeworks, built many fine homes over many years. So when the city of Portland declared a housing emergency in 2015, a move Ottawa would copy in 2020, and launched a review of single-family zoning—something that both British Columbia and Toronto later replicated—Eric was understandably nervous. He decided to get involved directly by joining a city advisory committee looking into the issue. Eric was wary of abandoning single-family zoning. After all, it had made Portland what it was, and making nice new houses for the city's top 5 percent of income earners had made Eric what he was—a successful businessman.

But Portland was starting to look less successful. To many eyes, the city long famous for roses and progressive politics was becoming synonymous with homelessness, poverty, and an ever-widening gap between rich and poor. To be fair, the same was said of most other west coast cities, including Los Angeles, San Diego, San Francisco, and Seattle. It was also said of Vancouver and Victoria. A 2022 point-in-time homeless survey counted more than 6,600 homeless people in Metro Portland, a number that had grown by more than 1,500 since the start of the pandemic. Makeshift shelters, tents, and rundown RVs were becoming an increasingly common sight. And there were rising concerns about crime and public safety too. Jason Bolt, the founder of an eyeglass lens company called Revant, noticed more and more unhoused people sheltering in the neighbourhood around his company's headquarters. When the company moved to the light industrial area a few years before the start of the pandemic, it had seemed safe enough. By 2022, he didn't feel safe anymore. His worry morphed into reality one day while he was walking down the street with a colleague. "As soon as we got around the corner, a guy ran out of an RV with a knife and came at us." Jason and his colleague were okay, but he realized his community was not. Garbage seemed to be everywhere, and makeshift bicycle chop shops were visible on almost every corner. A group of business owners in the area were so fed up that they threatened to leave the city if Portland didn't do something. The city responded with what it called a ninety-day reset, which was basically a sweep of the neighbourhood. People with no homes would be chased out of the area, until they found somewhere new to shelter and the whole process had to be repeated.

A lack of affordable housing wasn't the only contributor to homelessness, but social service agencies said it played a significant role. The city saw some of the fastest rises in house prices and rents in the United States. A survey by the real estate company Redfern found rents climbed 40 percent between the spring of 2021 and the spring of 2022. All of which left tens of thousands of people in Portland, and across Oregon, barely hanging on to their homes. The Housing Oregon non-profit counted almost 250,000 families across the state who made less than $33,000 a year and needed subsidized affordable housing. But only 143,000 units were available.

As property prices continued to rise in Portland, and across Oregon, Eric Thompson saw the writing on the wall. Housing was just too expensive to stick to the status quo. When the city asked for public comment on how it should change single-family zoning, it received more than fifteen thousand comments. Instead of fighting change, Eric decided to embrace it by building a different type of housing.

The first big shift that enabled builders and communities to change came in 2019 when the state of Oregon effectively banned single-family zoning in most cities. Housing advocates framed it differently, in an effort to make the change seem less radical, by saying the state had "re-legalized fourplexes," which were much more common a century ago, before the state allowed municipal governments to introduce single-family zoning in the 1920s. Almost a century later, Oregon lawmakers were effectively announcing a major reversal. In cities where there's a housing shortage, they said, it isn't fair to stop landowners from building more homes. In one fell swoop the state quadrupled the number of homes that could be built on the vast majority of residential lots.

Two years later, the city of Portland went a step further by allowing property owners to build as many as six units on what used to be a single-family lot if three of those units were designated as affordable, with rents tied to a city affordability formula. The "deep affordability bonus" would require units to be within reach of households earning up to 60 percent of the median family income in the city. None of this stopped people from building single-family houses, though it did shrink the maximum size of those to about 2,500 square feet. And it made it much, much easier for builders and landowners to replace small, old houses with four or even six new homes at a time.

Eric Thompson and his company, Oregon Homeworks, looked at the changes and built themselves a new business model. Instead of the big, beautiful houses of 3,000 square feet or more, the homes they built would be smaller, though still appealing and energy-efficient. And they would build more of them. The company had already started building smaller accessory dwelling units, known as ADUs (essentially, separate studio apartments), in the backyards of single-family homes. Eric saw there was strong demand for those, so when the new zoning allowed fourplexes, Oregon Homeworks was ready to go, having already established designs and plans for smaller square footage. A year after the zoning changes went into effect, the company had dozens of new homes under construction. The most popular option by far was the fourplex. It was more profitable than duplexes or triplexes, and Eric said it was easier to build fourplexes than to adjust to the city's affordability requirements that went along with a sixplex. Eric was excited by the demand for fourplexes. But what really energized him was another new option—cottage clusters.

As the name suggests, cottage clusters are small groupings of small houses on a single lot. In Portland, the footprint of the building can't be larger than 900 square feet, it can't be less than five feet from the property line, and there must be at least six feet between structures for fire safety reasons. The cottages also have to stay small; the average size of the cottages in a cluster can't exceed 1,400 square feet. Most of the new units that Oregon Homeworks build have two bedrooms and two bathrooms, and total about 900 or 1,000 square feet. "That's just a really efficient plan," Eric says. Cottage clusters also have the potential to become mini communities of small homes surrounding a shared courtyard. Some buyers may prefer to have their own small fenced yard, and changes to Oregon laws now allow relatively simple subdivision of single-family lots to create new small lots for each cottage. So if a single-family lot is divided, a cottage could be sold on a 1,500-square-foot lot as a fee-simple property (what's typically called freehold ownership in Canada, where a landowner has access to the property indefinitely and only needs to obey laws, bylaws, and zoning). The owner wouldn't have to contend with any condo fees or rules; they'd simply own their own, very small house on a very small lot.

Cottages like this one built by Oregon Homeworks are considerably smaller than traditional single-family homes, but they are considerably more affordable for middle-class Portland residents.

This is a significant change in the city, and it doesn't come without challenges. For example, Eric says city bylaws allowed all the cottages in a cluster to share the same storm drain but required each of them to have its own sewer line. Not only does that add to the cost of every unit, it could cause problems for the municipal sewer lines to have so many different taps being added to existing mains. City inspectors told Eric they were "working on it," and he hoped a new guideline would soon be introduced to allow shared sewer drains. He said different buildings can share a main trunk line if it's designed properly. He also points out that the cottage clusters are built to a high environmental standard, with monthly utility bills for each unit averaging around $40, which includes heating and electricity.

But the purchase price wasn't cheap. Most sold for between $400,000 and $500,000. Eric is quick to point out that's still not affordable for many young buyers, or those with lower incomes. But he says it's attainable for a lot of other people who previously would have had to look for somewhere to live a long drive away, in the outer suburbs of Portland. They want established, walkable neighbourhoods where they don't need to hop in their car to do everything. He mentions one family—a teacher and a restaurant manager with two young kids—who bought a small, detached two-bedroom home. Eric says they're typical of many of the new buyers he meets, who tell him they're looking for smaller units in order to live where and how they want to live. "They chose that home because they prioritized location and a yard and architectural design over square footage."

About one-third of the buyers moving into the smaller homes that Oregon Homeworks now builds are older buyers with no mortgage who want to downsize. Eric says the other two-thirds are almost exclusively young, first-time homebuyers with middle-class jobs—firefighters, teachers, and people who work in the service industry.

They're people who wouldn't have been able to afford the houses he built a decade ago, or the neighbourhoods they're now moving into. "So if they can now live here, I feel really good about what we're doing," he says. "I don't know if we're making a huge difference for the city as a whole, but for the people who buy our houses, we're making a big difference."

Of course, Oregon Homeworks isn't the only company building smaller new homes in Portland. Other builders took advantage of the new zoning and submitted hundreds of new building applications. But in a city of about 640,000—at the centre of a metro area of about 2.2 million people—the impact wasn't dramatic. Housing researcher Michael Andersen looked at the data for the first year that multiplexes were allowed in the city of Portland, before cottage clusters were permitted, and calculated an extra 200 to 300 homes were built because of the change. On its own, he doesn't think this type of infill will be enough to address the shortage of affordable housing in Portland. "It's certainly not a finish line on either housing poor people or on building enough homes." But Michael says the infill policy is a key component of making the city somewhat more affordable, and it's an effective way to evolve gradually. He thinks the benefits will become more and more apparent over time. "The bigger effect is in the long term. As every unit in the city reaches the end of its useful life, under the new law it's very likely to be replaced by a handful of less expensive, though nice, new units." Michael says that will help with affordability, but also with social integration in the city. "I think it's just a good way to scatter people of different incomes through neighbourhoods."

It seems clear that it will take more than missing-middle infill housing to address the lack of affordable accommodation in Portland. In 2018, voters in the three most populous of the counties that make up Portland approved an affordable housing bond worth more than $650 million to build permanently affordable homes for more than twelve thousand people. Over the following few years, the Portland Housing Bureau, which was founded in 2010, either built new affordable housing or bought and refurbished existing units. The city-funded bureau partnered with several local non-profits that helped find housing for families with young children, refugees, and people at risk of becoming homeless. They made a priority of helping groups representing Black and Indigenous people. The bureau pointed out that the average income for Black households in the city wasn't enough to make two-bedroom apartments affordable in any Portland neighbourhood. It was also aware of a long history of Black people and other minority groups being disadvantaged by single-family zoning in Portland, and in countless other American cities.

In the early 1900s, several cities in the eastern and southern US created racial zoning ordinances to segregate residents based on skin colour. These were overturned by the Supreme Court in 1917, and there's no evidence that the city of Portland ever enacted such explicit rules. But there are several examples of overtly racist policies in the local housing market. In 1919, the Portland Realty Board declared it unethical for an agent to "sell property to either Negro or Chinese people in a White neighborhood." The language remained in the board's Code of Ethics until 1956. During those decades, more discreet forms of racism put Portland's minority groups at a distinct disadvantage in the housing market. Portland introduced its first zoning codes in 1924: single-family, multi-family, business-manufacturing, and unrestricted. At first, most neighbourhoods were zoned for multi-family use. Only fifteen neighbourhoods were granted the exclusive status of being single-family, and all had organized requests by local residents to receive that designation. Many more areas were rezoned to single-family in the 1930s and 1940s, to both protect real estate values and make it easier for buyers to receive loans that were insured by the Federal Housing Administration. At around the same time, many private developers put racially restrictive covenants on new properties. These legal clauses restricted who could live in a home based on their race. In the leafy Portland neighbourhood of Laurelhurst, for instance, a covenant from 1913 stated: ". . . nor shall the same or any part thereof be in any manner used or occupied by Chinese, Japanese or negroes, except that persons of said races may be employed as servants by residents." The US Supreme Court declared the covenants unenforceable in 1948, but some can still be found on the deeds of homes in older Portland neighbourhoods.

These and other practices had the effect of keeping most of Portland's nicer neighbourhoods almost exclusively white. For much of the first half of the twentieth century, African Americans could buy a home only in Albina—a working-class collection of neighbourhoods close to both the docks and the railway tracks, where immigrants had lived for decades. Many Black shipbuilders moved to Portland during the Second World War, and moved into a new public housing project, called Vanport, along the shores of the Columbia River. But when those homes were swept away by a flood in 1948, the housing project was abandoned, leaving its residents searching for new homes. The racial covenants that were still common prevented them from moving into most of Portland's neighbourhoods, which meant most had to move to Albina. But a federal government lending practice, called "redlining," kept out Black buyers even if they had steady work.

Since the 1930s, the US government's Home Owners' Loan Corporation had assessed neighbourhoods across America and lumped them into colour categories for lending—green, blue, yellow, and red. Homes inside the green lines were considered a sound investment, and loans were relatively easy to obtain for their purchase. Inside the blue lines, there were a few concerns, but still many homes worth financing. But buying a house inside the yellow lines was extremely difficult if bank financing was needed, and people wanting to buy homes in redlined areas found it either extremely difficult or impossible to obtain home loans. Not surprisingly, Albina was redlined. In 1937, an appraiser described Lower Albina this way: "This area constitutes Portland's 'Melting Pot' and is the nearest approach to a 'slum district' in the city. Three-quarters of the negro population of the city reside here and in addition there are some 300 Orientals, 1000 Southern Europeans and Russians." In 1968, the US government hoped to end unfair practices like this with the establishment of the Fair Housing Act. But the Portland Housing Bureau found evidence that "it remained common for banks to practice redlining in Portland until the 1990s." A 2019 report for the city's Bureau of Planning and Sustainability concluded that white households have experienced "inequitable benefits from homeownership. White households in single-family neighborhoods have accumulated wealth through rising home values, further contributing to racial disparities in wealth."

Canadians shouldn't feel smug in comparison; explicitly racist covenants existed in cities across Canada as well. Covenants were placed on several homes in West Vancouver in the 1930s that excluded anyone "of the African or Asiatic race, or of African or Asiatic descent, except servants of the occupier of the premises and residence," just as in Portland. In 1948 the sale of a cottage near Grand Bend, on the shores of Lake Huron, revealed a registered restriction from 1933 barring the sale, use, occupation, or rental "by any person of the Jewish, Hebrew, Semitic, Negro or coloured race or blood." Both the purchaser, a prominent Jewish businessman named Bernard Wolf, and the seller agreed the restriction should be declared void, but it took Wolf two years and appeals all the way to the Supreme Court of Canada to have the covenant struck down, because lower courts upheld its validity. The Supreme Court also ruled it was an illegal restraint on an owner's right to sell.

While racist laws have been eliminated on both sides of the border, the disparity between rich and poor endures, and it continues to grow in Portland and other American cities. Housing advocates hope a combination of municipal zoning reform, new construction, and new lending rules will help make the market more affordable, and by extension perhaps more equitable. In May 2022, President Joe Biden introduced a Housing Action Plan that he said would "close the housing supply gap within five years" by building and preserving hundreds of thousands of affordable housing units. It also ordered the government agencies that steer lending to create new options for loans on smaller multi-family buildings, accessory dwelling units, and single properties with as many as four separate units. In making the announcement, Biden mentioned the national housing deficit in the United States of roughly 1.5 million homes, saying "this shortfall burdens family budgets, drives up inflation, limits economic growth, maintains residential segregation, and exacerbates climate change." That's a convincing claim, and a sobering one for Canada. If a country with more than eight times our population is worried about a deficit of 1.5 million homes, how should Canadians feel about a predicted deficit of 3.5 million homes by 2030?

SEARCHING FOR SANCTUARY

Calgary

THE SYRMAN FAMILY—DMYTRO, ANASTASIIA, and their four-year-old daughter, Varvara—first set foot on Canadian soil in March 2023. It had been a year since Russian soldiers bombed their way into the Syrmans' hometown of Dniprorudne in southern Ukraine. The city of seventeen thousand is located along the southern banks of the Dnieper River, and was strategically important because of its many mines. The Russians captured the small city just a few weeks after launching their invasion of Ukraine, and Dmytro and Anastasiia decided they would have to leave, despite the fact Dmytro still had a good job as a human resources manager at an iron factory. "We started all of this because we were scared for Varvara," he recalls in halting English. "When Russian bombs were falling near our city, it was really scary." Six months after the war started, Dmytro and Anastasiia packed their car and left Dniprorudne. "We lost everything," Dmytro says. They drove three thousand kilometres over six days, before finally finding a safe place to stay in

Poland. They weren't alone. Millions of Ukrainians were leaving the country, seeking safety elsewhere. Poland accepted millions, but with the country stretched to the breaking point, many Ukrainians realized they needed to look elsewhere. So Dmytro and Anastasiia started the paperwork to come to Canada, under the Canada-Ukraine Authorization for Emergency Travel, and eventually received the necessary approvals.

When the family arrived in Calgary, they were part of another Ukrainian wave. Immigrant settlement officials in the city estimated that 450 Ukrainians were moving to the city every week. That's not necessarily surprising, given Calgary's relatively affordable rents when compared with Vancouver and Toronto. The city also already had thousands of people with Ukrainian ancestry. Hundreds of Calgarians responded by opening the doors of their homes.

The Centre for Newcomers, a non-profit immigrant settlement agency, placed the Syrman family with Calgary resident Jeff Vosburgh and his family. "It was just out of the desire to help and also the desire to give people a chance to build a strong life in Canada," Jeff says. The Ukrainian family would stay with their Canadian hosts for a month, which they hoped would be enough time to find a place of their own. In return, the Vosburghs had the satisfaction of helping another family in their time of need. Twelve-year-old Jenson Vosburgh was excited to have the Syrmans move in for the month. "I think it's probably one of the best things we've ever done."

The Vosburgh family wasn't alone. All across the city, Calgarians responded generously, making quick commitments to welcome families into their homes before they'd even met them. Ed Koshka had enough space in his basement for a family of four. When his church started a coordinated effort to house Ukrainians, he stepped forward. "I am of Ukrainian descent and that's my heritage, my culture. I attend a Ukrainian church. I just feel compelled to do that."

Other Calgarians, like Laura Lazarick, turned to social media with direct offers of shelter. Laura offered a one-bedroom condo for two to three months, for free. "Ukraine is my ancestral motherland," she wrote. "All I ask for in return is a pierogi making lesson."

Others assisted in different ways. Tammy Brigidear helped more than thirty Ukrainian families find their bearings. Ann Kucheriava and her family had already arrived in Calgary when she met Tammy. The introduction came in a note that one of Ann's three daughters brought home from school, welcoming the family to Calgary and offering help. Ann's family had been on holiday in the Czech Republic when the war broke out. They never went back to their home in the city of Dnipro. As a result, they didn't have many clothes, let alone the many items a family of five needs to make a home. Tammy came to the rescue with donated clothes and other essential items. But other families had greater needs. Some had to sleep on the floor. Others needed rides or help filling out documents. The recipients of that generosity often give what they can of themselves. Ann learned English quickly and then secured a job at a registry where she helps many other new immigrants get their documents in order. "I love my work," she says with a smile. "I am explaining the rules. Many people don't even understand how to write 'Calgary.' I feel useful now."

Calgary's warm welcome of Ukrainian refugees has been a success story on many levels, but as is the case in so many other Canadian cities, housing is a huge barrier. The rapid influx of many Ukrainians made finding affordable places to live extremely difficult, even in a wealthy, growing city of 1.4 million people. By April 2023, rents had risen 25 percent for one-bedroom units newly listed on Rentals.ca as compared with April 2022. The average rent for new one-bedroom listings had risen to $1,686 a month. The average three-bedroom was advertised at $2,393. Those rents were expensive enough for Ukrainian evacuees, but the common request from many landlords for an additional month's rent as a security deposit proved too much for a lot of new arrivals from Ukraine. Before even moving into their new home, Ukrainian evacuees wanting a one-bedroom apartment would have to pay more than $3,300. Families wanting three bedrooms had to cough up nearly $4,800. Given the soaring rents, it's perhaps not surprising that local food bank usage shot up dramatically as well. Calgary food banks reported a 34 percent increase in demand in just one year. Meanwhile, Calgary's unemployment rate of 6.6 percent was higher than the national average of 5 percent, and while that had actually come down from a year earlier, many new arrivals reported serious difficulty finding work in the city.

Anna Martyniuk and her husband, Serhii, arrived in Calgary in January 2023, after spending many months in Poland. They spent a similar length of time looking for work in Calgary, with no luck. Serhii is a mechanic, but he couldn't find a job in his new home even after going to more than twenty interviews. Anna said it was because he doesn't speak English. "Please," she implored, "give some chance to some people." Anna hadn't found a job either, despite having a PhD and having taught at a university in Ukraine. Like countless immigrants before them, Anna and Serhii found the skills from their home country were of little use to them in Canada. And while Alberta, Ontario, and other provinces are now trying to do more to recognize work experience from other countries, it didn't help many newcomers in 2023.

While employment was a huge concern, housing remained the first hurdle for most newcomers. For many, it was the biggest. Kelly Ernst, the chief program officer at the Centre for Newcomers, said the supply of rental housing in Calgary just couldn't keep up with the new surge in demand. "We're in a desperate, dire need at the moment for host homes to try to accommodate the evacuees coming from Ukraine. It's reaching the proportions of being a crisis moment."

The federal government had already set aside seventy-five hotel rooms in Calgary, and twenty-five in Edmonton, as temporary accommodation for new Ukrainians when they first arrived. The Alberta government later provided more than $4 million to cover transportation costs to hotels, and more hotel rooms in Lethbridge, Medicine Hat, and Red Deer. The Centre for Newcomers also had access to two other hotels, thanks to help from private donors. But with more newcomers landing every day, those were all full. "When you have more than 600 people on a list and nowhere to house those people, the future may be very bleak for housing," Kelly Ernst said. "The stereotype is people are coming with accommodation, with resources to pay for those hotels, and very often they do not have those resources and they may be fleeing and not have any accommodation set up prior to fleeing."

While many Ukrainians were greeted at the airport by Canadian hosts, some were not so lucky. Immigrant support workers came to the aid of several new arrivals who had spent two or three nights in the Calgary airport because they had nowhere else to go. They found other Ukrainians sleeping in tents in city parks. Some, like the Kovalenko family, even ended up in local homeless shelters because they couldn't find housing. The Kovalenkos had left their home in Zaporizhzhia in the first few months of the war. Speaking through an interpreter, Yuri said they made a "split-second decision to take all of their bags, to lock up the apartment, and just to leave." Yuri was a veterinarian in Ukraine. He had a good life with his wife, Iullia, and their three kids. But the war and their flight to Canada all happened so rapidly that they didn't have time to make arrangements before they arrived. Once they did, they couldn't find a place to rent. So they ended up sleeping in Calgary's Inn from the Cold emergency shelter. After that, with the help of local churches, they found a host family to take them in for a longer spell. They hoped that would give them enough time to find jobs, schools, and more permanent housing. But that arrangement was very definitely a temporary one.

"It puts stress on the whole shelter system," Kelly Ernst said, "and it means more and more people are [living] rough in the streets." Nataliia Shen, the housing coordinator for vulnerable populations at the Centre for Newcomers, shares that frustration. "Our waiting list is growing extra every day, and every day I get requests from Ukrainians directly to my inbox saying that we need temporary accommodation."

Yulia Gorbach saw that pressure every day. As the chair of the Calgary Ukrainian Evacuee Welcome Committee, she played a pivotal role in welcoming thousands of Ukrainians to the city. The group met newcomers at St. Vladimir's Ukrainian Orthodox Sobor church, handing out blankets, pillows, toothbrushes, and emergency food hampers. "When they come here, it's like a deer in the headlights. Can you imagine coming to a foreign country with no language whatsoever?" Yulia worried the $3,000 that the federal government's Canada-Ukraine Authorization for Emergency Travel was providing for every Ukrainian adult, along with $1,500 for every child, simply wasn't enough to help them pay a few months' rent and skyrocketing grocery bills. While refugees arriving in Canada are normally given a year to settle, the program treated Ukrainian evacuees differently, expecting them to settle in and find jobs much more quickly. "It's not right," Yulia said. "Those people don't have the time, don't have income support, don't have anything."

It's true that refugees receive more financial support than Ukrainians receive from the federal government. Still, they also struggle to find affordable housing in Calgary. Fatima Tabish is one of the thousands of Afghan refugees who arrived in Calgary in the year following the return of the Taliban to power in 2021. She moved into a hotel squeezed between Macleod Trail, a major road, and the

CTrain LRT line. The hotel became a temporary community for Fatima and dozens of other refugees, who stayed there while they looked for more permanent housing. "Life is so nice in Canada, especially in Calgary," she says with a smile. "People are so good, so kind, but the challenge is the rent. It's expensive." Refugees like Fatima received $1,200 per month from the federal government to pay their rent. But they found it just wasn't enough in Calgary. "We are looking for homes, but the big problem is the rents are going up, higher and higher. Everything is so expensive." Fatima knew she would need a good job to afford a home. In Afghanistan, she worked as a teacher. Despite that experience, and a business administration degree, she knew there were no guarantees. She admitted to feeling anxious as she started looking for a home to rent and a job to pay for it. But she did her best to remain optimistic, and volunteered as an interpreter. It was an important role. Fatima helped other Afghan refugees settle in their new community and look for somewhere to live.

Unfortunately, many Afghans found themselves looking for a more permanent home and not finding it. Sohail Shafaq knows how hard that is, first-hand. The former TV journalist had to flee Afghanistan when the Taliban returned to power. Apart from the low vacancy rate and high costs, he had to contend with some landlords who didn't want to rent their properties to Afghans. "The owner of the home said, 'Where are you from?'" Sohail recalled, the day after viewing an apartment he wanted to rent. "We said, 'Afghanistan,' and they said, 'Oh, I was thinking you are from Ukraine.' Like that, they rejected us directly." With nowhere to rent, Sohail was stuck couch surfing in a friend's apartment. In total, he spent seven months searching for a home in Calgary before finding an apartment he could afford. He eventually moved into a two-bedroom apartment for $1,300, close to the college where he was studying English. Sohail moved in with a roommate, so he paid only $650 a month in rent, plus about $95 for utilities. It would be incredibly tight, but Sohail hoped he could make ends meet until his English improved and he could find a job. Even then, with rents so high, he wondered how he would ever manage to save money and get ahead.

While Sohail and Fatima grappled with their new lives, a growing number of newcomers were joining them and stretching Calgary to its limits. In 2022 the city received a record number of new residents from elsewhere in Canada, some of them enticed perhaps by Alberta's aggressive marketing campaign that wallpapered Toronto's busiest subway station with high-resolution photographs of the Calgary skyline and the Rocky Mountains. It also featured eye-catching slogans like BIGGER PAYCHEQUES. SMALLER RENT CHEQUES and FIND THINGS YOU'D NEVER EXPECT. LIKE AN AFFORDABLE HOUSE. Calgary also received a record number of global immigrants from other countries. By 2023 city officials estimated sixty-two people were moving to Calgary every day, and they predicted that rate of growth would continue for several years. In total, they estimated the city would add another 110,000 people by 2027.

Calgary has certainly been a popular city for Ukrainian evacuees, and for many others. But it's not alone. Statistics Canada data showed unprecedented population growth in cities across the country due to immigration in 2022. For the first time ever, Canada's population grew by more than 1 million in a single year. At 2.7 percent, the annual growth rate was the highest it had been since 1957, when the population increased by 3.3 percent thanks to a double-barrelled demographic explosion of both the postwar baby boom and a flood of refugees following the Hungarian Revolution a year earlier. In 2022, immigration accounted for nearly 96 percent of all growth recorded in Canada. This country had the leading growth rate of all G7 members, as it has done for many years. In fact, Canada's annual growth rate put it in the top twenty across the world—prompting

Statistics Canada to note that almost all the countries with a higher growth rate were in Africa. At this pace, Canada's population would double in just twenty-six years. It's worth noting that of the new arrivals, fewer than half were permanent residents. More than 600,000 were non-permanent residents—a staggering number that StatsCan attributed to an effort to "help fulfill employment needs across the country and the program created to welcome people fleeing the Russian invasion of Ukraine."

Of course, it's never been easy to leave a country in crisis and start a new life in a new country with a different language and customs. It has almost always required a huge amount of hard work and sacrifice. But for much of its history, Canada was a significantly more affordable place to find a home than it is now. When Croatian refugee Veselko Dodig disembarked at Pier 21 in Halifax in 1961, the median price for a single-family home in Canadian cities was a little less than $15,000. At the same time, the median income for a family of four was a little more than $5,000. Veselko was excited to leave his old life in Communist Yugoslavia behind and build a new life for himself in Canada. He switched his name to Bill, found a job, and worked hard. His wife followed three years later, and they soon had a home of their own. "They were able to save and buy a home in just a few years," their son, Victor Dodig, recalls. "In many respects, they lived the dream." Victor continued his father's dream by rising to the top of the Canadian business establishment, becoming president and CEO of Canadian Imperial Bank of Commerce. But he worries the country that welcomed his parents is now financially inhospitable for most immigrants. Many of them have difficulty finding good jobs, often due to the lack of recognition of foreign credentials. His other big worry is the shortage of affordable housing in Canada. In early 2023, the average national home price was hovering around $700,000, when the median after-tax income for

Canadian households was a little more than $73,000. The end result, Victor Dodig believes, is that it's now much more difficult for newcomers to build themselves a good life in Canada. "Today, that dream is at risk."

18

A MODULAR RESPONSE

Cork, Ireland

THE BIG, HEAVY TRUCK—called a lorry in Ireland—turned carefully onto the construction site, in the pleasant Cork suburb of Mahon. The waterside neighbourhood has been growing in recent years, as more new houses rise up around the sprawling Mahon Point shopping mall, with its fashion outlets and multiplex cinema. Once in the construction zone, the lorry lumbered down a gravel road surrounded by modest single-storey homes still under construction but almost complete. The lorry driver took his time, as the heavy load he was pulling was another one of those modest single-storey homes. There would be sixty-four in total, and his was one of the last. He drove even slower as he approached his final destination, and parked exactly where he was instructed. Then a giant red crawler crane rumbled up alongside, before construction workers unfastened the giant load from the trailer and attached the crane's steel cables. When the workers were satisfied that everything was connected as it should be, the crane lifted the structure off the trailer and pivoted slowly towards the concrete footings where it would be lowered. The crane operator and his colleagues on the ground worked in unison, and before long this prefabricated home was standing where it will remain for many years. With one careful manoeuvre of the crane, the new house was almost finished.

Watching with interest, just down the road, was local resident Michelle Buckley, a leader at the Mahon branch of the Irish youth organization Foróige. She'd moved to the neighbourhood in 1981, at the age of nine, and wanted to make sure the incoming Ukrainians felt as welcome as she did more than forty years ago. "When Mahon was being developed in the 1980s, the people who already lived here welcomed us, and I don't see why we shouldn't be doing the same now. We're a very small community but we have a massive big heart." She was confident that local clubs like Foróige would help new arrivals integrate into the community as soon as the buildings were finished. That wouldn't take long.

Construction crews would need only a few weeks to finish the exterior and connect all the utilities, at which point displaced Ukrainian families would move in and make this modular house their new home. Modular housing is a broad term that describes homes whose components are built inside factories before being moved to a building site to be assembled in a much shorter time than it would take to build entirely on-site. Modular housing includes various different types of construction, from wood frame to steel to concrete. It includes tiny homes that are self-contained single units all the way up to high rise residential buildings where each individual apartment was built off-site. The modules can also be separate parts of a building that are assembled and finished at the building site. Also called prefabricated housing, or prefab, this relatively new method of construction has been adopted on a small scale in various countries. But Ireland has really started to embrace modular construction in recent years.

After construction inside a factory, this modular housing unit is loaded onto a truck for delivery to the building site.

Before the Ukrainian evacuees arrived, Ireland's largest non-profit housing provider, Clúid ("to include" in Gaelic), was using modular units to build subsidized housing quickly. Standing in front of a new development of family homes in Cavan Town, in the northeast of Ireland, Chief Commercial Officer Eibhlin O'Connor describes what the construction process looked like. "These houses arrived on-site almost like Lego blocks. So the bottom floor arrived, and then the top floor was clipped on." Eibhlin says modular homes aren't cheaper, but they are faster to build. "If you can deliver the serviced sites, you can turn a project like this around in less than twelve months. Whereas a traditional procurement could take three years."

But Ireland didn't have a lot of time to build more housing. In 2022 the country took in more refugees per capita than either France or the United Kingdom, at a time when it was already struggling with high housing costs and low supply. Ireland had volunteered in 2015 to take part in European Union refugee settlement programs, following the migrant crisis sparked by the Syrian civil war. It was a noble commitment, but not an easy one to implement. At last count, Ireland had the lowest number of dwellings per person in the OECD, and average house prices are eight times the mean income. According to the National Youth Council of Ireland, 70 percent of the nation's young people have considered leaving the country due to the high cost of living, and the high cost of housing in particular. All of this put considerable pressure on the Irish government to find new shelter for refugees that wouldn't put even more strain on the already short supply.

The Irish government has had less trouble finding the modular homes themselves than the serviced sites where they'll stand. The Department of Integration and Office of Public Works needed several months to find suitable sites and prepare the utilities. Once they did, construction was quick. Buildwright Modular Concrete Homes in Monaghan builds houses that are fully fitted inside a factory. They're then transported by lorry to the building site, where the finishing touches are completed in a few weeks. The company was chosen to manufacture the modular homes in Monaghan, a town long known for furniture manufacturing that now has a growing home building industry. Construction takes place inside Monaghan's factory. It's dry, well-lit, climate controlled and set up for maximum efficiency. Managing Director Stephen Wright says it typically takes eight to ten weeks to build the basic concrete structure and finish the interior of the home. It's then transported to the site, where it needs another four to eight weeks to finish the exterior and connect all water, electrical, sewer, and gas lines. "So it could take six to nine months in total from order to occupancy."

But why are modular homes faster to build? After all, every home has to be built, whether it's on-site or in a factory somewhere, so why does it matter where it happens? Gaynor Tennant speaks for Offsite Alliance, a British industry group that was formed in 2019 to represent prefabricated building companies. She describes the traditional method of building homes from the ground up, at the construction site, as "bonkers." She says it's a broken and inefficient tradition that slows down the construction timeline when many countries can least afford delays. "In construction we drop a load of raw materials onto a site, with hand-drawn or hopefully digital drawings. And then we ask a team that have never met each other to assemble that into a product that resembles the drawings that they probably don't read very well, and then we redesign it to reflect what they did actually build."

At the construction site, individual modular units are assembled into the finished building in significantly less time than it takes to build a traditional structure.

Apart from being faster, modular home builders claim their method is more efficient with labour—an especially important consideration given the shortage of construction workers in countries like Canada. They claim building homes in factories requires fewer workers, and that the workforce can be more diverse because they're not required to move from building site to building site, town to town, in search of work. They also believe it's a preferable option for building homes in confined spaces in big cities, such as infill developments between existing homes or buildings. Critics complain both the quality and standards vary significantly from manufacturer to manufacturer because there are few widely accepted standards. But off-site construction companies in Ireland and Britain claim their standards have risen remarkably in recent years. They're lobbying governments to establish common standards, and they claim common standards will reduce costs and make the construction of new modular housing even faster.

There is certainly a need for speed when it comes to refugee accommodation. Ireland welcomed more than eighty thousand displaced Ukrainians in the fifteen months following Russia's invasion—a serious challenge for a country of only 5 million people. The Irish government used a variety of temporary accommodations—hotel rooms, school gyms, university dorm rooms during summer breaks, and emergency shelters. It even used an old airport hangar and two sports stadiums during the height of the influx. Thousands of Irish homeowners also offered rooms in their homes or vacation properties, which helped around three thousand people. But more space was needed, and as the war dragged on, it became clear that most of the Ukrainians would not be returning home any time soon. The Irish government decided it needed longer-term solutions—like modular homes. The Office of Public Works declared the provision of modular homes a "matter of extreme urgency" under European law, which meant the government could fast-track procurement and "allow exemptions to the planning regulations for a specific time to provide emergency homes for people fleeing the war in Ukraine."

The government identified more than a dozen sites in Dublin, Cork, Kildare, and Cavan that could accommodate five hundred new modular homes with space for two thousand people. It hoped that would be the start, and homes for thousands more would quickly follow. The new residents would primarily be women and children, and the sites would have roads, footpaths, street lighting, shared facilities, and green spaces. The estimated life of the buildings was sixty years, and the government insisted they had "the potential to be utilised to address other accommodation challenges, including social housing and student accommodation." But the immediate need for refugee housing was compelling. The head of the Irish office of the UNHCR (the United Nations' refugee agency), Enda O'Neill, said, "There's clearly a moral obligation, but also a legal obligation under national and European law to meet the basic needs of people coming here seeking protection, and we're talking about a humanitarian response, basic shelter and safety first and foremost."

By 2023 stories of asylum seekers who were neither safe nor sheltered became common. New arrivals from Ukraine and other countries found themselves pitching tents on Dublin sidewalks, or simply shivering in sleeping bags out in the open. One pregnant asylum seeker spent a few nights in a tent before finally being offered shelter indoors. Roughly sixty asylum seekers set up a makeshift tent camp in front of the International Protection Office in Dublin. "This is not good for anyone," one of them observed. "We need to start a life. We don't need to live like this." Enda O'Neill said the wet Irish weather wasn't the only concern. He worried asylum seekers sleeping rough were at greater risk of theft and assault. "This is particularly the case for asylum seekers who cannot access mainstream homeless services or emergency accommodation. In many cases they do not speak English, they are unfamiliar with the city and may be subject to racist or xenophobic attacks."

On a cold January morning in 2023, a group of homeless campers from several different countries was attacked by four Irish men and their dogs. The campers had set up about fifteen tents in a wooded area beside the River Tolka, in north Dublin. They hailed from a wide range of countries, including India, Portugal, and Poland. A Hungarian man, and another from Croatia, described being attacked by four men and their dogs, including a German shepherd, a pit bull, and a Rottweiler. "It was like a Blitzkrieg," the Hungarian man told the *Irish Times*. "From the moment when I see them coming with the dogs and starting to shout, within a minute they were on the other side of the camp. One had a baseball bat. It was hard to react. They were screaming: 'Get out. We'll burn the tents down. Get out now.'"

The two victims were treated in hospital and offered temporary indoor shelter overnight. "In all my eight years here," the Hungarian man said, "I have not seen so much racism as in the last few months."

Despite the backlash, many Irish people welcomed the visitors and offered to help. In the town of Fermoy, a half-hour drive north of the city of Cork, a local group of citizens came together to form Fermoy for All. Their effort has been called a "useful blueprint for communities nationally that want to help refugees and asylum seekers arriving in their towns." Volunteers visited an accommodation centre for refugees, inside a disused convent, to meet the newcomers face to face. Volunteer Kate O'Connell describes it simply: "We went up and said, 'We're your neighbours. We want to say that you're welcome, and we're going to keep coming here to help you figure out where all the things in the community are.'" Members of the group offered to help in various ways—offering directions to clinics and schools, or finding a free pair of football boots for kids with quickly growing feet. They also performed a crucial task in helping the new arrivals connect with volunteer groups, so the newcomers could show their gratitude to the country and community that had taken them in. Paul Kavanagh, who organizes a group called Fermoy Tidy Town, was happy to see new arrivals helping with efforts to clean up litter and plant flowers. "They want to give back to their community," he said. "We need more people to see that." The people of Fermoy for All showed there is an abundance of goodwill in their community. What's not so plentiful, of course, is housing.

By the spring of 2023, the Irish Department of Integration was looking for different forms of shelter that hadn't yet been tried. A spokesperson said it was "working hard on alternative solutions that will allow it to shelter people in the time ahead, including offers of floating accommodation." Cruise ships have been used to quickly offer accommodation in several countries under various circumstances. Barges have also been used. The British government leased a three-storey floating barge for eighteen months to house five hundred male refugees in Dorset. The floating accommodation is called *Bibby Stockholm* but was once named the *Floatel Stockholm*. It has provided short-term accommodation in a variety of scenarios. In the 1990s it housed asylum seekers in Hamburg. It later provided accommodation to construction workers building a gas plant on the Shetland Islands, and workers building a wind farm in Sweden.

While floatels and other makeshift forms of shelter could be crucial for immediate use, proponents of modular housing insist their method of off-site construction will be crucial in the middle ground between immediate, short-term shelter and slow, traditional construction. The modular resumé is getting longer, or higher, every year. The world's first modular high-rise was built in Brooklyn in 2016. The 32-storey tower contains 363 rental apartments in twenty-three different configurations. Like a giant Lego construction, the building is made up of 930 steel modules that were built inside a factory at the Brooklyn Navy Yard and delivered to the site by truck. Countertops, backsplashes, and appliances were all installed at the factory. The building took four years to complete, which is roughly comparable to how long a similar project using traditional construction might take. In this case, however, this was largely due to a dispute between the developer and a partner, which slowed construction. Even with the delay, proponents of off-site construction pointed to other benefits, like a reduction in noise and dust at the site.

The method proved popular, with more modular high-rises following. In 2019, a pair of even taller towers was finished in Singapore using prefabricated concrete modules. In 2021, another pair of modular high-rise buildings opened in Croydon, south London, the taller of which stood 44 storeys. Plans are under way for even higher modular high-rises in Croydon, with one set to reach 49 storeys. These larger projects provide significant boosts to local housing supply in dense urban areas, but they still take several years to finish. Low-rise modular housing can be set up more quickly.

As in Ireland, German authorities have turned to low-rise modular construction to house migrants. That was the case during the Syrian refugee crisis in 2015. And in 2022, with as many as a hundred migrants pouring into the port city of Hamburg every day, officials turned to modular once again. They knew it was one of the fastest ways of providing secure and stable housing. The biggest challenge was to find available land. In a densely populated city of nearly 2 million people, it's not always easy. But governments and other public agencies were able to find several relatively convenient spots. The first modular home project, managed by a local housing non-profit, was assembled at the Neue Huckepack (New Piggyback) train station in the central suburb of Rothenburgsort. Each of the rectangular units is a plain white shipping container that includes two bedrooms, with a small kitchen and bathroom in the middle. The containers were stacked into two-storey buildings. A few months later, the Red Cross opened 256 individual container homes on a former parade ground that's roughly the size of two soccer fields. While host countries embrace modular housing within their own borders, some have suggested those modular units could eventually be shipped overseas to help countries like Ukraine when they rebuild.

In fact, modular construction is already being used in those countries. In the village of Buzova, a half-hour's drive west of Ukraine's capital Kyiv, many homes were destroyed by Russian shelling and the fires that followed. But local residents returned after the Ukrainian military forced Russian forces back. For many people the biggest problem was that they had nowhere to live. So a donation of ninety-five modular homes from Denmark was welcomed in the village. The UNHCR assigned local families to these new portable homes. "The construction was done really fast," Oksana, one of the residents, observed on the day she moved into a brand-new modular unit. "Only a week and a half." After escaping to the safety of western Ukraine at the start of the war, Oksana and her family of five moved back to their village a few months later. When they returned home, they found a pile of bricks and rubble where their kitchen and a bedroom used to stand. Parts of the house remained standing; a painted yellow giraffe was still visible on one of the walls of Oksana's young daughter's bedroom, right beside a gaping hole that opened directly to the rubble-strewn backyard. It took the family all summer just to clean up the damage before they could even start modest repairs. But with the cold Ukrainian winter right around the corner, they needed to find shelter immediately. Oksana registered with the UNHCR, and by late October they were moving into two small modular homes that had been set up on their property. The houses are small and simple, but they have all the necessities—sink, fridge, and bed. Oksana's two young daughters were excited to sleep in the bunk beds. Oksana was relieved to have a shower and a heated home for the winter.

On the other side of the village, a grandmother named Nadiia moved into a modular house of her own. It was placed in her garden, next to her flower bed and the charred remains of her old home. Nadiia had been hiding in the cellar as explosions shook the ground above her. Two of those blasts made the cellar walls tremble, but Nadiaa stayed put. She didn't emerge until the shelling had stopped, when she heard the voice of a neighbour calling for her. Nadiia stayed with friends for months before registering with the UNHCR and being offered a temporary modular home. "After that call, the construction took only a few weeks. So quick!"

Nadiia, Oksana, and others can now rebuild their old homes and lives, and when they no longer need the modular homes, the units can be moved where they are required. In the meantime, the modular homes provide refugees with safety, warmth, and something else. "I cannot tell you how I missed the feeling of being at home," Nadiaa says. "Everything I love and need is here."

19

AN RV BY THE SEA

Annapolis Valley, Nova Scotia

THE DUNROMIN CAMPGROUND SITS in a lovely spot on the shore of the Annapolis Basin, with a sandy beach for summer swimming or paddling. People have sought shelter there for as long as anyone can remember. The Mi'kmaq lived and traded in the area for countless generations before cartographer Samuel de Champlain sailed there with a French expedition in 1605. For the last half century, families have come to spend their holidays in tents, cabins, and recreational vehicles. Some are drawn by the fishing—mackerel, when they're running, and striped bass on a really good day. Others prefer watching wildlife—loons, seals, sea otters, and occasionally porpoises. It all adds up to a nice holiday, and Dunromin was named one of the 25 Best Family Campgrounds in the country by *Parenting Canada*. But a stay at Dunromin offers more reprieve than relaxation for the Durling family. Andrea, Matthew, and their three sons aged three to 15 were on the verge of homelessness, and a vacant RV at the campground became their temporary home.

Before moving into the RV, the Durlings spent six months in a motel room in the town of Middleton, forty minutes up Highway 1. They paid for the room themselves until their money ran out. After that, Nova Scotia's Department of Community Services paid, through an Income Assistance program that helps low-income families pay rent, food, and other essential costs. But when the motel filled up with summer visitors, the Durlings had to leave. They found another motel room twenty minutes away, in Bridgetown. But eight nights later they had to leave yet again. When campground staff heard about the family's desperate situation, they offered them an RV for three nights. The younger kids threw Frisbees on the lush green campground lawn while their parents sat at a picnic table and discussed what to do next. It might have been a welcome vacation if they had known where they were going afterwards. In the end, their stay was simply more uncertainty dumped on top of too much stress. "I'm a mess mentally," Andrea admitted. "But we have to stay strong around the kids. We're doing our best to stay as optimistic as we can."

The Durlings had applied to move into public housing six months earlier, but were put on a wait-list along with another six thousand applicants across Nova Scotia. The number of people waiting for an affordable home was especially sobering given that the province had only 11,202 public housing units at the time. The Durlings were worried they wouldn't be moving into one of those places any time soon, and a report from Nova Scotia's auditor general suggested their fears were well founded. "Public housing assets are underutilized during a time when waitlists are significant," it concluded, noting the average wait was longer than two years. The report also identified inconsistencies in tenant application and placement processes, and found the province "does not have an effective governance structure in place for public housing." Nova Scotia's housing minister, John Lohr, claimed officials might find housing for as many as a thousand people on the wait-list by reassessing who lives where. "We might have a single person living in a five-bedroom unit or four-bedroom unit." However, the minister wasn't convinced that building more public housing was the best use of government funds.

With the hours ticking down on the Durlings' three-day stay at the campground, the Nova Scotia Department of Community Services offered to move them into a third motel, in Yarmouth. The historic port town near the southern tip of Nova Scotia has a lot to offer, but it's also 108 minutes away by car from Middleton, where the Durlings' doctor is located. The family car was failing, and Andrea worried it might break down and make them miss an important medical appointment. It was just the latest struggle the family had faced since moving back home to Nova Scotia from Ontario more than six months earlier. They made the move to look after an ailing family member, and stayed with relatives at first. They soon had to move out on their own, but realized there were no affordable rentals to be found anywhere. It made an already difficult transition even worse. Matt had left a full-time factory job in Ontario, hoping to find work in Nova Scotia. But with rents rising faster than locals could ever remember, it proved difficult to find a job that paid enough.

The average price of a residential home in Nova Scotia peaked at over $450,000 in the spring of 2022—about $100,000 more than a year earlier, and roughly double the average price five years earlier. In Halifax-Dartmouth the average home price rose 78 percent in a little over two years. Sale prices started dropping in 2022, as interest rates rose. But as in most of Canada, rents kept rising across Nova Scotia. By the spring of 2023 the average rent in Halifax had gone up 8.9 percent—four times higher than the average annual growth rate in Halifax, according to Statistics Canada, and the biggest jump among Canadian cities. The most striking number in the StatsCan report was the whopping 28 percent difference between what existing renters were paying for the average two-bedroom apartment and what landlords were asking for new two-bedroom rentals. With a vacancy rate of only 1 percent, there was little doubt most landlords would get what they were asking.

The rapid rise in rents happened in a province with temporary rent controls, introduced by the former Nova Scotia Liberal government during the pandemic, that capped annual increases for renters at 2 percent. But landlords faced no such restrictions when switching from an old tenant to a new tenant, something that renter Elizabeth O'Hanley was shocked to discover while scrolling through rental ads on Kijiji. She had lived on the top floor of a triplex for seven years, and was paying $925 in rent. But she was evicted, along with the renter in the main-floor suite, when the landlord informed them that he and his mother would be moving into those two units. Elizabeth was prepared to have to pay $1,500 a month in rent, but she was alarmed to find even that might not be enough. "It was crisis mode," she said. "I started looking for apartments there were absolutely no options. My neighbour downstairs was in the exact same situation as me." Elizabeth was then shocked to find an ad for the main-floor apartment in her triplex—the one her downstairs neighbour had just been evicted from—at a rent of $2,350 a month. "I don't think anything's worth that price," she said. The landlord did, obviously, and both suites were rented within days.

Facing growing political pressure to act on rents, Nova Scotia's Progressive Conservative government extended the rent cap of 2 percent annually until the end of 2023, and raised it to 5 percent until the end of 2025. The move was a compromise between renters who wanted the cap to remain the same and landlords who wanted it removed entirely. Peter Polley, whose company Polycorp Properties Inc. managed five hundred units in the Halifax area and the Annapolis Valley, said the cap would prevent landlords from keeping up with inflation. "It's not good for anybody—it's long-term negative for the housing industry."

Landlords weren't hearing much sympathy coming from tenants like Andrea and Matthew Durling. The couple finally found a home to rent, but they say it is so expensive that they can barely afford anything else. Not only that, but they live in perpetual fear that they could be evicted if either of them, or any of their three sons, does anything to upset the landlord. "He knows he can have someone else in here if we are inconvenient to him," Andrea says. That would have been a concern in years past, but with prices soaring and vacancy rates plummeting, Andrea worries they might find themselves on the verge of homelessness again. She calls the situation "astonishingly scary," and her fears are not theoretical. All around her she sees housed families like hers struggling just to pay rent, and sees several hotels filled with unhoused families and their kids. "We never had a homeless problem like this before," she says, pointing to new homeless encampments up and down the Annapolis Valley. "Now there are camps in Kingston and Aylesford. Berwick has an encampment, Kentville too, and the towns that don't will soon."

Homelessness is a growing concern in rural communities and small cities across Nova Scotia. What was once a largely invisible problem is now plain to see in the form of tent encampments in parks, ravines, and wooded areas. In Sydney, the non-profit Ally Centre of Cape Breton was handing out tents and sleeping bags as fast as they could find them in 2022. "People have nowhere to go," executive director Christine Porter said, "and frankly, a tent is their only option at this point in time." People pitched those tents in the Ally Centre's parking lot, empty lots along the harbour, and local parks. Police even received a complaint of someone camping in a cemetery. The Ally Centre handed out fifty tents in the summer of 2022, twice as many as the year before. Things got worse in September, when post-tropical storm Fiona barrelled through town, toppling trees, washing away roads, and cutting electricity for hundreds of thousands of people. Despite losing power for six days, Christine and the staff at the Ally Centre kept their doors open, if only to offer their homeless neighbours somewhere safe to get out of the lashing wind and rain. Some tents were destroyed, and the Ally Centre did its best to find replacements.

While people across Atlantic Canada cleaned up, climate researchers like Blair Feltmate, at the Intact Centre on Climate Adaptation, warned that Fiona was an omen of future problems. "We really need to understand that, due to climate change, we're going to experience more extreme weather in this country, and we need to prepare by way of adaptation, very rapidly, for that extreme weather." In addition to reducing carbon emissions, he said Canada needs to "put measures in place to cope with the problems and lessen the impacts, through a large-scale effort [to adapt]." But, he concluded, those measures aren't coming fast enough. "What's missing in Canada is a proper sense of appreciation for the need to act [with great urgency]."

While Canada's response to climate change has lacked urgency, the same can be said of this country's response to the housing crisis. But Christine Porter doesn't think it's entirely the federal government's fault. She's seen the local municipal council try to thwart a project to build twenty-four units of supportive housing in Sydney. She's also seen the local university welcome thousands of international students without assessing whether there was enough housing supply to accommodate them all. As Sydney residents cleaned up after Fiona, she worried the housing crisis was about to get worse. "It's just going to escalate, especially once the students all arrive and the rooming houses are full and the weather is getting colder."

The students in this case are international post-secondary students enrolled at Cape Breton University. A wave of new students from overseas started to arrive in 2018, after the university began recruiting internationally as part of a strategic effort to balance its books. The COVID-19 pandemic put immigration on hold, with the effect that a double cohort of students arrived in 2022. More than six thousand students from seventy countries were studying at the university. Fully two-thirds of the student population came from overseas—the highest rate in Atlantic Canada, and more than double the 30 percent share of enrolment that foreign students made up at the University of Prince Edward Island, which ranked second on the list. "And that's fine," Christine said. "We want them and we need them. However, we don't have the infrastructure to accommodate them, and it wasn't very well thought out."

As the local homeless population in Sydney grew rapidly, a wide range of area residents expressed the same opinion, including international students and university administrators. In an open letter, university president David Dingwall acknowledged that the rapid growth came with its challenges. "These challenges include the need for affordable housing, which is a national issue, as well as unemployment, which has always challenged this region." The letter promised the university would develop a Strategic Enrolment Management Plan that would determine "the most appropriate number of students for our campus," while many local residents and newly arrived students wondered why that hadn't happened already. In a frustrated post on Facebook, first-year international student Vrinda Katore urged the university to "stop offering enrollment letters." Vrinda also made a direct appeal to students in other countries—"If you're listening to this video, trust me, right now, this place is not equipped for you to come in."

New students found it just as difficult to find affordable

accommodation as lifelong residents, and many squeezed in wherever they could find space. One university student was killed when the duplex he was sharing with six other students caught fire. Rajesh Kumar Gollapudi was a business analytics student. The 33-year-old had left his wife and daughter in India to pursue a better life in Canada. His six roommates in Sydney, along with an extended family of five next door, were left homeless after the blaze, less than a week before Christmas. They were moved into a local motel after that, resigned to paying roughly three times the monthly rent they'd paid before the fire, until they could find a safer place to live. In the meantime, fire investigators went to work trying to determine the cause of the blaze, but displaced students like Siddharth Balachandar couldn't help but wonder if it was connected to overcrowding. "After this incident, we don't want to risk any of [those] sorts of accommodations and we don't want to go to a crowded place again."

Christine Porter says that kind of crowded living arrangement has become common as rents rise and people accept almost anything with a roof over it. For now, she'll continue to hand out tents and help the homeless in whatever way she can. And she'll also worry about her own situation. "I worry about my place all the time," she says, her voice rising to reveal a serious anxiety. "The owners are working out west, so if they decide to sell, well, what am I going to do? I'm a 60-year-old woman and I'm looking after my two grandkids. So I'm scared all the time. I mean, where would we go?"

The solution to the problem, Christine believes, is to build a lot more housing as quickly as possible. "We need all kinds of housing— one-bedroom, two-bedroom, supportive housing, everything! And until we get it, nothing's going to improve." Christine hasn't lost hope that that will happen. The Ally Centre and the non-profit New Dawn Agency have teamed up to construct a new building with twenty-four units of supportive housing, right in the centre of Sydney. But the need goes much further than that, she says. "We need to build so much more housing, and it's just not happening fast enough."

Jeff Karabanow agrees that more public housing is desperately needed in Nova Scotia. A professor of social work at Dalhousie University, he's followed the issue closely for decades. He points out that most of the existing public housing was built before the 1970s. "You can't just pick up where you've left off for years," he says. "There has to be a very concerted effort [from] both public and federal levels. We have to recognize that the private market cannot provide enough affordable housing." Jeff also co-founded the Out of the Cold emergency shelter in Halifax, and has spent many years talking to people who are homeless and studying the root causes of homelessness. He knows all too well the myriad factors that can lead to it—racism, marginalization, addiction, and a shortage of adequate social support. But he insists the hardship is compounded by an acute lack of affordable housing. "We've moved beyond crisis to a disaster zone! Housing support workers have nowhere to send people. Forget affordability, there's not even availability. You go to a showing for a rental and everyone is offering above price. So municipal governments have resorted to handing out tent kits for shelter. It's heartbreaking!"

For now, many stranded renters are left to make the best of a bad situation. When 57-year-old grandmother Terri Smith-Fraser was renovicted from her apartment in the Halifax suburb of Spryfield, she wondered what she would do. The older apartment she'd called home for nine years had been affordable, but the new rental listings she found were not. Most advertised apartments that cost more than double what she'd been paying. Her $49,000 annual salary as a nursing assistant had always been enough. Suddenly, it wasn't. "I find it very unfair that I don't make enough to rent a place in the city I've worked in for the last thirty years as a health care worker."

Terri wiped away her tears and made a decision. She would not move in with her adult daughters, or find a roommate to share costs. Instead, she bought a 24-year-old GMC Savana cargo van and moved into that. Savanas are now being converted into campers by a growing number of people across North America who either want or need to sleep in them. Terri had already planned to buy a van when she retired, to visit grandkids in Ontario and family on Prince Edward Island. So the idea wasn't unimaginable for her. But it was never supposed to be her permanent home. However, the lack of affordable housing in Halifax forced her hand.

Terri Smith-Fraser has called this GMC Savana van home through all seasons in Halifax.

Terri kept working at the hospital while living in her tiny new home on four wheels. It was a rough start. "When I first moved into the van," she recalls, "I was really miserable." She found it difficult to keep warm. Plus, she didn't like the layout, which had the kitchen at the back of the vehicle, blocking natural light from the rear windows. And then there was the question of safety. One night, while she was parked downtown, someone tried to break into Terri's van. She froze and hoped he'd leave. When it became clear he wasn't going to, she yelled in her deepest voice, scaring the would-be thief away. So Terri made a series of changes to make life inside the van better. She bought a diesel heater for cold nights, switched the kitchen with her bed to make it brighter inside, and decided to park in safer neighbourhoods or the driveways of people who needed a housesitter. She also kept a screwdriver and a can of wasp spray within reach, just in case anyone ever forced their way inside. None of it's ideal, of course, but at least she can afford it. When she adds up all the gas and maintenance, Terri estimates she spends as much on van life every month as she used to spend on rent, before she was renovicted and local rents skyrocketed.

Despite her impressive persistence and adaptability, Terri concedes that the situation has made her sad. At some of the more popular parking lots, like Walmarts or libraries, she has noticed other Haligonians living in vehicles. There was a single man who slept in his SUV for months. And then there was the older couple who slept in their car every night. At bedtime, the man would hold up a sheet to give his wife some privacy while she changed her clothes. "It's sad," Terri admits. "I didn't realize there are as many people living in vehicles as there are."

The reconfigured interior of the Savana van.

3-D PRINTING HOMES
FOR THE FUTURE

Nacajuca, Mexico

HARDSHIP IS A WAY of life in Nacajuca. The city of 150,000 straddles the flood-prone river Samaría, in the humid heart of Tabasco state. Major floods over the years have forced the evacuation of countless homes across the city. But a regular succession of smaller floods make life difficult for the city's poor residents on a much more frequent basis. Many locals spend six months of every year either cleaning up the muddy mess from the last inundation or worrying about the next. To make life more difficult, Nacajuca lies in a seismically active region that produces earthquakes, like the magnitude-7.4 event that shook much of southern Mexico in 2020. And if the threat of natural disasters wasn't challenging enough, more than half the city's population lives below the poverty line. Most of their houses could be better described as rudimentary shelter—rusting corrugated tin roofs, walls made of rough-cut fence boards, and tarps to keep out some of the wind and rain. But fighting the flooding is a losing battle for many, and often extends beyond bailing. Many residents also fight a near-constant battle against mould and mildew in their homes.

Petrona Hernández and her husband, Pedro, lived in one of these tiny makeshift houses with their daughter, Yareli. It had dirt floors that quickly turned to mud whenever it flooded. There was a rudimentary pump toilet and an improvised kitchen for cooking food, but all in all the house was too small and life too much of a struggle for the family. Pedro did his carpentry job from inside their house, and a fine sprinkling of dust from his work coated every surface. That work earned Pedro only the equivalent of a few hundred Canadian dollars every month. But things were looking up for the Hernández family in 2019, because they had qualified to move into a brand-new development of homes being built on the outskirts of town.

The project was a collaboration between different levels of government, two housing non-profits, and an innovative new construction materials company. The Tabasco government provided some of the funding through a new statewide program called Firm Floor that aimed to provide at least 80 percent of the state's residents with cement floors. The city provided the land and the utilities for the homes. Meanwhile, the Mexican social housing provider, ¡Échale a tu casa! (Build Your Own Home), picked the families based on a few key criteria: they had to have a low monthly income and live in a home that both had structural problems and experienced flood damage frequently. After enduring much hardship, the Hernández family's struggles suddenly became their assets. They qualified to own one of the homes that would be built in the innovative new development. Of all the many reasons to be happy, Pedro was mostly relieved for his daughter, Yareli, who was studying to be a nurse. "When we receive the house, my daughter will be able to rely on it. She won't have to worry anymore."

Ownership of the house wouldn't go to Yareli, but it wouldn't go to her father either. Échale granted ownership of the homes to the woman of the house. "It's to protect the family," Francesco Piazzesi, the founder of Échale, said. "A man will sell a house if they need to. A woman will do whatever she needs to do to save the house for her children and her family." No doubt that broad generalization doesn't apply to all men or all women, but Francesco formed that opinion over decades of helping impoverished Mexican families secure stable housing. He's convinced that the first step in helping people rise out of poverty is to provide them with a safe home. "If we want a better world, it's what we have to do." Échale has worked in twenty-eight Mexican states, collaborating on more than 250,000 houses that are now home to more than a million people. It's also helped rebuild homes after natural disasters. In 2013, Échale helped relocate and rebuild a town devastated by hurricanes Ingrid and Manuel. It also helped rebuild nearly 2,300 homes destroyed by the devastating 2017 Puebla earthquake, which left 370 people dead and more than 6,000 injured. Échale has been successful in building so many houses for two main reasons: it used an innovative building material and it trained the communities that needed better housing to use that innovation themselves.

Échale's building innovation was relatively simple. It developed a new form and type of building material called an Ecoblock. Though it looks much like a traditional concrete block, 90 percent of the Ecoblock is composed of local clay and soils, with the remaining 10 percent being a mix of cement, lime, sand, and water. Francesco says it offers excellent insulation, both thermal and acoustic, and is 30 to 40 percent stronger than traditional fired bricks or concrete blocks because it is compressed under high pressure rather than left to solidify through chemical change as it dries. Best of all, though, it can be made locally at a fraction of the cost of transporting cement blocks to a community. The portable hydraulic press that's used to make the blocks isn't much bigger than a large fridge.

The idea first came to Francesco in the 1980s while he was working for his father's company, which imported concrete block–making machines from Italy. He saw that communities that lacked the tool to make basic blocks also lacked the ability to build better lives for themselves. "It's like saying that a fisherman is dying of hunger." Now communities across Mexico can press their own blocks, instead of bringing in more expensive, less sustainable products from farther afield. Apart from saving money on shipping, Échale claims the process also reduces the company's carbon footprint by about 30 percent compared with what it would be if they were to use conventional cinder block. Ecoblocks have become the key building blocks in countless Échale projects across Mexico, as they were once again in the new Nacajuca development in 2019. But alongside this now-established construction form, a new building technology was being used—one with the potential to change the future of rapid construction as much as or more than the Ecoblock.

3-D printing, or additive manufacturing as it's also known, has been around for more than forty years. But it's only in the last decade that it's become accessible to millions of people. Simply put, 3-D printing is a mechanized method of creating a three-dimensional object, layer by layer, using a computer-created design. Almost anyone can now order a 3-D printer online, some for less than $200. People use them to print all sorts of things—jewellery, toys, figurines, architectural models, and much more. During the COVID-19 pandemic they proved invaluable in some hospitals, allowing staff to make their own masks and other personal protective equipment, test swabs, or other key medical devices. In Nacajuca, 3-D printing would employ cement instead of plastic, and it would be used for a much bigger product—a house.

The 3-D printed houses were built by a Texas construction technology company called Icon, in partnership with Échale and New Story, a San Francisco housing non-profit. The idea was simple: instead of building new homes with Ecoblocks, some of them would be manufactured with an oversized 3-D printer built by Icon, called the Vulcan II. The machine looks more like something you'd find in a very large computer server room than on a house construction site. But the Vulcan II is designed specifically to print single-storey homes, and it does it quickly and efficiently.

The printer is composed of two towers that stand 11 feet 5 inches (3.5 metres) tall. Each of those towers glides back and forth along base rails that are set down on opposite sides of the house's concrete foundation. The towers are connected by long rails that can be extended across the foundation to a total width of 28 feet (8.5 metres). One of those rails acts as a sort of track for the printer head to move back and forth as it squeezes a steady stream of cement mix through a nozzle, in a process reminiscent of soft-serve ice cream circling its way into a cone, or icing being squeezed out of a pastry bag. The printer follows a preprogrammed route according to the digital design of the house. It moves along at a speed of 5 to 7 inches (13 to 18 centimetres) per second, which adds only a couple of inches in height to the house at any given moment but adds up quickly because the printer just keeps going and going and going. It's equipped with lights so members of the building crew can keep inspecting the results through the night as the printer makes all the home's walls, both interior and exterior. The end result is that a small two-bedroom house can be printed in twenty-four hours or less.

This giant house printer, known as the Vulcan II, can print single-family homes as large as 3,000 square feet.

Only three to six people are needed to operate the Vulcan II. One of those people is the printer operator, who uses a tablet or smartphone to monitor the flow of concrete. Another is the "designated magma operator," who watches the flow and consistency of the concrete, which is made in real time, and whose ingredients will need subtle but important changes depending on the immediate atmospheric conditions (a downpour versus a sunny day). The other members of the work crew carry out various supporting tasks.

If the labour required in 3-D printed construction is minimal, the strength of the building is not. The printer uses a Portland cement–based product called Lavacrete, a high-strength concrete developed specifically for 3-D printing that's capable of supporting 6,000 psi (pounds per square inch). The result is high-quality housing, built strong, fast, and cheap. New Story estimated each 3-D printed house in Nacajuca cost US$10,000 to build.

Icon is quick to point out that cost can't be replicated in countries like Canada or the US because labour is so much cheaper in Mexico, and building standards for key components like the concrete foundation are more demanding north of the Rio Grande. Still, the new 3-D printing method of home construction appears to be considerably cheaper than traditional practices; Icon claims 3-D printed walls cost roughly half as much as walls with wood studs and drywall. Not only that, but the company notes its method drastically reduces construction waste, because it puts down only what's needed; there are no offcuts of excess lumber and no excess concrete that was mixed but not needed.

However, 3-D printing has its environmental critics who object to the fact that it uses concrete. Roughly 8 percent of global CO_2 emissions come from the manufacture of Portland cement, the most common type of cement used globally, when the world desperately needs to reduce greenhouse gas emissions while building a lot more housing. Independent studies have demonstrated that construction of 3-D printed concrete homes has a smaller carbon footprint than traditional concrete construction. One study from Malawi claimed 3-D printing reduced CO_2 emissions by 70 percent. And Icon claims its carbon emissions are lower than for all other forms of construction, primarily because it is so efficient and creates so little waste. Still, there's little doubt that all segments of the construction industry need to reduce emissions, and the company says it has a sustainability department working on doing exactly that with its cement mix.

Once the walls were printed on the first house in Nacajuca, local workers got busy adding the roof, windows, and indoor appliances, and the house was soon finished. At five hundred square feet, it's small by Canadian standards. But the bright, modern home was a dream come true for its new occupants. When Petrona Hernández finally moved in, she had a huge smile on her face. "The truth is that I did not expect it," she said, beaming. "I still do not believe it." From the front, the small home looks like something a child might draw—a perfect rectangle with a door centred between two plain upright windows. The main roof is flat, and there's a short slanted roof to shade the front veranda. But a closer look reveals some of the small home's charms: the four corners of the house curve elegantly, the windows are capped with classic lattices, and the clean white walls show dozens of horizontal lines from the concrete layers, like grooves in a vinyl record or striations on a cliff face. The front door opens straight into the small living room, which features the same lined concrete walls. Both bedrooms are also small, as are the kitchen and bathroom. But the house is sturdy, well insulated, and safe. It's everything its occupants' former home was not. This faster, more affordable form of construction is still in its infancy, but its proponents say it has the potential to change the world.

"It's time for the built environment to join the digital, automated, robotic revolution!" Jason Ballard, the CEO of Icon, said during a passionate presentation to an audience at South by Southwest, the annual collection of creative conferences in Austin, Texas. Wearing a black buttoned shirt and a bright-white cowboy hat, his appearance projected some of his less obvious contrasts. His field is construction, one of the oldest trades in the world, yet his focus is on using 3-D printers and other new technologies in building. And while he aims to lead one of the world's top tech companies, he seems more preoccupied with the timeless goal of helping people rise out of poverty. "People freak out when they hear about robots doing the work," Jason said of some of the early reactions to 3-D printed houses. "I wish they would freak out about the housing crisis like I'm freaking out about the housing crisis!" He doesn't deny that a rapid adoption of 3-D printing in the construction industry would benefit his company, but he insists it has the best chance at making a meaningful dent in the world's estimated shortage of roughly 1.6 billion homes. "We have a few dozen printers, but eventually there will need to be millions of construction systems."

Jason's interest in housing is older than the company he now leads. His first job after college was as a paid employee at a homeless shelter in Boulder, Colorado. He later trained to become a priest, but decided he could do more good for people in need of a home by working to change how housing is built. As CEO of Icon, he now receives emails from people who desperately need a home they can afford, and they wonder if he can help. "Those emails are coming from homeless veterans. They're coming from people after hurricanes. They're coming from people living under bridges. They're coming from working people—teachers, artists, musicians—who cannot afford to live in the cities where they work. So we've got to keep going and get to work."

Icon has been growing, building more 3-D printers for homes and announcing new partnerships with established construction companies. And it's not the only company doing so. The first 3-D printed office buildings opened in Dubai in 2016. The buildings were made in China, using a 20-foot (6-metre) tall 3-D printer, before being shipped to Dubai. Their round corners and futuristic design received a lot of attention. But so did their height—or rather their lack of height. Surrounded by high-rises, the single-storey office buildings managed somehow to look old-fashioned, despite their design, because they were so short.

3-D printing is especially well-suited to single-storey construction, and that's been one of the complaints against it. In an era when we need to build up rather than out, the thinking goes, no technology that makes mostly low-rise structures can be considered truly sustainable. But the company that built those one-storey offices,

Winsun Decoration Design Engineering Co., was also looking up. It built a five-storey apartment building in China's Jiangsu province using the same 20-foot printer that built the Dubai offices. The apartment building comprised individual components that were later assembled on-site. If the recent rise in modular towers is anything to go by, we might expect to see 3-D printed towers going higher still. But the most immediate benefit of 3-D printing might be the rapid construction of small, low-rise homes for some of the world's poorest people.

In Kenya, a company called 14Trees built a community of fifty-two 3-D printed homes in the coastal community of Kilifi in 2023. At six hundred square feet, the two-bedroom homes were only a little bigger than the efficient dwellings in Nacajuca. 14Trees planned to make slightly larger three-bedroom houses as well. And as was the case in Nacajuca, construction was quick: it took eighteen hours to print the walls of the two-bedroom homes. In total, each house took about a week to build, with the addition of appliances, utility connections, and roofs. The homes were listed for sale at US$27,000 each—not affordable for many Kenyans, but attainable for members of the working middle class, and much cheaper than similar new homes built using traditional construction methods. Like Échale in Mexico, 14Trees had already employed a type of block that used local soil and had a smaller carbon footprint than concrete. But managing director François Perrot said 14Trees switched to 3-D printers in 2020 because they are so much faster. "If we truly wanted to have a massive impact on the school and housing backlog, we needed to change the way we build—more disruptively. That's when we came to the conclusion that the only technology which would do that is 3-D printing."

While 3-D printed housing has an obvious appeal in developing countries, it will likely become more popular in countries like Canada and the US as well. Habitat for Humanity, the American non-profit housing provider, built the first 3-D printed owner-occupied house in the United States in 2021. The three-bedroom, two-bathroom house was 1,200 square feet in total. The construction company, Alquist 3D, needed just twenty-eight hours to print the walls. That home was built in Williamsburg, Virginia, and Habitat for Humanity is now expanding the use of 3-D printing across the US.

In Tempe, Marcus and Shawn Shivers moved into a beautiful new home that was the first 3-D printed house in Arizona. The couple had their kids when they were young, and spent most of their income raising their three sons. Marcus works as a bank courier and painter; Shawn works in a doctor's office, assessing patients' medication needs and liaising with nurses and insurance companies. So it took them years to save up enough money for a home of their own. By the time their kids were older, the listing prices for fixer-uppers was getting close to half a million dollars. They just couldn't afford it. So they applied to buy a new home through Habitat for Humanity's no-interest mortgage program. The couple were visibly emotional as they walked into the finished home for the first time. "It's a very beautiful home," Marcus observed. "And why not us?"

Meanwhile, Habitat for Humanity Arizona CEO Jason Barlow expects the non-profit will build a lot more 3-D printed homes in the future. "Once we work out a few of the bugs, and we can bring the cost down even more, I'm convinced that we can build entire neighbourhoods with this technology."

Jason Ballard of Icon Building agrees. "We are going to have to innovate like our life depends on it," he says. "It's not a bright human future if we can't shelter ourselves appropriately."

AFTERWORD

A New Way Forward

THE FIRST TASK FOR CONSTRUCTION crews working on the massive new housing project was to dig up the old railbed, near Vancouver's False Creek, to remove contaminated soil. The task was a drop in the bucket, so to speak, in the overall scope of what will be the largest Indigenous-led economic project in Canadian history. The giant development will include six thousand new homes in a neighbourhood of high-rises—enough to house ten thousand people—on the site of an old village called Sen'áḵw. Located smack dab in the heart of Vancouver, the project isn't being led by the city, the province, or the federal government. The Squamish Nation is in charge of this ambitious plan that seeks to address past injustices and build a better future for the Squamish people and many of their neighbours.

The village of Sen'áḵw was established long before Europeans first arrived in what is now Vancouver in 1791. Squamish families would travel to the village every year because the land and waters at the site were perfect for fishing, harvesting, and hunting. Beaver, deer, duck, and elk were found in abundance. The waters teemed with salmon, and the forests were full of giant cedar, which offered rot-resistant wood for building and carving, as well as tough, fibrous bark for weaving baskets. The Squamish built longhouses there, and welcomed traders from various nations. But colonization changed the village drastically. The federal government established what it called Kitsilano Indian Reserve no. 6, under the Indian Act, in 1877. Less than a decade later, it started carving up the reserve. In 1886, 3.5 acres were expropriated from the reserve when the Canadian Pacific Railway first arrived. Another seven acres were taken away in 1901. Mills followed the trains, and False Creek soon became the industrial heart of Vancouver. In 1913, the government of British Columbia decided the Squamish people had to leave once and for all. It offered residents of Sen̓áḵw some money, in an attempt to justify the eviction as a land sale. Many residents of the village were sent on a barge to other Squamish reserves, and all of the former village was swallowed into the swelling city. But the Squamish people never forgot. In 1977, they launched what would become a long, long legal challenge that finally saw the Federal Court of Canada return a portion of the original reserve land to the Squamish Nation in 2003. It was only 10.48 acres of the original 80, but Squamish leaders were determined to put it to good use.

The L-shaped parcel sits in an ideal position. It's the perfect example of the old mantra about what matters most in real estate— location, location, location. Sen̓áḵw has all three. The city of Vancouver called it "one of the most desired locations on the planet." It stands on the south side of the busy Burrard Street Bridge, and stretches east to the Granville Street Bridge, with a stunning north view of False Creek, Vancouver's glass high-rises, and the snow-capped North Shore Mountains above. The south side of False Creek, where Sen'áḵw is located, has more mid- and low-rise buildings, right in the middle of a city with a chronic housing shortage. So the Squamish Nation decided to put their ancestral village to good use in the future by reimagining it as a modern district that stretches up to the sky. They're now building new housing, and building a lot of it. The housing will be a mix of condominiums and rental apartments, as well as roughly three hundred affordable homes reserved for members of the Squamish First Nation. Though surrounded by the city of Vancouver, residents of Sen'áḵw will pay property taxes to the First Nation. The neighbourhood is exempt from conforming to city of Vancouver zoning regulations, according to the court ruling. It will be much more densely populated and built more quickly.

This rendering shows how the giant Squamish Nation–led Sen'áḵw housing development will change the appearance of Vancouver, and provide thousands of homes in the process.

Though many Vancouver residents welcomed the new development and the thousands of new homes it will create, others were opposed. The Kits Point Residents' Association said it was concerned about the "size, density, heights of towers and the effect on the neighbouring residential area," which included nearby Vanier Park. There's no doubt the development will be tall. The eleven towers will range in height from twelve to fifty-eight storeys. And there's little doubt it will be one of the densest areas in Vancouver, even though there is no rapid transit line running through it. Initial plans called for only 886 parking spaces for cars, with more than 4,400 for bikes. But the Squamish Nation said it would work with the city and the transit operator, TransLink, to improve service. The chair of the Squamish Nation Council, Khelsilem, said he's determined to continue down that road because housing is so desperately needed by the city as a whole, and by the Squamish Nation in particular. "The investment will build many needed rental apartments and generate long-term wealth for Squamish people across many generations. The wealth generated from these lands can then be recirculated into our local economies and communities to address our people's urgent needs for affordable housing, education, and social services."

Khelsilem says the Squamish Nation isn't bound by as many rules as most municipal councils are, and has now approved three large projects relatively quickly. He says that's possible, in part, because Squamish Nation leaders have considerable "social capital." The nation needs roughly a thousand more homes for its members, he says, and there's widespread agreement they need to be built as quickly as possible. Meanwhile, Metro Vancouver needs a lot more housing, and some local politicians now look to First Nations to make the most progress on new housing construction across the region. "Municipalities are encouraging us to be bold, because they know we can be. They know we can do it."

The Squamish Nation is working on Senáḵw with the Westbank Group, a developer that describes itself as "Canada's leading luxury residential and mixed-use real estate development company." The Squamish Nation also partnered with two neighbouring nations, the Musqueam and Tsleil-Waututh, to form the MST Development Corporation, which has acquired significantly more land through federal land dispositions. The partnership was described as "an historic joint venture," with the three First Nations collectively owning 50 percent of the corporation and the other half held by the Canada Lands Company, a federal Crown corporation. Together, they now own six prime properties in Metro Vancouver that add up to 160 acres and are worth an estimated $5 billion.

That includes 92 acres of former military land in the affluent oceanside neighbourhood of West Point Grey, called the Jericho Lands. Once the largest military training base in western Canada, the giant property was home to four large airplane hangars for flying boats and seaplanes, and a squadron of other buildings, including barracks for pilots and other personnel. In the early days, those pilots chased rum-runners and mapped coastlines. During the Second World War they flew reconnaissance missions, searching for enemy submarines. But over time Canada's military needs diminished. The site that was originally a Musqueam village, then a logging camp, before becoming a military base, would change yet again. After the war, the federal government decommissioned the base and leased the land to the city of Vancouver to use as a park. The barracks building, just a stone's throw from Jericho Beach, was taken over by hippies in 1970. Despite it having only one shower and six toilets, as many as four hundred people moved into the former barracks, naming their makeshift home Cool Aid. Vancouver's mayor described them as "hippies, drug pushers and draft dodgers" not long before the police came to kick them out later that year. The *Vancouver Sun* called the eviction the Battle of Jericho, and reported 250 police officers and an army unit were needed to pull the last of the squatters out of the building. A year later, the city leased the property to the Canadian Youth Hostels Association, which repurposed the barracks into a 300-bed hostel, the largest in North America.

In the decades that followed, as Metro Vancouver's population grew steadily, the housing supply in the comfortable neighbourhoods nearby failed to keep up. Yes, new condo towers have sprung up in several locations across Vancouver's west side, but a huge swath of this major metropolitan expanse is still dominated by single-family homes. A quick search of MLS listings in 2023 shows the cheapest single-family home in the area listed at $2.1 million. The three First Nations that make up the MST Development Corporation are now planning a major change for the neighbourhood. Initial plans envisioned 10,000 new homes for 20,000 new residents—more than Point Grey's current population of 14,000. Some current residents expressed a hope that the new development would be capped at eight storeys, but that seemed unlikely. The city simply doesn't have enough housing, and MST planners were confident that if they build it, residents will come.

MST is also planning another big housing development in Vancouver, making a total of three major new Vancouver developments that are Indigenous led. The Heather Lands, as the 21-acre property is known, is a former RCMP headquarters near BC Children's Hospital. David Negrin of MST Developments said the housing that will be built there should help middle-class Vancouverites. "A large portion of our development will be affordable, attainable and workforce housing." MST was involved in negotiations with the city, the province, and the federal government to provide dedicated workforce housing that would be offered at a discount of up to 25 percent. So nurses at BC Children's Hospital, for instance, might pay less for housing close to where they live. Whether nurses and other health care workers can ultimately afford it, however, remains to be seen. And from a community standpoint, the question that will likely determine whether the development is a success is how many truly affordable homes it provides, not how many storeys high it is.

Despite concerns from long-time residents about the scale of new development, there's little doubt Vancouver needs a lot more housing. The truth is, Metro Vancouver needs even more new homes than these three ambitious projects (Sen̓áḵw/False Creek, Jericho Lands, and Heather Lands) will provide. And though the need varies from community to community, the same can be said for most of Canada's cities, and many smaller towns as well.

For all the work that needs to be done, there are positive signs that communities are becoming more receptive to change. In October 2023, the British Columbia government announced new restrictions on short-term rentals, to come into effect in 2024, that would only allow them in a host's primary residence, secondary suite, or accessory dwelling unit in most towns and cities with more than 10,000 people. A month later, the federal Housing Minister, Sean Fraser, hinted he may follow suit with similar rules that applied nationally. The federal government also announced owners of short-term rentals that do not comply with local laws could no longer claim expenses against rental income. At around the same time Ontario updated its definition of affordable housing so more construction projects could cash in on discounts and tax breaks. In Calgary, vacant downtown office buildings have been repurposed as apartments. The city of Edmonton got rid of almost all parking requirements in 2020, with the exception of accessible parking spaces that must still be provided for people living with disabilities. A year later Toronto followed suit, removing minimum parking requirements for new condos in a city where the average underground parking space cost between $48,000 and $160,000 to build. Medicine Hat, Alberta, adopted the Housing First approach to ending homelessness. In Montreal, an old paint factory was converted into a social housing co-op with thirty affordable and accessible units. The City of Toronto is opening hundreds of prefabricated modular homes on several city-owned lots to help homeless people. These changes, and many more across the country, are helping. But so much more is needed.

Governments will also need to rethink zoning, as both British Columbia and Toronto have done by effectively ending single-family zoning in many neighbourhoods. But infill construction of new townhomes in old neighbourhoods won't provide enough affordable homes. Many more policy changes are needed at all levels of government, and many more innovations are required across the country in zoning, financing, construction, public subsidies, and policy. A growing number of people are calling on the federal government to make sure its investments in housing keep pace with the annual immigration targets it sets. BC's housing minister, Ravi Kahlon, urged his federal counterpart to create a direct tie between federal funding for affordable housing and immigration targets for each province. That recommendation is not a veiled excuse to reduce the number of immigrants who come to Canada. It's understandable that many Canadians might be leery of any talk of immigration in connection with rising house prices, given some of the discriminatory immigration measures in our history. But many housing analysts say Canadians should address the connection directly, because the long history of immigrants settling successfully in this country is due in large part to the historic availability of affordable housing. If immigration is going to continue to be a success, they say, we will need a lot more affordable housing. "There is a responsibility to these new immigrants," Andy Yan at Simon Fraser University's City Program told me, "to ensure that coming to Canada is a viable option that isn't simply a future of indebtedness." In fact, many people in this country believe we should welcome more immigrants. Whatever the number of new arrivals, it seems fair to expect the federal government to incorporate housing supply into all its future immigration plans. That's an important change, but again, it's only one of many that are needed to repair our crumbling foundation. While government policies are key, our attitudes and expectations will also likely have to change.

"We'll have to accept that the white picket fence is gone," Leo Spalteholz, the Victoria housing analyst, believes, referring to the stereotypical expectation of a nice single-family home that millions of Canadians have long held. "But we should be able to figure out how we can make it affordable to have a comfortable home, in a condo at least." Canada is going to need a lot more homes, and most of them will probably be smaller than the spaces our parents called home when they were young.

Khelsilem agrees that making housing more accessible to Canadians is crucial, but not simply to give everyone adequate shelter. He says the current housing crisis is robbing young people in particular of opportunity. "Both rents and housing prices have become unfair," he believes. "No matter what income level your household [has], very few households in urban areas now are getting a fair deal. And that's impacted a whole generation in terms of the future of who we are as a country—the ability to have a life, have a home, grow your wealth, especially if you come from an impoverished background. We're creating a whole economic class where one side has property, and the other is just locked out."

Locked out. Those two words describe millions of Canadians perfectly. It will be up to our political leaders at all levels to unlock the door that has slammed shut on so many. And imagine what

Canada will look like if they don't. Imagine more homeless camps, more seniors living in vans, more families priced out of their home-towns, and more young people growing up convinced they'll never find a stable home. That doesn't have to be Canada's future. There are numerous examples from around the world, and many from this country, of specific policies and practices that can lead to the con-struction of more housing that's affordable for more people. But if the facts related in this book demonstrate anything, they show that the list of repairs needed to fix Canada's broken housing system is a long one. Like an overwhelmed homebuyer reading the inspection report on the old fixer-upper they've just bought, Canadians *should* feel overwhelmed. We have an awful lot of deferred maintenance, to borrow a popular real estate term. And as any homeowner who's ever had a leaky roof, a rotten deck, or serious cracks in the founda-tion knows, those problems won't fix themselves. So if this really is the beginning of the housing crisis, not the end, we need to get to work on the repairs. Now.

November, 2023

APPENDIX A

A List of Repairs

CANADA'S HOUSING CRISIS is an exceptionally complex problem that can't be fixed with one easy prescription. Simply reducing red tape at city halls won't do it, not on its own. The same can be said for banning foreign buyers, reinvesting in social housing, restricting short-term vacation rentals, and various other proposed measures—none will work in isolation. All are needed. Here's a list of measures to address Canada's housing crisis, based on the research that acted as the foundation for this book:

1. Build more housing! The Canada Mortgage and Housing Corporation (CMHC) says this country will need 3.5 million additional units by 2030. That's on top of the 2.3 million already projected to be built between 2021 and 2030.
2. Build more public housing. The federal government was a major home builder for decades after the Second World War, but that ended in the 1990s. The feds need to get back into housing in a

much bigger way, beyond what the current federal government has committed to do.

3. Retain vacant public land and transfer it to provincial housing ministries, non-profit housing providers, and municipal governments for the specific purpose of building affordable housing developments.

4. Reinvest in housing co-ops. A quarter of a million Canadians live in non-profit housing co-ops, but renewed investment from all levels of government could house hundreds of thousands more. If we're looking for a target, we could copy Germany, where co-op housing makes up 5 percent of the country's housing stock. If we doubled the number of co-op housing units that currently exist, we could house another quarter of a million Canadians.

5. Fund provincial housing agencies, like BC Housing and the Ontario Housing Corporation, to ramp up construction capacity and build significantly more subsidized housing units.

6. Protect existing affordable housing stock through first right of refusal. Provincial governments can give local governments and housing authorities the first chance to purchase existing affordable rental apartment buildings that are likely to be bought by REITs and renovated to make more expensive rentals or condos. Provinces can also protect disused schools and other public buildings that might be repurposed into housing.

7. End single-family zoning. Municipal governments with growing populations and high prices (most Canadian cities) could end the dominance of single-family homes. Changing local laws to allow townhouses and multiplexes to be built on the same lots that are now reserved for single-family homes would allow builders to add more homes as older houses are torn down and replaced with new buildings.

8. Allow for even greater density of new developments if affordability

commitments are made. This strategy has been adopted in Portland, Oregon, so that four units are allowed on every lot but up to six are permitted if half the units are designated as affordable, according to a formula tied to the city's median income.

9. Increase federal building subsidies to homeowners and private builders who take advantage of the above recommendation and other initiatives that create affordable housing.

10. The federal government should offer increased tax breaks, such as GST exemptions, to builders who create more affordable homes.

11. The federal government could offer no-interest or low-interest loans through CMHC to builders who create more affordable homes.

12. Increase public investment by billions in the National Housing Co-Investment Fund so it can pay for more housing construction in a time of higher interest rates.

13. Introduce new federal subsidies to cities and towns that approve new construction quickly, in a predetermined time frame. Vancouver developer Bob Rennie suggests $10,000 per rental apartment, $15,000 for a unit of social housing, and $7,500 per single-family house under $1 million. This would help cities pay for more staff to process building applications quickly.

14. Cities could have off-the-shelf housing designs for multiplexes and townhouses, available to all property owners who apply for building permits. This would save considerable money on design and variance applications that add to property costs.

15. Cities could hold design competitions with prize money for architects to obtain the above-mentioned designs that meet city criteria. This would allow for more visual diversity by allowing residents to choose between multiple designs, while still lowering costs.

16. Tie federal funding for affordable housing directly to annual immigration numbers for each province. Federal investments in

housing in many provinces have not kept pace with local needs and the number of new people arriving every year.

17. Build housing for essential workers, like nurses and firefighters, and develop rental and purchase discounts so that they can live in the communities where they work. This can take many forms— dedicated rental apartments reserved for essential workers, rental supplements, purchase discounts, and exclusive property.

18. Build more Indigenous housing. Recent federal budgets have included some new investment, but with a projected 50 percent increase needed in on-nation housing, more will be needed. Both federal and provincial governments could boost spending on Indigenous housing and commit to specific housing targets, on- and off-reserve.

19. The federal government and provinces could partner to provide better support for homeless encampments to move people into housing with sufficient support services.

20. Repair and redevelop single-room occupancy hotels and rooming houses. Both federal and provincial governments could make significant investments to repair and redevelop the buildings that house the country's poorest residents, like the many SROs on Vancouver's Downtown Eastside.

21. Consider establishing rent control in between tenancies. Provinces that only have rent control for the duration of a tenancy could implement a cap on rent increases between tenants as well.

22. Create rental registries. Provincial governments can establish registries to keep track of how much rents go up between tenancies.

23. Build better transit, with frequent hub stations. Trains, LRT, rapid buses, and other fast, reliable transportation options will help move more people more efficiently, and make more dense, walkable neighbourhoods more accessible, which can help with affordability. Good public transit will also reduce the need for

parking spaces, which increase construction costs.

24. Ease parking requirements, especially for smaller suites and in dense areas that are well served by transit. Some municipalities are reducing minimum numbers of parking stalls per housing unit. Others are doing away with them completely, or replacing vehicle parking requirements with requirements for bike storage areas.

25. Provincial governments can introduce guaranteed permitting time frames, where a city is required to provide builders with permits within a predetermined time or face financial penalties.

26. Introduce restrictions on Airbnb, Vrbo, and other short-term vacation rentals to keep more homes open to long-term renters. They could be banned altogether, restricted to commercial areas, or limited to homes where the owner will always be present.

27. Where short-term vacation rentals are permitted, provinces and big cities can work with the companies offering the vacation rentals, establishing clear rules that put the onus for screening out rule-breakers on the companies that host the vacation rental ads in the first place.

28. Provinces and cities can introduce vacancy taxes, where property owners who don't rent out secondary homes pay more for the privilege. British Columbia says this type of tax put twenty thousand more apartments into the rental market. Other provinces could adopt similar measures.

29. Discourage house-flipping by implementing provincial anti-flipping taxes (on top of 50 percent federal capital gains tax on investment properties) on owners who sell property less than three years after buying it.

30. The federal government could extend the capital gains tax to primary residences, not just investment properties. This idea is bound to be unpopular with many homeowners, but would act as a financial disincentive against speculation. If not desired for

all homeowners, capital gains could apply to primary residences that are sold quickly—for instance, less than three years after they were purchased—as a disincentive against home-flipping for fast profit.

31. Consider banning foreign non-residents from buying property in Canada, as other countries have done. This should not target any single country or nationality and should not apply to any immigrants or non-citizens who live full-time in Canada—only to non-residents who buy properties here and keep them empty most of the year.

32. Provinces could appoint anti-money-laundering commissioners to prevent houses and condominiums from being purchased with the proceeds of crime.

33. The federal government could change the Proceeds of Crime (Money Laundering) and Terrorist Financing Act to include unregulated mortgage lenders, brokers, and insurers, as well as land registries.

34. Provinces could require beneficial owners, such as an adult student whose parents own a luxury mansion, to be identified and registered.

35. Universities can open house-sharing agencies. Simon Fraser University now operates a senior–student room-match service. Lonely seniors receive a little company, help around the house, and some extra income, while university students receive safe accommodation in a home that's registered with the university and police.

36. Provide government incentives to manufacturers and technology developers to commercialize and demonstrate innovative new construction methods that improve speed, environmental efficiency, and labour requirements of home building, such as 3-D printing, modular prefabrication, and more.

37. Study the feasibility of establishing a national mandated home savings plan, like Singapore's Central Provident Fund. Also study the capacity for the Canada Pension Plan or other large funds to be expanded for use on housing.

APPENDIX B

———

Craigie's Index

Percentage price rise of an average single-family home
in Canada from 2001 to 2021: 365

Percentage price rise of everything else: 43

Projected shortage, in millions, of homes across
Canada by 2030: 3.5

Number of empty homes in Japan in 2018: 8.5 million

Number of times Bank of Canada raised interest rates in 2022: 7

Percentage of average Canadian household income needed
to cover costs of average home sold in 2022: 62.7

Percentage in Toronto: 85.2

In Vancouver: 95.8

Average price of a detached house in
Metro Vancouver in 2001: $345,260

In 2021: $1,576,800

Percentage of Canadian households that own
their home in 2021: 66.5

Percentage of Torontonians in their thirties: 25

Median price of a single-family home in
Canadian cities in 1961: $15,000

Median income for a family of four in 1961: $5,000

Approximate average price for a Canadian home in 2023: $700,000

Median after-tax income for Canadian
households in 2023: $73,000

Record-breaking number of people who moved
to Canada in 2022: 1,050,110

Number of those immigrants estimated to be
non-permanent residents: 607,782

Approximate number of Ukrainians moving to
Calgary every week in 2022: 150

Percentage of Canada's 2022 population growth
attributed to immigration: 96

Rank of Canada among OECD countries
in population growth in 2022: 1

Percentage of housing in Paris considered
affordable for low-income people in 2021: 25

Target for 2035: 40

Average annual number of housing units
built in the Île-de-France region between
1994 and 2014: 43,000

In 2017: 98,000

New homes built in New York City that year: 20,000

In London: 19,000

Average number of purpose-built rental apartments across
Canada annually from 1990 to 2019: 19,200

Percentage of national rental vacancy rate
across Canada in 2022: 1.9

Victoria, BC, vacancy rate in 2021: 0.9

Approximate percentage of Germany's
population that live in co-op housing: 6

In Canada: 0.625

Percentage of Berlin's rental housing stock
comprised of co-op housing: 12

Number of Canadians who are homeless on
any given night: between 25,000 and 35,000

Approximate number of people experiencing
homelessness in Toronto in 2021: 7,347

Approximate number of people experiencing
homelessness in Finland in the mid-80s: 20,000

In 2021: 4,000

Number of supported housing units in Finland in 1985: 127

In 2016: 1,309

Number of shelter spaces in Finland in 1985: 2,121

In 2016: 42

Estimated annual savings to Finnish society by housing
homeless people with supports instead of leaving
them on the streets, per person: €15,000

Approximate number of homes taken out of Canada's
long-term rental market by Airbnb listings: 31,100

In Montreal: 6,000

What Airbnb claims visitors to its listings spent
in Montreal in 2018: $475 million

Percentage of Montreal housing units that
were rented in 2016 census: 63

Percentage share of host revenue collected
by 6% of Airbnb hosts in New York City in 2014: 37

Minimum number of days a visitor must spend in a
Santa Monica Airbnb if one of the primary residents does
not remain on-site for the duration of the visit: 30

Number of days lost per year due to absenteeism, fatigue, and
being late by commuters who travel more than an hour each way: 7

Percentage of Greater Toronto Area commuters who traveled
more than an hour each way in 2016: 16

Approximate number of essential workers in Toronto who earn
between $40,000 and $60,000 a year (too much to apply for social
housing but too little to afford a decent place to live): 90,000

Number of new housing units now allowed on former
single-family lots in Oregon: 4

Number of new units per lot in Portland, if half are
deemed affordable: 6

Number of storeys in world's first modular high-rise,
built in Brooklyn in 2016: 32

Percentage difference between existing
two-bedroom rental apartments in Halifax
versus new listings in 2023: 28

Maximum number of hours needed to "print"
a small two-bedroom house with an Icon Vulcan II printer: 24

SOURCES

Introduction: Just the Beginning

Interview: Marie-Josée Houle, Canada's first Federal Housing Advocate.

2 **Between 2001 and 2021 the average price:** Statistics Canada, Table 18-10-0005-01, "Consumer Price Index, annual average, not seasonally adjusted," January 17, 2023, https://doi.org/10.25318/1810000501-eng; Global Property Guide, "House prices in Canada, composite of 11 cities (March 1999=100)," May 29, 2023, www.globalpropertyguide .com/North-America/Canada/Home-Price-Trends.

2 **The Canada Mortgage and Housing Corporation:** "Canada's housing supply shortage: Restoring affordability by 2030," CMHC website, June 23, 2022, www.cmhc-schl.gc.ca/blog/2022/canadas-housing -variety-supply-shortage-restoring-affordability-2030.

4 **A Royal Bank report estimated:** Victoria Wells, "Posthaste: Canada's housing affordability crisis is worse than ever," Financial Post, December 21, 2022, financialpost.com/executive/executive-summary /housing-affordability-crisis-canada-worse.

4 Benjamin Tal, deputy chief economist at CIBC: Iva Poshnjari, "Real estate: Canada's housing crisis is just beginning, economist says," BNN Bloomberg, October 5, 2022, bnnbloomberg.ca/a-decline-in -home-prices-won-t-save-us-cibc-economist-says-1.1828462.

1. Priced Out: Vancouver

Interviews: Martin and Nicole Chiu; David Eby (while Housing Minister), January 2022; Andy Yan, SFU City Program; Thomas Davidoff, UBC Sauder School of Business, associate professor in the Real Estate Strategy and Business Economics group.

5 When Martin and Nicole Chiu got married: Andrea Yu, "This family left their parents' place in Vancouver for a Calgary townhouse," Maclean's, July 20, 2022, macleans.ca/economy/realestateeconomy /the-move-priced-out-of-vancouver/.

8 In 2021 approximately 77,000 households: City of Vancouver, Standing Committee on City Finance and Services report, April 6, 2022, council.vancouver.ca/20220427/documents/cfsc3.pdf.

9 Bob Rennie, a real estate marketer: Vancouver Sun, Q&A on B.C. Housing with David Eby, Bob Rennie, Joy MacPhail, and Bernd Christmas, June 19, 2022, vancouversun.com/business/real-estate /live-qa-bc-housing-affordability.

9 Yes, housing prices have shot up: Dirk Meissner, Canadian Press, "B.C. is the most unaffordable province for housing in Canada, census data shows," CBC News, September 21, 2022, cbc.ca/news/canada/british -columbia/bc-highest-rate-unaffordable-housing-canada -census-data-1.6590005.

9 In January, 2001 the price for a detached: Real Estate Board of Greater Vancouver, Monthly Market Report, January 2001, rebgv .org/market-watch/monthly-market-report/january-2001.html.

9 that price had jumped to $1,576,800: Real Estate Board of Greater Vancouver, Monthly Market Report, January 2021, rebgv.org/market

-watch/monthly-market-report/january-2021.html.

10 **The prices just kept soaring:** Real Estate Board of Greater Vancouver, Monthly Market Report, April 2022, rebgv.org/market-watch/monthly -market-report/april-2022.html.

2. Priced In: Tokyo

Interviews: Fri McWilliams; Susan Chen; John Hozack (email); Chris Corday; Andre Sorensen, Professor of Geography and Planning, University of Toronto; Jonathan Wakrat.

23 **In 2018, Japan had roughly 8.5 million:** Takanori Tani, "Japan's 'ghost houses' given second life as rural towns fight blight," Nikkei Asia, May 30, 2021, asia.nikkei.com/Business/Markets/Property/Japan-s -ghost-houses-given-second-life-as-rural-towns-fight-blight.

24 **The population in Japan's capital kept growing:** Robin Harding, "Why Tokyo is the land of rising home construction but not prices," Financial Times, August 3, 2016, ft.com/content/023562e2-54a6 -11e6-befd-2fc0c26b3c60.

24 **In 2021, Japan recorded:** OECD, Affordable Housing Database, "HM1.1. Housing Stock and Construction," October 18, 2022, oecd.org /els/family/HM1-1-Housing-stock-and-construction.pdf.

24 **one new home per 146 people in Japan:** Statista Research Department, "Number of construction starts of dwellings in Japan from 2013 to 2022," Statista, January 2023, statista.com/statistics /667913/japan-dwellings-construction-starts-2015/.

24 **The Urban Renaissance:** Prime Minister of Japan and His Cabinet, "Basic Policies for Urban Renaissance," April 16, 2004, japan.kantei .go.jp/policy/tosi/kettei/040416kihon_e.html.

3. Shattered Dreams: Golden Horseshoe

Interviews: Poornima Malisetty; anonymous home buyer in Brampton; Gurpreet Sander; Elan Weintraub, mortgage broker; Jeff Dakers.

30 **At the peak of the market:** Toronto Regional Real Estate Board, Market Watch, December 2021, trreb.ca/files/market-stats/market -watch/mw2112.pdf.

31 **"Paradise Developments makes business":** Ryan Patrick Jones, "They purchased homes right before the real estate downturn: Now, they're struggling to close," CBC News, December 19, 2022, ici.radio-canada .ca/rci/en/news/1942420/they-purchased-homes-right-before-the -real-estate-downturn-now-theyre-struggling-to-close.

33 **Across southern Ontario, homeowners were:** Jennifer Ferreira, "Canadians with fixed-rate mortgages 'terrified' in face of higher interest rates upon renewal," CTV News, December 13, 2022, ctvnews .ca/business/canadians-with-fixed-rate-mortgages-terrified-in-face -of-higher-interest-rates-upon-renewal-1.6191490.

33 **In Toronto, Rebecca Cossar had locked in:** Jones, "They purchased."

35 **Canada Mortgage and Housing Corporation forecast:** Jean-Francois Perreault, "Which province has the largest structural housing deficit?" Scotiabank, January 12, 2022, scotiabank.com/ca/en/about /economics/economics-publications/post.other-publications.housing .housing-note.housing-note--january-12-2022-.html.

35 **Housing Task Force set up by the provincial government:** Ontario Housing Affordability Task Force, Report, February 8, 2022,files .ontario.ca/mmah-housing-affordability-task-force-report-en-2022 -02-07-v2.pdf?_gl=1*12jakqb*_ga*NDgwNzI1NTMuMTY3MzQ2NDg 2NQ..*_ga_HLLEK4SB6V*MTY3MzQ2NDg2NC4xLjEuMTY3MzQ2 NjAoNy4wLjAuMA.; Colin Butler, "Ontario promised to build 1.5 million homes by 2031: A new report says that will likely never happen," CBC News, August 16, 2022, cbc.ca/news/canada/london/ontario-build -housing-crisis-1.6551546.

36 **Mike Moffat, the lead author:** M. Moffatt, A. Dudu, and M. Hosseini, Ontario's Need for 1.5 Million More Homes, Smart Prosperity Institute, August 2022, institute.smartprosperity.ca/sites/default

/files/Ontario%27s%20Need%20for%201.5m%20More%20Homes
-SPI%20August%202022.pdf.

36 **the Ontario housing market was reasonably affordable:** Statistics
Canada, "Housing in Canada: Key results from the 2016 Census,"
October 25, 2017, www150.statcan.gc.ca/n1/daily-quotidien
/171025/dq171025c-eng.htm?indid=14429-1&indgeo=0.

37 **Finance Minister Chrystia Freeland:** Sean Boynton, "Sky-high home
prices in Canada are 'intergenerational injustice,' Freeland says,"
Global News, April 11, 2022, globalnews.ca/news/8752309/canada
-home-prices-intergenerational-injustice-chrystia-freeland/.

37 **the housing crisis was back in the spotlight:** Mike Crawley, "Here are
the key promises Doug Ford made in the 2022 Ontario election
campaign," CBC News, June 7, 2022, cbc.ca/news/canada/toronto
/doug-ford-ontario-premier-election-campaign-promises-1.6478783.

39 **Gil Peñalosa—an urban planner and runner-up:** Laura Hanrahan,
"Denser homes, no development charges: How a Toronto mayoral
candidate wants to fix housing," Storeys, September 16, 2022, storeys
.com/gil-penalosa-toronto-mayor-housing-platform/.

40 **Between 2016 and 2021, Ontario:** Statistics Canada, "Land use,
Census of Agriculture historical data," May 11, 2022, www150.statcan
.gc.ca/t1/tbl1/en/tv.action?pid=3210015301&pickMembers%5B0%5D
=1.7&cubeTimeFrame.startYear=2001&cubeTimeFrame.endYear
=2021&referencePeriods=20010101%2C20210101.

4. Dreams Renewed: Paris

41 **Catherine Cortinovis felt overwhelmed:** AFP, "Above the luxury shops
of La Samaritaine, social housing with a view of Paris," Batinfo.com,
September 27, 2021, batinfo.com/en/actuality/au-dessus-des-boutiques
-de-luxe-de-la-samaritaine-logement-social-avec-vue-sur-paris_19174.

42 **The iconic Parisian department store:** Sophie Davies, "La
Samaritaine: The classic Paris department store returns in style,"

Paris Perfect, October 14, 2021, parisperfect.com/blog/2021/10/la
-samaritaine-paris/.

42 **But when it reopened in 2021, La Samaritaine:** Feargus O'Sullivan,
"For a lucky few, Paris debuts public housing in a pricey landmark,"
Bloomberg, September 25, 2021, bloomberg.com/news/articles/2021
-09-25/transforming-a-paris-landmark-into-public-housing.

44 **Zina Hadjab couldn't believe her luck:** Sébastien Thomas, "Qui sont
les locataires qui habitent les logements sociaux de la Samaritaine?"
Le Parisien, September 22, 2021, leparisien.fr/immobilier/qui-sont
-les-locataires-qui-habitent-les-logements-sociaux-de-la-samaritaine
-22-09-2021-4PR35IHYU5EXNOTS63W7B35R6Q.php.

44 **Her new home is what's known in Paris:** Marie Amelie Marchal, "À
quoi ressemblent les logements sociaux de la Samaritaine à Paris?"
actuParis, September 23, 2021, actu.fr/ile-de-france/paris_75056/photos
-a-quoi-ressemblent-les-logements-sociaux-de-la-samaritaine
-a-paris_45121212.html.

46 **Yonah Freemark, of the Urban Studies and Planning:** Yonah
Freemark, "Doubling housing production in the Paris region:
A multi-policy, multi-jurisdictional response," International Journal
of Housing Policy, December 19, 2019, https://doi.org/10.1080
/19491247.2019.1682233.

49 **In the suburb of Romainville:** Claire Ané, "Accession sociale à la
propriété: L'essor du bail réel solidaire," Le Monde, January 8, 2023,
lemonde.fr/societe/article/2023/01/08/accession-sociale-a-la-propriete
-l-essor-du-bail-reel-solidaire_6157032_3224.html.

50 **He loves the four-storey building:** "The roofs of Paris: unesco World
Heritage status," Guilbert Express website, April 20, 2020, express.fr/en
/pro-tips/roofing/the-roofs-of-paris-unesco-world-heritage-status/.

50 **Built between 1959 and 1962 as a public housing project:** Anne
Lacaton and Jean-Philippe Vassal, "Tour Bois le Prêtre:
Transformation of housing block, Paris 17," Archilovers, January 15,

2013, archilovers.com/projects/74486/tour-bois-le-pretre.html#info.

51 **The former Ministry of Defence headquarters:** Mathilde Riaud, "Pénurie de logements: Innover pour desserrer l'étau en Ile-de-France," Les Echos, December 5, 2022, lesechos.fr/thema/articles/penurie-de -logements-innover-pour-desserrer-letau-en-ile-de-france-1885778.

51 **The competition for private rentals:** Liz Rowlinson, "Beyond the boulevards: Homebuyers target a less sought-after Paris," Financial Times, October 21, 2022, ft.com/content/d3c4d80b-7587-468f -9f95-bcc22cce3733.

51 **But the trend in Paris seems to be headed:** Magda Maaoui, "Social contract: Parisian social housing," Architectural Review, June 30, 2022, architectural-review.com/buildings/housing/social-contract -parisian-social-housing.

5. Renters in a Dangerous Time: Ottawa

Interviews: lawyer representing Elsie Kalu (email); Ottawa city councillor Catherine McKenney; Joshua Hawley, housing advocate and Carleton University pHd candidate; Andy Yan, SFU City Program.

52 **Erin Hobson knew it was time:** Safiyah Marhnouj, "Renters facing record-high prices, dwindling options in Ottawa," CBC News, August 15, 2022, cbc.ca/news/canada/ottawa/ottawa-rent-high-prices -affordability-1.6545690.

52 **And then there was the bedroom closet:** "Ottawa resident says 'disheartening' apartment search has life on hold," CBC News, August 15, 2022, video, 1:43, cbc.ca/player/play/2061400643738,

53 **Rents kept rising, and by the end of the year:** Rentals.ca, "June 2023 Rental Report," Rentals.ca, rentals.ca/national-rent-report.; CMHC, Rental Market Report: January 2023 Edition, January 26, 2023, cmhc-schl. gc.ca/en/professionals/housing-markets-data-and-research/market reports/rental-market-reports-major-centres?utm_source=twitter&utm _medium=cmhc_ca&utm_content=organic&utm_campaign=RMR.

54 **In the town of Russell, a half-hour drive:** Nicole Williams, "These seniors face a 20% rent increase—and Ontario rules make it legal," CBC News, November 22, 2022, cbc.ca/news/canada/ottawa/seniors -20-rent-increase-ontario-rules-laws-1.6655181.

54 **What they didn't know was that:** Lucas Powers, "Ontario PCs slash spending and oversight, unveil tax cut and new LCBO hours in 1st economic plan," CBC News, November 15, 2018, cbc.ca/news/canada /toronto/ontario-pc-fall-economic-outlook-cuts-tax-lcbo-1.4906718.

56 **Affordability is certainly a challenge:** David Pugliese, "Military's intelligence command avoids posting staff to Ottawa because of region's high cost of living," Ottawa Citizen, July 11, 2022, ottawacitizen.com/news/national/defence-watch/militarys -intelligence-command-avoids-posting-staff-to-ottawa -because-of-regions-high-cost-of-living.

57 **When the new Canadian Forces Housing Differential:** "Canadian Forces Housing Differential soon to replace Post-Living Differential," Maple Leaf, March 21, 2023, canada.ca/en/department-national-defence /maple-leaf/defence/2023/03/canadian-forces-housing-differential.html.

57 **the average rent in the NCR had more than doubled:** CMHC, Report on the Ottawa Rental Market in 2010, n.d., publications.gc.ca/collec tions/collection_2010/schl-cmhc/nh12-77/NH12-77-2010-eng.pdf.

57 **But the change also cut off more than 7,700:** Ashley Burke, "Thousands of military members to be cut off as Ottawa introduces expanded housing benefit," CBC News, March 22, 2023, cbc.ca/news /politics/canadian-armed-forces-new-housing-benefit-1.6787686.

57 **Elsie Kalu found that out:** Priscilla Ki Sun Hwang, "Mom, daughter face homelessness after buying home and tenant refuses to leave," CBC News, October 24, 2022, cbc.ca/news/canada/ottawa/non -paying-tenant-ottawa-small-landlord-face-homelessness-1.6610660.

58 **The board finally granted an eviction:** Ontario Superior Court of Justice, court file no. CV-22-00000074-00CP, soloontario.ca/wp-content

/uploads/2022/12/Statement-of-Claim-Plaintiff-Kalu-22-DEC-2022.pdf.

59 **In a rundown row of old brick:** Blair Crawford, "Four Sandy Hill rooming house deaths highlight the tragedy of 'renovictions,'" Ottawa Citizen, May 13, 2022, ottawacitizen.com/news/local-news /coroner-investigating-four-deaths-at-downtown-rooming-house.

60 **Alexander William Faulkner:** Mattatall-Varner Funeral Home, "Alexander William 'Sandy Bill' Faulkner" (obituary), mattatallvarnerfh .com/obituaries/148031, accessed August 2, 2023.

60 **Robert Gagnon died the following winter:** Robert Gagnon (obituary), Daily Press (Timmins), February 20, 2021, timminspress. remembering.ca/obituary/robert-gagnon-1081656178.

6. A Co-operative Approach: Berlin

Interviews: Carlo Wahrmann (email); Andreas Mense, urban economist at the Institute for Employment Research in Nuremberg; Michael Voigtlander, real estate economist at German Economic Institute; Carol Schröder.

65 **The banks that were financing:** Paul F. Duwe, "Neubauprojekt am Gleisdreieck: 'Die Leute im Möckernkiez ticken anders,'" Tagesspiegel, March 27, 2018, tagesspiegel.de/wirtschaft /immobilien/die-leute-im-mockernkiez-ticken-anders-4963147. html.; Möckernkiez eG Berlin, sdg21, August 22, 2016, sdg21 .eu/en/db/moeckernkiez-eg-berlin.

66 **The building also has a giant common:** "A car free neighborhood in car-centric Berlin: Möckernkiez," YouTube, uploaded by cities4people, October 1, 2021, m.youtube.com/watch?v=v2GhxK3DUg0.

70 **Across Germany, about 5 percent:** OECD, German Policy Brief, June 2018, oecd.org/policy-briefs/Germany-plicy-brief-housing.pdf.

70 **In Canada, only a quarter of a million people:** Co-operative Housing Federation of Canada, "Facts and Figures," chfcanada.coop/about-co -op-housing/facts-and-figures/, accessed August 2, 2023.; Manuel

Lutz, "Practising solidarity in Europe's housing co-operatives," Assemble Papers, November 20, 2019, assemblepapers.com .au/2019/11/20/lived-solidarity-housing-co-operatives/.

73 **In a 2021 referendum Berlin voters:** Aggi Cantrill and Hayley Warren, "Berlin referendum could determine the future of the city's housing," Bloomberg, September 22, 2021, bloomberg.com/news /features/2021-09-23/berlin-referendum-targets-city-s-corporate -landlords.; Philip Oltermann, "Berlin's rental revolution: Activists push for properties to be nationalised," Guardian, April 4, 2019, theguardian.com/cities/2019/apr/04/berlins-rental-revolution -activists-push-for-properties-to-be-nationalised.; Dave Brancek, "Berliners voted for a radical solution to soaring rents: A year on, they are still waiting," Euronews, September 26, 2022, euronews.com /my-europe/2022/09/26/berliners-voted-for-a-radical-solution-to -soaring-rents-a-year-on-they-are-still-waiting.

74 **Still, Carolin Schröder says housing co-ops:** Carolin Schröder and Heike Walk, "Co-operatives and climate protection: Housing co-operatives in Germany," in Anthony Webster, Linda Shaw, and Rachael Vorberg-Rugh, eds., Mainstreaming Co-operation: An Alternative for the Twenty-First Century? (Manchester: Manchester University Press, 2016), researchgate.net/publication/309779447_Co-operatives_and _climate_protection_Housing_co-operatives_in_Germany.

7. Homeless: Duncan, BC

Interviews: Mayor Michele Staples; Councillor Stacy Middlemiss; Marc Lee; Carolina Ibarra, Pacifica Housing; Keith Simmonds, minister of the Duncan United Church.

76 **Gina Dias and her "hubby" Josh Derrah:** Sarah Simpson, "Cold weather shelter not open on night of homeless man's death in Duncan," Cowichan Valley Citizen, January 4, 2023, cowichanvalleycitizen.com/news/cold -weather-shelter-not-open-on-night-of-homeless-mans-death-in-duncan/.

77 **"I just wish I'd stayed with him":** Skye Ryan, "'I miss him so much': Widow of Duncan man found dead on freezing night speaks," CHEK News, December 31, 2022, cheknews.ca/i-miss-him-so-much-says -widow-of-duncan-man-found-dead-on-freezing-night-1128904/.

77 **the eighth year of the province's toxic:** BC Coroners Service, "Toxic-drug supply claims nearly 2,300 lives in 2022," news release, January 31, 2023, news.gov.bc.ca/releases/2023PSSG0008 -000109#:~:text=The%20number%20of%20deaths%20 being,lives%20each%20and%20every%20day.

77 **Adrian Sylvester—a member of:** Hannah Lepine, "Community believes cold weather played role in homeless persons death in Duncan," CHEK News, December 29, 2022, cheknews.ca/community-believes-cold -weather-played-role-in-homeless-persons-death-in-duncan-1128654/.

78 **Carolyn Lawson moved into:** Kendall Hanson, "Cowichan Valley campground and RV park price increases forcing tenants out," CHEK News, July 18, 2022, cheknews.ca/cowichan-valley-campground-and -rv-park-price-increases-forcing-tenants-out-1062863/.

78 **That happiness ended abruptly:** Riverside RV & Camping, riversidecampingduncan.com/, accessed August 2, 2023.

80 **bylaw officers started handing out:** Kathryn Marlowe, "Bylaw officers in the Cowichan Valley were writing more tickets for people living in RVs in 2022 than in previous years," CBC Radio News, February 9, 2022.

82 **federal government's 2023 update:** Government of Canada, "National Housing Strategy," placetocallhome.ca/what-is-the-strategy, accessed August 2, 2023.; Peter Zimonjic, "Liberals detail $40B for 10-year national housing strategy, introduce Canada Housing Benefit," CBC News, November 22, 2017, cbc.ca/news/politics/housing-national -benefit-1.4413615.

82 **it was already well behind its original targets:** Auditor General of Canada, 2022 Reports to Parliament. Report 5—Chronic Homelessness, oag-bvg.gc.ca/internet/English/att_ e_44159.html.

83 **Economist Marc Lee, at the Canadian:** Marc Lee, "How to build affordable rental housing in Vancouver," Canadian Centre for Policy Alternatives paper, March 2021, policyalternatives.ca/sites/default /files/uploads/publications/BC%20Office/2021/03/ccpa-bc _Affordable-Housing-March2021_report.pdf.

84 **At around the same time, the 52-unit:** David Minkow, "Community leaders call for urgent support to shelter unhoused people after recent deaths," Discourse, January 19, 2023, thediscourse.ca/cowichan -valley/call-for-support-to-shelter-unhoused-people.

8. Housing First: Helsinki

Interview: Juha Kahila, Head of International Affairs at the Y-Foundation.

86 **Pasi Hietanen started drinking:** Jenny Mäkinen, "Vuosia kadulla elänyt Pasi Hietanen kertoo, millaista on elämä ilman kotia: 'Minut on todettu kuolleeksi kahdeksan kertaa'" [Pasi Hietanen, who lived on the street for years, tells what life is like without a home: "I have been found dead eight times"], MTV Uutiset, October 16, 2022, mtvuutiset.fi/artikkeli/vuosia-kadulla-elanyt-pasi-hietanen -kertoo-millaista-on-elama-ilman-kotia-minut-on-todettu -kuolleeksi-kahdeksan-kertaa/8549836#gs.p1fo8i.

88 **They found Pasi an apartment:** Jenny Mäkinen, "Elämää katujen jälkeen: 'Itse olen ohjeistanut kerran nuorta miestä, että kuinka pyyhitään tiskipöytä'" [Life after the streets: "I once instructed a young man how to wipe the counter"], MTV Uutiset, October 16, 2022, www-mtvuutiset-fi.translate.goog/artikkeli/elamaa-katujen-jalkeen -itse-olen-ohjeistanut-kerran-nuorta-miesta-etta-kuinka-pyyhitaan-tiski poyta/8550156?_x_tr_sl=fi&_x_tr_tl=en&_x_tr_hl=en&_x_tr_pto=sc.

88 **Social workers and security staff keep watch:** "Vuosia kadulla elänyt Pasi Hietanen kertoo, millaista on elämä ilman kotia: 'Minut on todettu kuolleeksi kahdeksan kertaa'" [Pasi Hietanen, who lived on the street for years, tells what life is like without a home: "I have been

found dead eight times"], YouTube, uploaded by MTV Uutiset, October 19, 2022, youtube.com/watch?v=dE09Jru3ahM.

89 **"We decided to make the housing unconditional,":** Tahiat Mahboob, "Housing is a human right: How Finland is eradicating homelessness," CBC Radio, January 24, 2020, cbc.ca/radio/sunday/the-sunday-edition -for-january-26-2020-1.5429251/housing-is-a-human-right-how -finland-is-eradicating-homelessness-1.5437402.; Jon Henley, "'It's a miracle': Helsinki's radical solution to homelessness," Guardian, June 3, 2019, theguardian.com/cities/2019/jun/03/its-a-miracle-helsinkis -radical-solution-to-homelessness.

90 **The sight of people sleeping rough:** Ella Hancock, "Helsinki is still leading the way in ending homelessness—but how are they doing it?" World Habitat, October 6, 2022, world-habitat.org/news/our-blog /helsinki-is-still-leading-the-way-in-ending-homelessness-but-how -are-they-doing-it/.

91 **reviewed several studies that looked at the cost-benefit:** Angela Ly and Eric Latimer, "Housing First impact on costs and associated cost offsets: A review of the literature," Canadian Journal of Psychiatry 60, no. 11 (November 2015): 475–87, https://doi .org/10.1177/070674371506001103.

91 **The merit of Housing First is clear to the many people:** Y-Foundation, A Home of Your Own: Housing First and Ending Homelessness in Finland (Helsinki: Y-Foundation, 2017), ysaatio.fi /assets/files/2018/01/A_Home_of_Your_Own_lowres_spreads.pdf.

9. The Airbnb Effect: Montreal

Interviews: Guillaume Dostaler, coordinator of the tenants' rights group Entraide logement Hochelaga-Maisonneuve; Rebecca Bain.

96 **Jean-François Raymond wasn't expecting:** CBC News, "Some Montreal tenants are being evicted so their apartments can be turned into tourist rentals," CBC News, February 14, 2023, cbc.ca/news

/canada/montreal/montreal-eviction-hochelaga-maisonneuve
-tourism-rentals-1.6748299.

96 **However, the council permitted vacation rentals:** Olivia O'Malley,
"Montreal tenant receives eviction notice to make way for Airbnb,"
CTV News, February 19, 2023, montreal.ctvnews.ca/montreal-tenant
-receives-eviction-notice-to-make-way-for-airbnb-1.6280484.

97 **his neighbour, a 68-year-old man who had lived there:** Isabelle
Ducas, "Évincés pour faire place à des Airbnb," La Presse (Montreal),
February 14, 2023, lapresse.ca/actualites/grand-montreal
/2023-02-14/evinces-pour-faire-place-a-des-airbnb.php.

97 **rents were rising much faster:** Al Sciola, "Rent prices for two-bedroom
apartments in Montreal are 10% higher than last year," Daily Hive,
November 15, 2022, dailyhive.com/montreal/price-one-bedrooms-rent.

99 **Tourisme Montréal certainly thinks so:** "Hochelaga-Maisonneuve
Streets," Tourisme Montréal, mtl.org/en/what-to-do/heritage-and
-architecture/les-rues-d-hochelaga-maisonneuve-montreal.

100 **For some Montreal renters, like Félix Blanche:** Montreal Gazette,
"Montrealers, tourists discuss their experience with Airbnb,"
YouTube, July 15, 2019, youtube.com/watch?v=XEpawemNyvg.

100 **In 2018 it claimed that Airbnb visitors:** Airbnb, "Airbnb platform
attracts millions of dollars for Montreal tourism," news release,
August 21, 2018, newswire.ca/news-releases/airbnb-platform
-attracts-millions-of-dollars-for-montreal-tourism-691341761.html.

101 **Professor David Wachsmuth, at McGill University:** Steve Rukavina,
"Why Quebec's law designed to crack down on illegal Airbnbs isn't
working," CBC News, May 5, 2022, cbc.ca/news/canada/montreal
/quebec-airbnb-crackdown-not-working-1.6439867.

101 **led a study on the impact of short-term rentals in Canada:** "The
Impact of Short-term Rentals on Canadian Housing," CMHC website,
November 23, 2020, cmhc-schl.gc.ca/en/nhs/nhs-project-profiles
/2020-nhs-projects/impact-short-term-rentals-canadian-housing.

103 **Cloé St-Hilaire and her co-authors found:** Cloé St-Hilaire, Mikael Brunila, and David Wachsmuth, "High rises and housing stress: A spatial big data analysis of rental housing financialization," Journal of the American Planning Association, 2023, tandfonline.com/doi/epdf /10.1080/01944363.2022.2126382?needAccess=true&role=button.

103 **In 2022 it legislated a sixty-day right:** "Sell a building that is subject to the pre-emptive right," City of Montreal website, July 11, 2023, montreal.ca/en/how-to/sell-building-subject-to-pre-emptive-right.; Susan Schwartz, "Montreal moves to protect 78 rooming houses from speculators," Montreal Gazette, September 19, 2022, montrealgazette .com/news/embaragoed-montreal-is-using-its-right-of-first-refusal -to-protect-78-rooming-houses-from-speculators.

103 **Legault disclosed he'd moved into:** Canadian Press, "Quebec provincial party leaders reveal how much money they make, how many assets they have," CTV News, September 13, 2022, montreal.ctvnews .ca/quebec-provincial-party-leaders-reveal-how-much-money-they -make-how-many-assets-they-have-1.6066323.

104 **Legault had come under fire:** Daniel J. Rowe, "'Good luck finding that,' opposition party criticizes Legault response that apartments in Montreal go for $500-$600," CTV News, April 29, 2021, montreal. ctvnews.ca/good-luck-finding-that-opposition-party-criticizes -legault-response-that-apartments-in-montreal-go -for-500-600-1.5406952.

104 **The city of Montreal allows boroughs:** "Areas where operating a tourist home is authorized," City of Montreal website, April 13, 2023, montreal.ca/en/how-to/areas where-operating-tourist-home -authorized?arrondissement=MHM.

105 **A frat house atmosphere is described:** Christopher Curtis, "'This isn't the Holiday Inn': Montreal residents decry Airbnb rentals," Montreal Gazette, February 11, 2020, montrealgazette.com/news/local-news /this-isnt-the-holiday-inn-montreal-residents-decry-airbnb-rentals.

10. A Long-Term Strategy on Short-Term Rentals: Santa Monica, California

Interview: Kevin McKeown, former Santa Monica mayor.

108 **When Scott Shatford was laid off:** Scott Shatford, The Airbnb Expert's Playbook: Secrets to Making Six-Figures as a Rentalpreneur, Kindle ed., 2014.

110 **When Santa Monica city councillors met:** Sam Sanders, "Santa Monica cracks down on Airbnb, bans 'vacation rentals' under a month," NPR, May 13, 2015, npr.org/sections/thetwo-way /2015/05/13/406587575/santa-monica-cracks-down-on-airbnb-bans -vacation-rentals-under-a-month#:~:text=Tuesday%20night%2C %20the%20Santa%20Monica,law%20takes%20effect%20June%2015.

111 **The Home-Sharing Ordinance spelled out:** "Overview of the home-sharing ordinance," City of Santa Monica website, n.d., https://www.smgov.net/departments/pcd/permits/short-term -rental-home-share-ordinance/

112 **He pleaded no contest and:** Alison Griswold, "Airbnb is no longer the nice guy of the sharing economy," Quartz, December 5, 2016, qz.com/842996/what-happens-when-a-30-billion-startup-stops -being-nice-and-starts-being-real.

114 **A beautiful Spanish-style house:** Jorge Casuso, "Home rented as quasi hostel raises concerns about home-sharing law," Santa Monica Lookout, August 13, 2019, surfsantamonica.com/ssm_site/the_lookout /news/News-2019/August-2019/08_13_2019_Home_Rented_as _Quasi_Hostel_Raises_Concerns.html.

115 **After years of defending its laws:** Airbnb, "Airbnb and City of Santa Monica reach settlement agreement," news release, December 10, 2019, news.airbnb.com/airbnb-and-city-of-santa-monica-reach -settlement-agreement/.

115 **reserved for people with lower incomes:** City of Santa Monica, "2022 income and rent limits (30% affordability standard)," https://www

.smgov.net/uploadedFiles/Departments/HED/Housing_and
Redevelopment/Housing/Fee-_Affordable_Housing/2022
_Income_and_Rent_Limits_30_NOT%20Subject%20to
%20Ordinance%202429%20(1).pdf, accessed August 3, 2023.

115 **Each building had its own specific:** Erin Taylor, "New affordable
housing opens in Santa Monica," City of Santa Monica website,
December 12, 2022, santamonica.gov/blog/new-affordable-housing
-opens-in-santa-monica.; City of Santa Monica, "Support available to
additional low-income seniors through Preserving Our Diversity
program," news release, February 2, 2021, santamonica.gov
/press/2021/02/02/support-available-to-additional-low-income
-seniors-through-preserving-our-diversity-program.; "EAH
Housing begins construction on Southern California development,"
Affordable Housing Finance, August 23, 2022, housingfinance.com
/developments/eah-housing-begins-construction-on-southern
-california-development_0.; Jennifer Kennedy, "Another victory
for tenants," SMRR, May 20, 2021, smrr.org/2021/05/another
-victory-for-tenants.

117 **yet another challenge for the Home-Sharing:** Associated Press,
"Airbnb loses another legal challenge to Santa Monica's strict short-
term rental rules," KTLA5, March 13, 2019, ktla.com/news/local-
news/airbnb-loses-another-legal-challenge-to-santa-monicas-strict
-short-term-rental-rules/.; Maura Dolan, "Federal appeals court
upholds Santa Monica's ban on short-term vacation rentals," Los
Angeles Times, October 3, 2019, latimes.com/california/story/2019
-10-03/9th-circuit-santa-monica-airbnb.

117 **Meanwhile, Scott Shatford is still:** Building Wealth with Real Estate
with Chris Lopez, "Interview with AirDNA founder Scott Shatford,"
YouTube, October 5, 2021, https://www.youtube.com
/watch?v=4w9ovrIQr_Y

11. In Short Supply. St-Boniface, Quebec

Interviews: Diane Longpre; Mario Mercier, spokesperson for L'Association des locataires de Sherbrooke.

119 **As Quebec's annual July 1:** Celine Cooper, "Why do Quebecers put up with July 1 moving day hell?" Montreal Gazette, July 3, 2018, montrealgazette.com/opinion/columnists/celine-cooper-why -do-quebecers-put-up-with-july-1-moving-day-hell.

120 **But once again she was told:** Paule Vermot-Desroches, "Pénurie de logements: la crise qui gronde, à quelques jours du 1er juillet," Le Nouvelliste (Trois-Rivières), June 7, 2022, latribune.ca/2022/06/18 /penurie-de-logements-la-crise-qui-gronde-a-quelques-jours-du-1e -juillet-7f50e3a5b1cd23f34a53d1c50478eb71/.

121 **Diane was still professional and organized:** Rad, "La crise du logement, on règle ça comment?" YouTube, uploaded by Radio-Canada, September 15, 2022, youtube.com/watch?v=G3Uaf58×8qE.

121 **Karyne Cloutier found herself:** Rachel Lau, "Montreal single mother refused housing because she has 4 children," CTV News, July 2, 2022, montreal.ctvnews.ca/montreal-single-mother-refused-housing -because-she-has-4-children-1.5493235.

122 **Quebec's Charter of Human Rights and Freedoms:** "Housing: no discrimination allowed," Éducaloi website, educaloi.qc.ca/en/capsules /housing-no-discrimination-allowed/#:~:text=When%20it %20comes%20to%20housing,skin%20colour%2C%20religion %20or%20age, accessed August 3, 2023.

123 **A 2022 Léger survey of Quebecers:** Maxance Cloutier, "Les tout -petits pénalisés par la crise du logement," Le Devoir (Montreal), June 29, 2022, ledevoir.com/societe/728109/sondage-les-tout -petits-penalises-par-la-crise-du-logement.

123 **In 2021, the Pan-Canadian Women's Housing:** Kaitlin Schwan, Mary-Elizabeth Vaccaro, Luke Reid, Nadia Ali, and Khulud Baig, The Pan-Canadian Women's Housing & Homelessness Survey (Toronto:

Canadian Observatory on Homelessness, 2021), homelesshub.ca
/sites/default/files/attachments/EN-Pan-Canadian-Womens
-Housing-Homelessness-Survey-FINAL-28-Sept-2021.pdf.

123 **28 percent of women-led single-parent households:** Statistics
Canada, "Core housing need in Canada," September 21, 2022,
www150.statcan.gc.ca/n1/pub/11-627-m/11-627-m2022056-eng.htm.

124 **The average rent advertised on Kijiji:** Émilie Warren, "Housing situation still precarious in many Quebec regions ahead of Moving
Day," CBC News, June 30, 2022, cbc.ca/news/canada/montreal/
housing-crisis-in-quebec-regions-ahead-of-moving-day-1.6505669.

124 **In Cowansville—population twelve thousand:** Ruby Irene Pratka,
"Cowansville creates emergency fund for renters amid housing
crisis," Quebec Community Newspapers Association website, June 20,
2022, qcna.qc.ca/news/cowansville-creates-emergency-fund-for
-renters-amid-housing-crisis.

125 **an unusual offer of twenty tiny homeless shelters:** Maris Coulton,
"Why some Quebec towns are welcoming Mike Ward's tiny shelters—
and why advocates for homeless people object," CBC News, February
20, 2022, cbc.ca/news/canada/montreal/tiny-shelters-homeless
-drummondville-victoriaville-1.6357021.

126 **When 17-year-old Bianca Beaulne was accepted:** Michael Boriero,
"Housing headaches for new students in Lennoxville," Sherbrooke
Record, June 6, 2022, sherbrookerecord.com/housing-headaches
-for-new-students-in-lennoxville/.

126 **Bishop's University in Lennoxville:** Bishop's University, "Bishop's
University inaugurates new campus housing," news release, February
20, 2023, ubishops.ca/bishops-university-inaugurates-new
-campus-housing-2/.

127 **The students' housing advocacy group Unité de travail:** Frédéric
Lacroix-Couture, "Groups hold meeting to improve access to student
housing in Quebec," CTV News, April 11, 2023, montreal.ctvnews.ca

/groups-hold-meeting-to-improve-access-to-student-housing-in
-quebec-1.6351137.

127 **Akpelozim Lokoun, a student coordinator:** CBC News, "As school
year starts, students are being squeezed out of Quebec's rental
market," CBC News, August 22, 2022, cbc.ca/news/canada
/montreal/student-housing-quebec-1.6558176.

12. Subsidies for (Almost) Everyone: Singapore

Interview: Jove Nazatul.

129 **Liz and Ben were ready:** Your Own Economy, "Finally got keys to
our HDB BTO flat at Bidadari!!" YouTube, January 31, 2023, youtube
.com/watch?v=KbNBZ9iigKc.

130 **HDB flats, as they're known, are ubiquitous:** "Types of flats,"
Housing and Development Board, hdb.gov.sg/residential/buying-a
-flat/finding-a-flat/types-of-flats#:~:text=With%202%20bedrooms
%20with%20attached,Living%2F%20dining,
accessed August 3, 2023.

131 **Liz and Ben paid a little more:** Your Own Economy, "HDB BTO
process, welcoming residents of Woodleigh Hillside @ Bidadari—
Part 2," YouTube, November 20, 2022, youtube.com/watch
?v=GU4oMlbiQ1I.

131 **When they finally moved in:** Your Own Economy, "HDB BTO
process for OCS, EC, CPF, paying mortgage—Part 1," YouTube,
June 29, 2022, youtube.com/watch?v=6c4CowE9-eQ.

133 **the highly desirable and central Bidadari neighbourhood:** "Project
spec & review: Woodleigh Hillside," BTOHQ, btohq.com/bto
-project-spec/woodleigh-hillside, accessed August 3, 2023.

133 **The population grew rapidly in the first half of the twentieth:**
"Evolution of public housing in Singapore," Government of
Singapore website, June 9, 2020, gov.sg/article/evolution-of
-public-housing-in-singapore#:~:text=The%20Housing%20%26

%20Development%20Board%20was,basic%20amenities%20at%
20affordable%20prices.

134 **In its place he created the Housing and Development:** Wendell Cox,
Demographia International Housing Affordability, 2022 Edition
(Houston and Winnipeg: Urban Reform Institute and Frontier
Centre for Public Policy, 2022), urbanreforminstitute.org/wp-content
/uploads/2022/03/Demographia-International-Housing-Affordability
-2022-Edition.pdf.

135 **Economists, urban planners, frustrated renters:** PolyMatter, "How
Singapore solved housing," YouTube, May 1, 2020, youtube.com
/watch?app=desktop&v=3dBaE04QplQ.

135 **Singapore's "Housing Miracle,":** Abhas Jha, "'But what about
Singapore?' Lessons from the best public housing program in the
world," World Bank Blogs, January 31, 2018, blogs.worldbank.org
/sustainablecities/what-about-singapore-lessons-best-public
-housing-program-world.

135 **Singapore has strict ethnic quotas:** Haris Khan, "Building
Singapore: An exploration of public housing," PP&G Review,
November 25, 2016, ppgreview.ca/2016/11/25/building-singapore
-an-exploration-of-public-housing/.

136 **Singapore decriminalized sex between:** Agence France-Presse,
"Singapore lifts gay sex ban but blocks path toward marriage
equality," Guardian, November 20, 2022, theguardian.com
/world/2022/nov/30/singapore-lifts-gay-sex-ban-but-blocks
-path-toward-marriage-equality.

136 **Adrianna Tan is married:** Natalie Choy, "LGBTW Singaporeans may
find public housing access harder," Bloomberg, August 25, 2022,
time.com/6208496/singapore-lgbt-discrimination-rights-equality/.

137 **A single 24-year-old named Lisa:** Lisa's Adulting in Singapore, "How
I bought a resale HDB at 24 y/o as a single," YouTube, April 21, 2022,
youtube.com/watch?v=rBWNlgqXwRk&t=256s.

139 **In Greater Victoria, recent counts:** Community Social Planning
Council, "Point-in-time homeless count report 2020," news release,
March 12, 2020, communitycouncil.ca/point-in-time-homeless
-count-report-2020/.

139 **Singapore, with roughly thirteen times the population:** "530 rough
sleepers found in Singapore, 'significant decrease' from last count:
MSF," Channel News Asia, April 24, 2023, channelnewsasia.com
/singapore/homeless-rough-sleepers-sleeping-msf-530-street-count
-3439311#:~:text=The%20nationwide%2C%20single%2Dnight
%20street,the%20National%20University%20of%20Singapore.

13. An Essential Problem: Toronto
Interview: Nicola Montgomery.

143 **Of course, the people most affected:** City of Toronto website
https://www.toronto.ca/city-government/data-research-maps
/research-reports/housing-and-homelessness-research-and
-reports/shelter-system-flow-data/.

145 **a shortage of nurses is surely:** Owen Dyer, "Covid-19: Ontario
hospitals close wards as nursing shortage bites," British Medical
Journal 378 (2022): o1917, https://doi.org/10.1136/bmj.o1917.

146 **The Community Commitment Program for Nurses:** Dylan Dyson,
"Arnprior Hospital offering $25,000 to new nurse hires," CTV News,
September 9, 2022, ottawa.ctvnews.ca/arnprior-hospital-offering
-25-000-to-new-nurse-hires-1.6062626#:~:text=To%20be
%20eligible%2C%20the%20new,be%20receiving%20funding
%20from%20the.; "Community Commitment Program for Nurses
(CCPN)," HealthForce Ontario website, healthforceontario.ca/en
/Home/All_Programs/Community_Commitment_Program_for
_Nurses, accessed August 3, 2023.

147 **Deborah Buchanan-Walford teaches:** Tess Kalinowski, "Shortage of
affordable housing for workers costs GTA a 'staggering' $8 billion

annually," Toronto Star, July 20, 2021, vha.ca/news/toronto-star
-shortage-of-affordable-housing-for-workers-costs-the-gta-a
-staggering-8-billion-annually/.

147 **Care aides, education assistants, cleaners, dental assistants:**
"Toronto's Vital Signs Report 2019/20," Toronto Foundation website,
torontofoundation.ca/vitalsigns-issue-2/, accessed August 3, 2023.

148 **the Toronto Board of Trade and WoodGreen Housing:** Anna-Kay
Russell, Craig Ruttan, Stéphanie Bussière, Clément Bret, Nathalia
Marques, Tua Hytönen, and Michelle German, Housing a Generation
of Essential Workers 3 (Toronto: Toronto Region Board of Trade and
WoodGreen, 2022), workforcehousing3.trbot.ca/foreword/.

149 **Toronto's growth rate started to slow significantly:** Statistics
Canada, "Population and demographic factors of growth by census
metropolitan area or census agglomeration, Canada, 2017/2018,"
www150.statcan.gc.ca/n1/pub/91-214-x/2019001/tbl/tbl-1.1-eng.htm.

149 **the only major Canadian city to see its population drop:** Graeme
Bruce, "A visual look at how Canadians relocated during the pandemic,"
CBC News, October 26, 2022, cbc.ca/news/canada/relocating
-canada-pandemic-1.6630425.

149 **Mike Moffatt from the Ivey Business School:** Mike Moffatt,
"Examining the exodus out of Toronto," author website, March 29,
2019, mikepmoffatt.medium.com/examining-the-exodus-out-of
-toronto-b10384daffb5.

14. Key Worker Housing. London

Interview: Emily Bere.

151 **people who worked in essential jobs—nurses, firefighters:** "Key
worker success through Metropolitan Home Ownership scheme,"
Police Life, police-life.co.uk/property/key-worker-success-through
-metropolitan-home-ownership-scheme, accessed August 4, 2023.

151 **One offered subsidies to help key workers:** "Proud to provide home

to key worker during lockdown," Paradigm Housing website, August 24, 2020, paradigmhousing.co.uk/proud-provide-home-key-worker-lockdown/.

153 **it was time to bring back some key worker housing:** "Key Worker housing schemes 2022," Alexander Southwell Mortgage Services website, as-mortgages.co.uk/key-worker-housing-schemes-2022/, accessed August 4, 2023.

153 **a new equity share scheme offered by the local council:** "H&F gives keyworkers priority for local affordable homes," London Borough of Hammersmith & Fulham website, May 27, 2022, lbhf.gov.uk/articles/news/2022/05/hf-gives-keyworkers-priority-local-affordable-homes.

154 **"Before this I was in a private rental":** Royal Borough of Kensington and Chelsea, "Key workers move into homes fit for heroes," news release, May 12, 2021, rbkc.gov.uk/newsroom/key-workers-move-homes-fit-heroes.

154 **Physiotherapist Lydia Roderiques:** Canary Wharf Group, "NHS worker takes advantage of new affordable Canary Wharf homes," news release, March 14, 2022, group.canarywharf.com/press-release/nhs-worker-takes-advantage-of-new-affordable-canary-wharf-homes-140322/.

156 **The head of the local NHS Trust:** "Plans for key worker accommodation approved—November 2021," Spelthorne Borough Council website, December 6, 2022, spelthorne.gov.uk/article/21001/Plans-for-key-worker-accommodation-approved-November-2021.

157 **Kerry Parker was delighted:** "Key workers set to get priority at new £1.2m property development," Warrington Housing Association website, August 28, 2020, wha.org.uk/key-workers-set-to-get-priority-at-new-1-2m-property-development/.

158 **British key workers could take advantage:** Jack Airey and Sir Robin Wales, Revitalising Key Worker Housing (London: Policy Exchange, 2019), policyexchange.org.uk/wp-content/uploads/2019/11/Revitalising-Key-Worker-Housing.pdf. Key worker FAQs," Peabody Housing Association website, peabody.org.uk/find-a-home/key

-workers-regency/key-worker-faqs, accessed August 4, 2023.

158 **31-year-old Nurse Specialist Christine McLaren:** "Key worker escapes rental trap to buy dream home in Southport," Business Shows Group website, November 2, 2020, businessshowsgroup.co.uk/key -worker-escapes-rental-trap-to-buy-dream-home-in-southport/.

158 **The key one was called a Help to Buy Equity Loan:** City of Wolverhampton Council, "Covid heroes and other key workers can buy their brand new home for just £1," news release, October 15, 2021, wolverhampton.gov.uk/news/covid-heroes-and-other-key-workers -can-buy-their-brand-new-home-just-ps1.

15. Squeezed Out by Single-Family Zoning. Victoria

Interviews: Luke Mari; Leo Spalteholtz, real estate analyst.

161 **He now sits on the board of the Greater Victoria Housing:** "About Us," Greater Victoria Housing Society website, greatervichousing .org/about/, accessed August 4, 2023.

163 **Neighbouring Oak Bay took nine years:** Mary Griffin, "Oak Bay council rejects proposed condo development after nine years of planning," CHEK News, March 18, 2022, cheknews.ca/oak-bay-council -rejects-proposed-condo-development-after-nine-years-of-planning -992649/#:~:text=A%20proposed%20condo%20development%20 that,Quite%20honestly%2C%20I%20was%20speechless.

164 **the building code and new, stronger seismic:** Office of Housing and Construction Standards, "BC Building Code and earthquake safety," BC Government website, www2.gov.bc.ca/assets/gov/farming-natural -resources-and-industry/construction-industry/building-codes-and -standards/guides/fs_bcbc_seismic.pdf, accessed August 4, 2023.

167 **the BC Energy Step Code:** "Frequently Asked Questions," BC Energy Step Code Council website, energystepcode.ca/faq/#:~:text =What%20is%20the%20BC%20Energy,the%20base%20BC %20Building%20Code, accessed August 4, 2023.

167 **inclusionary housing contributions:** City of Victoria, Inclusionary Housing and Community Amenity Policy (Victoria: City of Victoria, 2023), victoria.ca/assets/Departments/Planning-Development /Community-Planning/Housing-Strategy/Inclusionary %20Housing%20and%20Community%20Amenity %20Policy_Adopted%20June%2027%202019.pdf.

170 **The municipally owned Cedar Hill Golf Course:** Megan Atkins-Baker, "Saanich looks at fee hikes, annual pass removal for Cedar Hill Golf Course," Saanich News, September 24, 2021, saanichnews.com /news/saanich-looks-at-fee-hikes-annual-pass-removal-for-cedar-hill -golf-course/.

16. Infills for Affordability: Portland, Oregon

Interviews: Eric Thompson, Oregon Homeworks; Michael Andersen, senior housing researcher at the non-profit Sightline Institute, Portland.

171 **the City of Portland declared:** City of Portland, "New housing report shows unprecedented affordable housing production, rising incomes, rent increases," news release, March 22, 2023, portland.gov/phb/news /2023/3/22/new-housing-report-shows-unprecedented-affordable -housing-production-rising.

172 **A 2022 point-in-time homeless survey:** David Mann, "Tri-counties release 1st count of Portland area's homeless population since 2019," KGW News, May 4, 2022, kgw.com/article/news/local/homeless /portland-point-in-time-count-2022/283-23908a65-a619-4373 -92bf-f01907ad1ad8.

172 **Jason Bolt, the founder of an eyeglass lens company:** Katia Riddle, "Portland finds it's hard to disentangle the rise in crime from the housing crisis," NPR, December 12, 2022, npr.org/2022/12/12 /1142171547/in-portland-it-s-impossible-to-disentangle-the -rise-in-crime-from-the-housing-cr.

174 **As the name suggests, cottage clusters:** "About the RIP2 Project," City of Portland website, portland.gov/bps/planning/rip2/about -rip2#:~:text=Cottage%20clusters,-Cottage%20cluster%20, accessed August 5, 2023.

177 **the infill policy is a key component:** "About the Residential Infill Project," City of Portland website, portland.gov/bps/planning/rip /about-project, accessed August 4, 2023.

178 **several examples of overtly racist policies:** Bureau of Planning and Sustainability, Historical Context of Racist Planning: A History of How Planning Segregated Portland (Portland: City of Portland, 2019), portland.gov/bps/documents/historical-context-racist -planning/download.

178 **The language remained in the board's Code of Ethics:** Portland Housing Bureau, "Displacement in North and Northeast Portland: An Historical Overview," City of Portland website, portlandoregon .gov/phb/article/655460, accessed August 5, 2023.

180 **explicitly racist covenants existed:** Bob Aaron, "Honouring Bernard Wolf, and his role in ending real-estate racism in Canada," Toronto Star, April 17, 2015, thestar.com/life/homes/2015/04/17/honouring -the-end-of-real-estate-racism-in-canada.html.; "Bernard Wolf Dead at 96," Jewish Telegraphic Agency, January 16, 1987, jta.org/archive/ bernard-wolf-dead-at-96.

180 **several homes in West Vancouver:** "West Vancouver makes racist land covenants history," CBC News, January 28, 2020, cbc.ca/news /canada/british-columbia/land-covenants-1.5442686.

181 **Biden mentioned the national housing deficit:** The White House, "President Biden announces new actions to ease the burden of housing costs," news release, May 16, 2022, whitehouse.gov/briefing -room/statements-releases/2022/05/16/president-biden-announces -new-actions-to-ease-the-burden-of-housing-costs/.

17. Searching for Sanctuary: Calgary
Interview: Sohail Shafaq (email).

183 **Millions of Ukrainians were leaving:** Statista Research Department, "Estimated number of refugees from Ukraine recorded in Europe and Asia since February 2022 as of July 11, 2023, by selected country," Statista, July 11, 2023, statista.com/statistics/1312584/ukrainian -refugees-by-country/.

183 **the Syrman family:** Bill Graveland, "'A crisis': Calgary charity seeks one-month homes for Ukrainian refugees after influx," CBC News, March 29, 2023, cbc.ca/news/canada/calgary/ukraine-war-calgary -refugee-newcomers-1.6795286.

184 **Ann Kucheriava and her family:** "Calgary couple help 30+ Ukrainian families settle in Calgary," Wildin, March 13, 2023, wildin.ca/tag/calgary/.

184 **The rapid influx of many Ukrainians:** Camae Marayag, "Massive influx has Calgary charity seeking one-month homes for Ukrainian refugees," CTV News, March 29, 2023, calgary.ctvnews.ca/massive -influx-has-calgary-charity-seeking-one-month-homes-for -ukrainian-refugees-1.6334310.

185 **Calgary's unemployment rate of 6.6%:** Statistics Canada, "Labour force characteristics by census metropolitan area, three-month moving average, seasonally adjusted," www150.statcan.gc.ca/n1/daily-quotidien /230406/t007a-eng.htm, accessed August 5, 2023.; Statistics Canada, "Labour force characteristics by census metropolitan area, three-month moving average, seasonally adjusted," www150.statcan.gc.ca/n1/daily -quotidien/220506/t007a-eng.htm, accessed August 5, 2023.

185 **Anna Martyniuk and her husband:** Bryan Labby, "Calgary's popula- tion surge: New arrivals struggle while 110,000 more expected by 2027," CBC News, April 24, 2023, cbc.ca/news/canada/calgary /calgary-newcomers-programs-demand-population-projection -1.6816845.

186 **The Alberta government later provided more than $4 million:**

Alejandro Melgar, "Alberta providing \$4.32M to help Ukrainians find temporary living," CityNews Calgary, March 31, 2023, calgary. citynews.ca/2023/03/31/alberta-ukrainian-temporary-living/.

187 **Nataliia Shen, the housing coordinator:** Aryn Toombs, "Need for temporary housing dire, with hundreds more Ukrainians expected to arrive in Calgary," Livewire Calgary, March 29, 2023, livewirecalgary .com/2023/03/29/need-for-temporary-housing-dire-with-hundreds -more-ukrainians-expected-to-arrive-in-calgary/.

187 **"When they come here, it's like a deer in the headlights":** Olivia Condon, "'Beyond capacity': Housing Ukrainian evacuees in Calgary a daily struggle for support organizations," Calgary Herald, January 11, 2023, calgaryherald.com/news/local-news/beyond-capacity-housing -ukrainian-evacuees-in-calgary-a-daily-struggle-for-support -organizations.; Carolyn Kury de Castillo, "Volunteers worry about housing as Ukrainian refugees in Calgary find housing in homeless shelter," Global News, June 16, 2022, globalnews.ca/news/8925411 /ukrainian-refugee-housing-calgary/.

187 **She moved into a hotel:** Dan McGarvey, "Refugee hotels fill up as surge in newcomers hits Calgary's tight rental market," CBC News, October 11, 2022, cbc.ca/news/canada/calgary/refugees-calgary -afghanistan-housing-newcomers-1.6610455.

188 **the rents are going up, higher and higher:** Rentals.ca, "June 2023 Rental Report," Rentals.ca, rentals.ca/national-rent-report.

189 **Toronto's busiest subway:** Lauren O'Neil, "Toronto's busiest subway station is currently a giant ad for Alberta," BlogTO, September 2022, blogto.com/city/2022/09/toronto-busiest-subway-station-giant -ad-alberta/.

189 **Canada's population grew by more than 1 million:** Statistics Canada, "Canada's population estimates: Record-high population growth in 2022," The Daily, March 22, 2023, www150.statcan.gc.ca /n1/daily-quotidien/230322/dq230322f-eng.htm.

190 **in 1961, the median price for a single-family home:** Central
   Mortgage and Housing Corporation, Canadian Housing Statistics
   1963 (Ottawa: CMHC, 1964), publications.gc.ca/collections
   /collection_2016/schl-cmhc/nh12-1/NH12-1-1963.pdf.

190 **At the same time, the median income:** Dominion Bureau of
   Statistics, 1961 Census of Canada: Earnings and Income Distribution
   (Ottawa: Queen's Printer, 1967), publications.gc.ca/collections
   /collection_2017/statcan/CS99-524-1961.pdf.

190 **Victor Dodig, recalls:** Victor Dodig, "Victor Dodig: Canada must
   urgently address affordability, housing woes so immigrants can
   thrive," Financial Post, October 24, 2022, financialpost.com/news
   /economy/victor-dodig-canada-immigration-housing-affordability
   /wcm/d074cc1a-5517-44de-bfec-d3db3480c6a8/amp/.

190 **In early 2023, the average national home price:** Canadian Real
   Estate Association, "Canadian home sales continue to pick up steam
   in May," CREA website, June 15, 2023, stats.crea.ca/en-CA/.

190 **when the median after-tax income:** Statistics Canada, "Focus on
   Geography Series, 2021 Census of Population," December 16, 2022,
   www12.statcan.gc.ca/census-recensement/2021/as-sa/fogs-spg/page
   .cfm?topic=5&lang=E&dguid=2021A000011124.

18. A Modular Response: Cork, Ireland

192 **the construction site, in the pleasant Cork suburb:** Laura Hogan,
   "First modular homes for Ukrainian refugees ready by June," RTE,
   April 29, 2023, rte.ie/news/2023/0429/1379876-housing-modular
   -homes/.; Department of the Taoiseach, "Rapid build housing,"
   Government of Ireland website, November 4, 2022, gov.ie/en
   /publication/ef882-rapid-build-housing/.

193 **the new house was almost finished:** John Bohane, "Modular homes
   in Cork city for Ukrainian families ready in two weeks," Echo Live,
   May 3, 2023, echolive.ie/corknews/arid-41131102.html.

193 **Ukrainian families would move in:** Eoin English, "First look inside Cork's modular homes as Mahon prepares to welcome Ukrainian families," Irish Examiner, June 9, 2023, irishexaminer.com/news /arid-41158930.html.

193 **Modular housing is a broad term:** Ciaran Brennan, "Taking modular construction mainstream, with Gaynor Tennant of the Offsite Alliance," Time & Materials Podcast, February 24, 2023, irepod.com /podcast/the-ciaran-brennan-podcast/taking-modular-constructionv -mainstream-with-gaynor.

193 **Modular housing includes various:** Kristina Smith, "Can modular go mainstream?" Construction Management, April 24, 2023, constructionmanagement.co.uk/can-modular-go-mainstream/.

194 **In 2022 the country took in more refugees:** Sonya Ciesnik, "How Ireland's housing crisis affects refugees and migrants," InfoMigrants, April 3, 2023, infomigrants.net/fr/post/47716/how-irelands-housing -crisis-affects-refugees-and-migrants.

195 **70 percent of the nation's young people:** "Young people considering emigration for better quality of life than in Ireland," National Youth Council of Ireland website, September 12, 2022, youth.ie/articles /young-people-considering-emigration-for-better-quality-of-life -than-in-ireland/.

196 **modular home builders claim their method:** Who will be the builders? Modulars role in solving the housing labour crisis. A Make UK Modular report. March, 2023. https://www.makeuk.org/insights /reports/who-will-be-the-builders-modulars-role-in-solving-the -housing-labour-crisis.

197 **It even used an old airport hangar:** Cormac McQuinn, Jack Horgan-Jones, and Anne Lucey, "Modular homes to be built to house refugees, with sites across four counties selected," Irish Times, July 28, 2022, irishtimes.com/ireland/2022/07/28/five-locations-across-four-counties -selected-as-sites-for-modular-homes-to-house-refugees/.

198 **a legal obligation under national and European:** European
Commission, "Ireland's participation in EU schemes to relocate and
resettle refugees," EC Factsheet, February 28, 2021, ireland
.representation.ec.europa.eu/news-and-events/news/ireland
-voluntarily-agrees-take-part-eu-schemes-resettle-refugees
-2021-02-28_en#:~:text=The%20EU%20has%20never%20forced
,measures%20under%20the%20Lisbon%20Treaty.

198 **stories of asylum seekers who were neither safe nor sheltered:**
Laura Fletcher, "'Grim milestone' as 501 new asylum seekers without
State accommodation," RTE, May 18, 2023, rte.ie/news
/ireland/2023/0412/1376527-asylum-seekers/.

198 **Roughly sixty asylum seekers set up:** Andrei Scintian and Mostafa
Darwish, "Asylum seekers in 'Tent City'—living on the street in Dublin—
tell us 'we need to start a life,'" Irish Mirror, May 12, 2023, irishmirror.ie
/news/irish-news/watch-asylum-seekers-tent-city-29964662.

199 **a group of homeless campers from several different:** Kitty Holland,
"Ashtown camp allegedly threatened by 'four men' hours before
attack, migrants say," Irish Times, February 4, 2023, irishtimes.com
/ireland/social-affairs/2023/02/04/ashtown-camp-allegedly
-threatened-by-four-men-hours-before-attack-migrants-say/.

199 **a local group of citizens came together to form Fermoy:** Liz
Dunphy, "How a Cork town opened its arms to refugees: 'You just
need to love your community,'" Irish Examiner, March 5, 2023,
irishexaminer.com/news/munster/arid-41085379.html.

200 **it housed asylum seekers in Hamburg:** Marion MacGregor,
"'Creative solutions' to a refugee housing problem in Hamburg,"
InfoMigrants, December 13, 2022, infomigrants.net/en/post/45366
/creative-solutions-to-a-refugee-housing-problem-in-hamburg.

200 **The world's first modular high-rise:** Jenna McKnight, "World's
tallest modular high-rise by SHoP Architects opens in Brooklyn,"
Dezeen, November 18, 2016, dezeen.com/2016/11/18/worlds-tallest

-modular-prefabricated-apartment-tower-shop-architects
-brooklyn-new-york/.

201 **In 2019 a pair of even taller towers was finished in Singapore:**
India Block, "World's tallest modular tower is now Clement Canopy
in Singapore," Dezeen, July 2, 2019, dezeen.com/2019/07/02
/clement-canopy-worlds-tallest-modular-tower-bouygues/.

201 **In 2021, another pair of modular high-rise buildings:** "World's
tallest modular housing scheme completed in Croydon," PBC Today,
May 17, 2021, pbctoday.co.uk/news/mmc-news/ten-degrees
-croydon/93494/.

201 **the Red Cross opened 256 individual container homes:** "DRK
eröffnet neue Unterkunft für Geflüchtete," German Red Cross website, March 4, 2023, drk-harburg.hamburg/details/drk-eroeffnet
-neue-unterkunft-fuer-gefluechtete.

203 **a grandmother named Nadiia moved into a modular house:**
Victoria Andrievska, "UNHCR Modular homes help people whose
homes were destroyed or severely damaged to stay in their
communities," October 26, 2022, UNHCR website, unhcr.org/ua
/en/50937-modular-homes-help-people-whose-homes-were
-destroyed-or-severely-damaged-to-stay-in-their-communities.html.

19. An RV by the Sea: Annapolis Valley, Nova Scotia
Interviews: Andrea Durling (email); Christine Porter, Executive Director,
Ally Centre of Cape Breton; Jeff Karabanow, Dalhousie Social Work
Professor.

204 **Dunromin was named one of the 25 Best:** "Dunromin Campsite and
Cabins," Government of Nova Scotia website, novascotia.com/places
-to-stay/campgrounds/dunromin-campsite-and-cabins/52,
accessed August 6, 2023.

204 **Andrea, Matthew, and their three sons:** Andrew Rankin, "The
Tory turn: Nova Scotia's affordable-housing crisis worsens," Saltwire,

August 29, 2022, saltwire.com/atlantic-canada/news/the-tory-turn
-nova-scotias-affordable-housing-crisis-worsens-100767029/#.

205 **and a report from Nova Scotia's auditor general:** Office of the
Auditor General of Nova Scotia, "Oversight and management of
government owned public housing," Independent Auditor's Report,
June 2022, oag-ns.ca/sites/default/files/publications
/2022HousingHighlights.pdf.

206 **The average price of a residential home:** Statista Research
Department, "Average house price in Nova Scotia, Canada from 2018
to 2022, with a forecast until 2024 (in Canadian dollars)," Statista,
January 2023, statista.com/statistics/604264/median-house-prices
-nova-scotia/#:~:text=The%20average%20house%20price%20in
,and%20exceed%20432%2C000%20Canadian%20dollars.

206 **In Halifax-Dartmouth the average home price rose:** Daniel Crook,
"The pandemic effect: A two-year retrospective on Canadian real
estate prices," Zoocasa, March 31, 2022, zoocasa.com/blog/canada
-home-prices-jan-2020-vs-feb-2022/.

206 **By the spring of 2023 the average rent in Halifax:** CMHC, Rental
Market Report: January 2023 Edition, assets.cmhc-schl.gc.ca/sites
/cmhc/professional/housing-markets-data-and-research/market
-reports/rental-market-report/rental-market-report-2022-en
.pdf?rev=ff8ebfd2-961f-4589-8ae2-fac01d1aedac,
accessed August 6, 2023.

207 **But landlords faced no such restrictions:** Nicola Seguin, "With
some rents doubling between tenants, Nova Scotians want to know if
rent cap is staying," CBC News, March 15, 2023, cbc.ca/news/canada
/nova-scotia/rent-cap-nova-scotia-expires-dec-2023-1.6778218.;
Nova Scotia government press release - Rent Cap Extended - March
22, 2023 Government of Nova Scotia, "Rent cap extended," news
release, novascotia.ca/news/release/?id=20230322001.

207 **Facing growing political pressure to act:** Michael Gorman, "Nova

Scotia government extends cap on rent increases to the end of 2025, raising it to 5%," CBC News, March 22, 2023, cbc.ca/news/canada/nova-scotia/rent-cap-housing-colton-leblanc-1.6787084.

208 **"People have nowhere to go":** Tom Ayers, "Cape Breton police taking gentle approach to tenting in public places," CBC News, June 20, 2022, cbc.ca/news/canada/nova-scotia/cape-breton-police-tenting-in-public-places-1.6494854.

209 **climate researchers like Blair Feltmate:** Alex Cooke, "Fiona reminds us climate change is here—and Canada must adapt now: expert," Global News, September 29, 2022, globalnews.ca/news/9164593/climate-change-adaptation-needed-fiona/.

210 **The students in this case are international:** Josefa Cameron, "Cape Breton university responds to concerns over international student enrolment," CBC News, December 22, 2022, cbc.ca/news/canada/nova-scotia/cbu-international-students-housing-crisis-1.6695753.

211 **One university student was killed when:** Josefa Cameron, "12 people displaced after fatal weekend fire in Sydney duplex," CBC News, December 20, 2022, cbc.ca/news/canada/nova-scotia/fire-displaced-international-student-dead-1.6692390.; Josefa Cameron, "Some CBU students choose hotel over crowded housing after fatal fire in Sydney," CBC News, January 4, 2023, cbc.ca/news/canada/nova-scotia/fire-housing-crisis-international-students-cbu-1.6702494.

212 **57-year-old grandmother Terri Smith-Fraser:** Suzanne Rent, "Halifax woman living the van life gets a closer look at the housing crisis in the city," Halifax Examiner, October 13, 2022, halifaxexaminer.ca/housing/priced-out/halifax-woman-living-the-van-life-gets-a-closer-look-at-the-housing-crisis-in-the-city/.

213 **she bought a 24-year-old GMC Savana cargo van:** Lindsay Jones, "This 57-year-old grandmother didn't choose the van life: The housing crisis chose it for her," Globe and Mail, May 23, 2023, theglobeandmail.com/canada/article-halifax-housing-van-life/.

20. 3-D Printing Homes for the Future: Nacajuca, Mexico

216 **Major floods over the years have forced the evacuation:** New Story, "This is Nacajuca," YouTube, December 8, 2020, youtube.com /watch?v=ifsZkGgjmlc.

216 **fighting the flooding is a losing battle for many:** Sarah Lee, "Impact, innovation, partnerships," New Story, December 14, 2021, newstoryhomes.org/nacajuca-mexico.

217 **Petrona Hernández and her husband:** "Las casas sustentables y antisismos en Nacajuca," El Universal (Mexico City), November 27, 2021, eluniversal.com.mx/estados/las-casas-sustentables-y-antisismos-en-nacajuca/.; Debra Kamin, "How an 11-foot-tall 3-D printer is helping to create a community," New York Times, September 28, 2021, nytimes.com/2021/09/28/business/3D-printing-homes.html.

217 **But things were looking up for the Hernández family:** "Construyen casas con impresora 3D en Tabasco—En Punto," YouTube, uploaded by NMás, December 16, 2019, youtube.com /watch?v=ElN8vs5eWYM.

217 **The Tabasco government provided some of the funding:** Government of Tabasco, "Pone en marcha Adán Augusto desarrollo de primera Comunidad Sostenible 2030," September 22, 2019, tabasco.gob.mx/noticias/pone-en-marcha-adan-augusto-desarrollo -de-primera-comunidad-sostenible-2030.

218 **Échale has worked in twenty-eight:** Ricardo Treviño and José Longino Torres, "From blocks to 3D printed houses: This social entrepreneur's journey," Conecta, October 27, 2021, conecta.tec.mx /en/news/national/entrepreneurs/blocks-3d-printed-houses-social -entrepreneurs-journey.

218 **It also helped rebuild nearly 2,300 homes:** "Échale, the Mexican social enterprise that facilitates access to housing," Red Social Innovation website, January 25, 2023, red-social-innovation.com/es /solution/echale-facilitating-access-to-housing/.

218 **Though it looks much like a traditional concrete block:**
"Ecoblock," Échale website, echale.mx/en/ecoblock/,
accessed August 6, 2023.

218 **Francesco says it offers excellent insulation:** "Calakmul Rural
Housing Programme," World Habitat Awards website, world-habitat
.org/world-habitat-awards/winners-and-finalists/calakmul-rural
-housing-programme/, accessed August 6, 2023.

220 **the Vulcan II is designed specifically to print:** Carlota V., "ICON
unveils its new robotic home 3D printer, Vulcan II," 3Dnatives, March
14, 2019, 3dnatives.com/en/vulcan-ii-140320195/#.

220 **The printer is composed of two towers that stand:** "3D home community, Nacajuca, Mexico," World Housing website, worldhousing
.org/communities/3d-home-community-nacajuca-mexico/,
accessed August 6, 2023.

220 **icing being squeezed out of a pastry bag:** Karina Andrew Herrera,
"Impresora gigante 3D construye casas en Tabasco resistentes a
desastres naturales," Noticieras Televisa, December 17, 2019, noticieros
.televisa.com/ultimas-noticias/casas-tabasco-3d-impresora
-construye-resistentes-desastres-naturales/.

222 **the company notes its method drastically:** Buchanan, Craig &
Gardner, Leroy. (2019). Metal 3D printing in construction: A review
of methods, research, applications, opportunities and challenges.
Engineering Structures. 180. 332-348. 10.1016/j.engstruct.2018
.11.045. https://spiral.imperial.ac.uk/bitstream/10044/1/66422/2
/Metal%203D%20printing%20in%20construction%20-%20LG.pdf

222 **One study from Malawi claimed 3-D printing:** Media Release.
"14Trees Pioneers 3D Printing Technology in Africa for Affordable
Housing and Schools." Holcim. December, 16, 2020. https://www
.holcim.com/media/company-news/14trees-first-construction
-3d-printer-africa#:~:text=Iroko%20will%20help%20scale
%20up,footprint%20by%20up%20to%2070%25.

223 **The main roof is flat:** New Story + ICON + Échale, "3D printed housing for those who need it most," YouTube, uploaded by New Story, December 11, 2019, youtube.com/watch?v=PbgCuoaUobE.

223 **"It's time for the built environment to join:** Jason Ballard, "It's time to build," YouTube, uploaded by ICON, April 7, 2022, youtube.com /watch?v=63uhYWkictE&feature=youtu.be.

224 **The first 3-D printed office buildings opened:** Hallie Busta, "Gensler completes the world's first 3D-printed office building," Architect Magazine, June 1, 2016, architectmagazine.com/technology /gensler-designs-the-worlds-first-3d-printed-office-building-in -dubai_o.; Hadeer Abdalla, Kazi Parvez Fattah, Mohamed Abdallah, and Adil K. Tamimi, "Environmental footprint and economics of a full-scale 3D-printed house," Sustainability 13 (2021): 11978, https://doi.org/10.3390/su132111978.

225 **It built a 5-storey apartment building:** Michelle Star, "World's first 3D-printed apartment building constructed in China," CNET, January 19, 2015, cnet.com/culture/worlds-first-3d-printed-apartment -building-constructed-in-china/.

225 **But the most immediate benefit of 3-D printing:** Luis Triveno and Olivia Nielsen, "Can 3D printing become a sustainable way to close the global housing gap?" World Bank Blogs, May 12, 2022, blogs. worldbank.org/sustainablecities/can-3d-printing-become -sustainable-way-close-global-housing-gap.

225 **In Kenya, a company called 14Trees:** Brittany Chang, "A 52-home community starting is now being 3D-printed in Kenya: Take a look around Mvule Gardens," Yahoo! News, March 23, 2023, ca.news. yahoo.com/52-home-community-starting-now-090000234 .html?guccounter=1&guce_referrer=aHR0cHM6Ly93d3cuZ2 9vZ2xlLmNvbS8&guce_referrer_sig=AQAAAJeMdGwsIeLG7 _YcTeR7geSgA9hubhoB7BehDRVfT_VaTOvN6yxtn7JeURkNajj 3Q7u7QK8j5_walQtSiqM_ttAoA65zHerofl-Nn5roOptiJOu2EIP

5geO1OmMmdtZmBLyPYGcbqESsvNxKEpcrF47sLp5ZZ
YmcgLx6ix5eBQ8N.

226 **In Tempe, Marcus and Shawn Shivers:** Madeleine P., "Habitat for
Humanity building an affordable 3D printed home in Arizona," 3D
Natives, June 14, 2021, 3dnatives.com/en/habitat-for-humanity-
3d-printed-home-arizona-140620215/. ; Habitat for Humanity Central
Arizona, "Why not us? Habitat's 3D-printed home in Tempe,
Arizona," YouTube, April 20, 2022, youtube.com
/watch?v=T6HXB5suZIE&t=497s.

Afterword: A New Way Forward
Interviews: Khelsilem, chairperson, Squamish Nation Council; Ravi
Kahlon, BC Housing Minister.

227 **The task was a drop in the bucket:** Grant Cameron, "Largest
Indigenous-led economic project in Canadian history underway in
Vancouver," Journal of Commerce, October 26, 2022, canada.construct
connect.com/joc/news/projects/2022/10/largest-indigenous-led
-economic-project-in-canadian-history-underway-in-vancouver.

227 **The village of Sen̓áḵw was established:** Westbank Projects Corp.,
"History of the Sen̓áḵw lands," Sen̓áḵw, senakw.com/history,
accessed August 7, 2023.

228 **were sent on a barge to other Squamish:** Angela Sterritt, "The little-
known history of Squamish Nation land in Vancouver," CBC News,
April 21, 2019, cbc.ca/news/canada/british-columbia/little-known-
history-of-squamish-nation-land-in-vancouver-1.5104584.

230 **The Kits Point Residents' Association:** "Residents' association
takes Vancouver to court over agreement for Squamish Nation-led
development," CBC News, October 6, 2022, cbc.ca/news/canada
/british-columbia/kits-point-judicial-review-vancouver-squamish
-nation-senakw-1.6608352.

230 **The eleven towers will range in height:** Nelson Bennett, "First
Nations address Vancouver's housing shortage," Business in

Vancouver, May 27, 2022, biv.com/article/2022/05/first-nations
-address-vancouvers-housing-shortage.

231 **The Squamish Nation also partnered with:** The three First Nations
are referenced by their English translation. The Indigenous names of
each nation are as follows: xʷməθkwəy̓əm (Musqueam),
Skwxwú7mesh (Squamish), and səlilwətaɫ/Selilwitulh (Tsleil-Waututh).
https://www.caut.ca/content/guide-acknowledging-first-peoples
-traditional-territory

231 **Once the largest military training base:** "Remembering the Jericho
Beach Air Station," Jericho Sailing Centre website, November 7, 2015,
jsca.bc.ca/2015/11/07/remembering-the-jericho-beach-air-station/.

231 **the federal government decommissioned the base:** Vancouver
Heritage Foundation, "Jericho Beach: 1860's onward," Spacing,
February 17, 2014, spacing.ca/vancouver/2014/02/17/jericho
-beach-1860s-onward/.

231 The Vancouver Sun **called the eviction the Battle of Jericho:** "HI
Vancouver Jericho Beach celebrates its 50th birthday," HI Canada
website, July 6, 2021, hihostels.ca/en/magazine/hi-vancouver-jericho
-beach-celebrates-its-50th-birthday.

233 **there's little doubt Vancouver needs a lot more:** "Future Cities
Canada Spotlight: Housing Innovations," CMHC website, September
13, 2021, cmhc-schl.gc.ca/en/nhs/nhs-project-profiles/2020-nhs
-projects/future-cities-canada-spotlight-housing-innovations.

233 **In Calgary, vacant downtown office buildings:** Karina Zapata,
"Another office-to-residential conversion is underway in downtown
Calgary—this time with balconies," CBC News, January 17, 2023,
cbc.ca/news/canada/calgary/office-to-residential-the-cornerstone-1
.6716211?__vfz=medium%3Dsharebar&fbclid=IwAR2RpOIbU9NAn
TAHzR-k2fQnMgrbhO6YMnpoi2VNd595F7xRkV8CruLtdsk
&mibextid=Zxz2cZ.

233 **The City of Edmonton got rid of almost:** Madeleine Cummings,

"Edmonton got rid of parking minimums 2 years ago: What has happened since then?" CBC News, December 12, 2022, cbc.ca/news/canada/edmonton/edmonton-got-rid-of-parking-minimums-2-years-ago-what-has-happened-since-then-1.6680750.

233 **A year later Toronto followed suit:** City of Toronto, "Toronto removed minimum parking requirements on new condos: City Council approves changes to regulations for car and bike parking spaces in new developments," news release, December 15, 2021, toronto.ca/news/city-council-approves-changes-to-regulations-for-car-and-bike-parking-spaces-in-new-developments/#:~:text=%E2%80%9CToday%2C%20City%20Council%20took%20real,car%20to%20purchase%20a%20home.%E2%80%9D.

234 **The City of Toronto is opening hundreds:** "Toronto modular housing sites: Modular Housing Initiative," City of Toronto website, toronto.ca/community-people/housing-shelter/affordable-housing-developments/modular-housing-initiative/, accessed August 7, 2023.

234 **BC's Housing Minister, Ravi Kahlon, urged:** Bullet point presentation from BC housing minister Ravi Kahlon to federal housing minister Ahmed Hussen in 2023.

PHOTO CREDITS

1. Vancouver Special. The author.
2. La Samaritaine. Arthur Weidmann—Own work, CC BY-SA 4.0, https://commons.wikimedia.org/w/index.php?curid=116991157.
3. Ottawa rooming house. Joshua Hawley.
4. Co-op evening at Möckernkiez. Carlo Wahrmann.
5. Victoria single-family house. The author.
6. Portland cottage. RE PIXS.
7, 8. Modular home assembly and completion. Courtesy Centrepoint UK.
9, 10. Halifax van. Terri Smith-Fraser.
11. 3-D house printer. By ICON Team, https://3dprintingindustry.com/news/icon-unveils-plans-for-improved-next-generation-vulcan-3d-printer-190706/, CC BY-SA 4.0, https://commons.wikimedia.org/w/index.php?curid=126652246.
12. Sen̓áḵw. Rendering courtesy of the Squamish Nation. Design Architect: Revery Architecture. Architect of Record: Kasian Architecture, Interior Design and Planning. Renderings: Tandem Studios.

ACKNOWLEDGEMENTS

I'M GRATEFUL TO MANY people who helped me write this book. Firstly, to those who shared their time with me to answer my questions directly. That includes those who study the issue or work in a related field, like housing advocacy, construction, or policy. I'm especially grateful to the people who shared their personal experiences with me. It would be easy and understandable to keep your own struggles to yourself, but all of the people quoted in this book who spoke to me directly expressed a hope that doing so could help bring about some kind of improvement in housing affordability in this country. I hope they're right.

I'm also grateful to Anne Collins, who was so encouraging when I first approached Penguin Random House Canada, and to Deirdre Molina, who took on the editing responsibilities with an enthusiasm that reflected the importance of this subject. Writing about an evolving topic that affects so many people—and doing it on a relatively tight deadline—is a significant challenge, and one that I could not have done without Deirdre's encouragement, humour, and passion for this issue.

And finally, my family. Thank you, Becky, for always demonstrating what it really means to help the people around us. Thanks to my kids, who listened to their dad's fretting about housing but still believe me when I tell them that Canada can improve. I've long been indebted to my sister, Gillian, for reminding me to always try to make things better, and to my mum, Betty, for always listening.

INDEX

(Page numbers in italic represent photos.)

GREGOR CRAIGIE is a writer and journalist who has worked for more than twenty-five years for the *BBC World Service, CBC News, CBS Radio,* and *Public Radio International.* His curiosity led him to dozens of countries on five continents, honing his skill as a story-teller in feature pieces on a wide variety of topics ranging from the identification of missing Bosnian Muslim men in mass graves to the massive seal hunt in southern Africa. He has been the host of *On The Island* on CBC Radio One in Victoria, BC, since 2007, and in that role has interviewed thousands of people on hundreds of different topics. His first book, *On Borrowed Time: North America's Next Big Quake,* was a finalist for both the Balsillie Prize for Public Policy and the City of Victoria Book Prize, and was a *Globe and Mail* Top 100 book in 2021. Craigie has also written non-fiction books for young readers, including *Why Humans Build Up: The Rise of Towers, Temples and Skyscrapers.* His first novel, *Radio Jet Lag,* was published in 2023.